HISPANIC CLASSICS
Modern Drama

Antonio Buero Vallejo

THE SHOT

(*La detonación*)

Second Spanish edition
translated with an introduction and notes
by

DAVID JOHNSTON

ARIS & PHILLIPS – WARMINSTER – ENGLAND

© *La detonación* Antonio Buero Vallejo, 1989.

British library CIP data

British Library Cataloguing in Publication Data
Buero Vallejo, Antonio
    The shot (La detonación). - (Hispanic classes).
    1. Drama in Spanish, 1945 - - English texts
    I. Title II. Johnston, D. (David) III. Series IV.
    Detonación. *English*
    862'.64

ISBNS   cloth   085668 455 4
         limp   085668 456 2

ISSN (Hispanic Classics) 0953 797 X

The publishers wish to acknowledge with thanks the financial assistance of the Dirección General del Libro y Bibliotecas of the Ministerio de Cultura de España with the translation.

Printed and published in England by Aris & Phillips Ltd, Teddington House, Warminster, Wiltshire BA12 8PQ.

CONTENTS

To Amalia and Mariano

ACKNOWLEDGEMENTS

I am glad to have this opportunity to acknowledge publicly two long-standing debts. Firstly, to Guadalupe Martínez Lacalle, who was the first to help me see that there is much more to the modern Spanish stage than perhaps at first meets the eye. Secondly, to Antonio Buero Vallejo, both for his incalculable help in the preparation of this book and for his unfailing courtesy and patience in answering the many questions with which I have bombarded him over the years – courtesy and patience which very often my queries certainly did not deserve. Finally, a word of thanks is also due to John Lyon for his wise suggestions and encouragement when this translation was still in its infancy.

PREFACE

Antonio Buero Vallejo, born in Guadalajara, 1916, has been the leading playwright in Spain and the Spanish-speaking world since the première of his first play in 1949. It is universally agreed that this play, *Historia de una escalera* (*Story of a staircase*) restored serious and worthwhile drama virtually at a stroke to a Spanish stage which was dominated since the end of the Civil War by officially sanctioned escapism and mediocrity. The scale of this achievement can only be fully appreciated when one takes into account the fact that Buero Vallejo had been a political prisoner in one of Franco's concentration camps since the end of the war until 1946. Indeed, eight months of this period were spent under sentence of death for his part in the defence of Spanish democracy.

Originally a painter by vocation, upon his release he turned to the theatre as the most appropriate vehicle for expressing his ideas and vision with force and immediacy. Since 1949 Buero Vallejo has had twenty-five plays performed in Spain and abroad, a body of work whose deep moral substance and concern for human rights has earned for its author the reputation of being the moral conscience of his country. Between 1949 and 1975, the year in which Franco died, he gave public and compassionate voice to the frustration and anger of millions of Spaniards. His is very much the theatre of a "vencido", one of the defeated of the Civil War, but it is the work of a "vencido" who has never ceased to struggle, who has consistently defended the values of freedom and civilisation in the face of authoritarianism. His theatre was to become a mirror for its times, in spite of the social and political blindfold which Francoism had sought to place round the country's eyes. Accordingly, he once defined his plays as "gafas para cegatos que quisieran ver" ("glasses for those who are blind but who want to see"), meaning by this that the theatre can serve to clarify the hidden or supressed realities of both national and individual life.

Since 1975 Buero has continued to write, producing plays at roughly the rate of one every two years. Although offered an important political appointment in recognition of his unflinching support for human rights throughout the Franco years, Buero has preferred to speak solely through the theatre. His plays continue to be generally well received by the public for whom they have been written, and some of the most recent ones in particular have been rewarded with comparatively long runs. It is certainly true to say that he enjoys – if that is the correct word – a mixed

relationship with the critics, some of whom now seem to doubt wheth
tragedy (Buero's chosen genre) and his particular style of writing are viab
at a time when spectacle rather than text is in vogue. Be that as it ma
the solid literary quality of the construction of his plays (why should t
fact that a play is considered "well made" be taken as a damni
criticism?) coupled with his extraordinary sense of theatrical innovati
have attracted scholarly and media attention all over the world. His pla
have been translated into sixteen languages and performed in ma
countries. Individual plays have always attracted awards and prizes.
particular, in 1973 Buero was elected to the Spanish Academy and in 19
he was awarded the National Prize for Literature for the fourth tim
More recently, in 1986 he became the first dramatist to win the prestigio
Cervantes Prize, the Hispanic world's equivalent of the Nobel Priz
Recent homages have been organised in theatres and universities in Spa
Germany and the United States of America, and a vast and growing critic
bibliography produced by theatre critics and Hispanists from ma
countries attests to the quality of Buero's theatre, achieved in spite of t
difficult conditions under which he has laboured.

In the final analysis this is the real measure of Buero's success as
professional man of the theatre. At a time when it would have been mo
lucrative to follow the example of dramatists like Alfonso Paso a
produce simple escapist drama, Buero wrote and triumphed with serio
pieces which the Francoists were quick to denounce as the vision of
"amargado", of a man "embittered". It is an undeserved reputation whi
he has found difficult to shake off, in spite of the fact that his plays, as
himself has put it, "are not the attempt to find a solution to anything, t
simply seek to restate the problem with hope and compassion". E
throughout his career, in common with all those who work in the Span
independent theatre, Buero has also had to contend with extremely po
resourcing (with all the technical, administrative and artistic problems tl
this entails). It is a sad reflection on the state of the theatre in Spa
even today, that some of the best stagings of Buero plays have taken pla
outside his native land.

David Johnston
Glasgow, October 1989

FURTHER READING

It would be impossible to give anything like an exhaustive bibliography in the space available here. For further information consult Marsh Forys, *Antonio Buero Vallejo and Alfonso Sastre. An Annotated Bibliography*, London, 1988.

A. VV.: *Antonio Buero Vallejo, Premio 'Miguel de Cervantes' 1986*, Barcelona, 1987.

Borel, Jean-Paul: *El teatro de lo imposible*, Madrid, 1966.

Doménech, Ricardo: *El teatro de Buero Vallejo*, Madrid, 1969.

Estreno, 5, 1979. Special number devoted to Buero's theatre.

García Pavón, Francisco: "Introducción", Buero Vallejo, *La detonación*, Madrid 1978.

González-Cobos Dávila, Carmen: *Antonio Buero Vallejo: el hombre y su obra*, Salamanca, 1979.

Halsey, Martha, T.: *Antonio Buero Vallejo*, New York, 1973.

Iglesias Feijoo, Luis: *La trayectoria dramática de Antonio Buero Vallejo*, Santiago, 1982.

Johnston, David: "Posibles paralelos entre la obra de Unamuno y el teatro 'histórico' de Buero", *Cuadernos Hispanoamericanos*, 386, 1982, pp. 340–364.

Nicholas, Robert L.: *The tragic stages of Buero Vallejo*, N. Carolina, 1972.

Paco, Mariano de (Ed.): *Estudios sobre Buero Vallejo*, Murcia, 1884.

Paco, Mariano de (Ed.): *Buero Vallejo (Cuarenta años de teatro)*, Murcia, 1989.

Pajón Mecloy, Enrique: *Buero Vallejo y el antihéroe. Una crítica de la razón creadora*, Madrid 1986.

Pérez-Stansfield, Maria Pilar: *Direcciones del Teatro Español de Posguerra*, Madrid, 1983.

Puente Samiego, Pilar de la: *A. Buero Vallejo: Proceso a la historia de España*, Salamanca, 1989.

Ruggeri Marchetti, Magda: *Il teatro di Antonio Buero Vallejo o il processo verso la verità*, Rome 1981.

Verdú de Gregorio, Joaquín: *La luz y la oscuridad en el teatro de Buero Vallejo*, Barcelona 1977.

Antonio Buero Vallejo

INTRODUCTION

The premiere of *La detonación* in the autumn of 1977 was an event eagerly awaited by the Madrid theatre-going public. Of course, the appearance of any new play by Antonio Buero Vallejo, generally considered since 1949 to be Spain's foremost living dramatist and the spearhead of cultural resistance to Francoism, had always tended to excite a marked degree of public interest and speculation. Broadly speaking, in a country characterized by draconian restrictions on freedom of expression, Buero's theatre consistently offered Spaniards one of their few opportunities to reflect upon their own national reality, past and present. Accordingly, many people looked towards the theatre of Buero as a potent source of imagery of their political dispossession. Moreover, Buero's plays tend to approach issues of a collective nature by concentrating upon the problems of the individual so that his theatre becomes a meaningful and accessible commentary upon the most immediate difficulties arising out of everyday living. In this way, and under difficult political circumstances, Buero Vallejo has created a social theatre which focuses precisely upon the moment of personal confrontation with external circumstances and which seeks to assess, and perhaps help to galvanise, the moral force which the individual has to muster if he or she is to interact meaningfully with these circumstances. In broad terms, Buero's work is concerned both to portray and to recuperate the significance of the life of the individual in a system which preached and imposed a stifling conformism. It is for this reason that the critic Ricardo Doménech has referred to Buero as the writer who, in the climate of repression of post-Civil War Spain, has been most successful in giving "such immediate, accurate and profound expression to the existence of ordinary Spaniards and to the most hidden depths of national life".[1]

But there were other factors that autumn of 1977 which served to sharpen the sense of expectation normally aroused by any new play from the pen of Buero Vallejo. General Franco had been dead for less than two years and the country as a whole was treading a knife-edge path, poised between hopes for a democratic future and the fear of a brooding military past. It was a moment to take stock, both to re-examine national history, which had been subject to a process of Francoist revisionism and distortion, and to prepare the conditons by which Spain could develope as a modern democratic nation. *La detonación* was the first play written by Buero under these new circumstances, his first play to be produced without

having to make provision for the sluggish and unwelcome attentions of the censor's blue pencil. At this clear turning point in Spanish history, many looked to Buero as an important commentator on national affairs, a dramatist who could be relied upon to confront with integrity and intelligence the burning issues of the moment.

In the event, Buero was to produce in *La detonación* a play which, on one level, both reflects immediate events in Spain and analyses the castrating influence of censorship with a clarity which would previously have been unwise, if not impossible. Nonetheless, it still refused to take advantage of the new climate of freedom to shout to the rooftops those political home truths that clearly characterised its author's everyday experience of life in Franco's Spain. Perhaps one could have expected Buero at this time to have indulged in the kind of bluntness of expression and outspoken protest that we normally associate with agitprop drama. But Buero has never had any wish to create a theatre which is little more than a political megaphone. So, in this his first real moment of creative freedom, he chose to write a play which celebrates those artistic and intellectual virtues which are particularly necessary for any writer who seeks to circumvent the censor, but which are also the universal prerequisites of all good literature. In *La detonación*, the writer in question is Mariano José de Larra (1809–1837), the satirist who pilloried the establishment of his time in spite of the beady and, at times, dangerous surveillance of the censor, a writer whose response to the shortcomings and failures of his Spain was as immediate and implacable as Buero's own.

In choosing to focus on the life and times of Larra in this way, of course, Buero is quite clearly justifying his own stance as a writer during the Francoist years. First and foremost, by emphasising what Larra considered to be his moral obligation to produce even under the dead hand of censorship, Buero is impatiently refuting the charge that the publication of any manuscript previously submitted to the censor is tantamount to active collaboration with the régime. The tension between Larra and Clemente Díaz, which moves rapidly from the arena of cultural politics into that of a deep-rooted personal animosity, is an unequivocal version of the bitter polemic between Buero and Alfonso Sastre which polarised the Spanish theatre-world in the early nineteen sixties.[2] Faced with Sastre's declaration that he would cultivate an "impossibilist theatre" by writing plays whose refusal to compromise would render them unperformable in Spain until after the removal of political censorship, Buero replied that his work had always been, and would continue to be, "possibilist", meaning by this that he considered that the subtlety of expression required to get round the censor was not a necessary defect but a source of literary strength in

itself. The evident moral superiority of Larra over Díaz is Buero's vindication of his own "possibilist" stance, as well as an assertion that many of the acknowledged masterpieces of Spanish literature were produced under political circumstances no less difficult than those in sway in Franco's Spain.[3] In other words, Buero is describing the existence of an independent radical tradition of Spanish writers, of whom Larra is a notable representative (the seventeenth-century poet Quevedo is also mentioned in the play), a tradition from which Buero sees himself as deriving and to which he contributes.

All of this means, as Buero himself has recognised, that *La detonación* is quite possibly his most autobiographical piece of work.[4] There are many reasons why the figure of Larra should have attracted him both as a suitable vehicle for the analysis of the problems of the writer struggling against authoritarianism, and as a role model for his own position in Franco's Spain. Larra was the best prose stylist of his generation, a writer of clear intelligence and sensitivity who "adopted a critical, independent attitude towards official authority, traditional prejudices and conventional values".[5] This impressive battery of attributes he directed towards one particular end: the regeneration of his country. This is why Larra has a significance in Spanish culture which goes far beyond his purely journalistic and literary achievements. To the Spanish radical tradition he has become a symbol of resistance to the conventional values of authority, a potent voice, as Buero has Larra himself declare at several moments in the play, for those elements of national life stifled under the facade of official history, the official version of things propounded by an unchanging establishment. This "Spanish Voltaire", as Larra has been called, clearly saw the need to cut through the shams and myths of his society, to puncture with his trenchant satire the lies which maintained its power structures.[6] Moreover, the fact that Larra extends this spirit of protest against the shortcomings and failures of national life to form an attack on those who retreat from commitment to the real world into a series of totally private concerns gives his work a contemporary air which finds sympathetic echoes in many writers of the modern period.

This central notion of exposing those national and personal truths which have been overlaid by the rhetoric of authority and of personal expediency is no less important in the work of Antonio Buero Vallejo, as is quite clear from even the most cursory glance at his plays, from the first-written, *En la ardiente oscuridad (In the burning darkness)*, to the most recent, *Lázaro en el laberinto (Lazarus in the labyrinth)*. When he has Larra refer to the motor force of his work as simply the "passion for truth", Buero is also describing what we might call the central cognitive

urge of his own theatre, that is the need to disentangle the truth of life from the plausible and comfortable falsehoods woven around it. Couched in these terms, it all sounds very metaphysical. Indeed, there is a strong metaphysical strand in much of Buero's work which is, in many ways, the direct result of hi being imprisoned and condemned to death in the cruel aftermath of the Civil War. But his Larra passes over metaphysical speculation very quickly, almost impatiently, and in those final moments before suicide he recreates his life as a systematic attempt to peel away the various levels of political and moral deceit which characterised the world in which he lived.

In this way, the Larra of *La detonación* provides an unmistakeable image of Buero's essentially corrective relationship with his own society. That for Buero this is the most honest and direct response of a writer working in such circumstances is made crystal clear, in particular, through the first conversation that Larra has with Mesonero. The latter's fearful withdrawal from a clear-sighted engagement with the pressing immediacy of political circumstances, and his cultivation of what is little more than the folkloric description of social customs, is an unequivocal indictment of those writers and artists of Franco's Spain who devoted their talents to the pursuit of the "typically Spanish" – even when, in the nineteen-sixties and seventies especially, that particular product was expressed most notably through the clichéd image of national sexual frustration. In direct opposition to this insistence on the "stagey" images of national life, of "the Spain of tinpot bands and the tambourine" as the great poet Antonio Machado put it, Buero clearly intends his audience to view Larra's crusading zeal and spirit of protest as the only meaningful public voice that literature can raise in times of oppression. So much so that through the use of masks he transforms what we might call Larra's ethic of exposure, which lies at the heart of all worthwhile satire, into one of the defining scenic elements of the play. The mask, a sign of the falseness and hypocrisy of the world, was central to one of Larra's most powerful pieces, the article entitled "All the world's a mask", which was published in March 1833, a small fragment of which Buero incorporates bodily into the text of his play. Ostensibly a Mesonero-like piece in that it describes the masked ball which is traditionally held in Madrid at Carnival time, the article is principally concerned to "disenchant", as Larra himself writes, to present the mask not as an occasional source of innocent diversion but as the symbol of a society constantly avoiding its own truth.

Apart from its undeniable theatrical effectiveness, the mask is a symbol which works on a variety of levels. On one hand, it alludes to the social roles and types into which people comfortably tend to slot, behind

which they are content to conceal their individual identity – in this sense, it is a variation on the theme of the uniform, which Buero also exploits, in Brechtian fashion, to suggest the fundamental sameness of all the men of power who make their brief appearances in the play. Clearly related to this is the sense that the mask enables human beings to be dishonest not only with each other but also with themselves. In this way the mask is a pyschosocial motif which illustrates, in the most graphic manner, the divorce between truth and the lie in both the community and individual life. In particular, in the highly self-conscious world of Madrid café-life – above all in a café where, as Buero's Larra remarks, all of Spain is present in miniature – the mask is a symbol both of the posturing which obviates the need to concern oneself genuinely with issues and of the hypocrisy which allows people to dissimulate responses which are simply unfashionable. Finally, the masks lend a hallucinatory quality to the play which is wholly appropriate to the intensity of Larra's last few moments on earth and to the fact that everything that happens on stage takes place inside the theatre of his fevered consciousness. It is perhaps important to note here that all those elements that seem deliberately theatrical – the carefully contrived changes of lighting, confusions of historical chronology, the rich interweaving of dream and apparent reality, of memories that are both recreated and imagined – are in fact the result of the spectator being plunged wholly into the reeling mind of the man who is about to take his own life.[7]

Running just beneath the surface of Larra's sociopolitical intentions (which I have referred to as the public voice of his work), there is a clearly defined subjective element. In his important article "All Souls' Day, 1836", which once again Buero adapts to fine dramatic effect in the play, Larra depicts himself as wandering through the cemetery of national life. He notes finally:

> I was filled with a violent urge to leave that horrible
> cemetery. I sought refuge in my own heart, filled of late
> with life, dreams, desires. God in Heaven! Just another
> cemetery. My heart is but another grave. What is written there?
> Let us read it. Who has died here? Terrible words. *Here lies*
> *hope!* Silence, silence!

It is this note of personal anguish, especially when considered in conjunction with his three tormented love affairs, all of which Buero makes reference to in *La detonación*, and his subsequent suicide, which has given Larra the posthumous reputation of being the quintessential romantic. It is temptingly easy to see Larra as the victim of his own depressive nature and emotional instability, and this view is still not uncommon among both

critics and the general public. It is a view which in the words of Juan Luis Alborg has "motivated many glosses in the pages of high-flown and easy literature... It could be said that Larra was a romantic in some of his attitudes towards life, attitudes which can be reduced virtually to the anecdotal, but he was a great deal less so, in fact hardly at all, in the deepest roots of his thought".[8]

These words reflect the spirit of Buero's recreation of Larra. Although the dramatist is concerned to depict his character as very much a creature of his times, the romanticism of Buero's Larra is rarely more than an attention to appearance, an awareness of fashion. Much more romantic in his attitudes is Larra's friend, the poet Espronceda, and Buero is very careful to show how his political efficacy is seriously eroded by a juvenile impulsiveness. Moreover, at the moment at which Larra's feelings might be expected to be at a pitch of intensity, just when his mistress has finally left him and only the option of suicide remains open, Buero's Larra is suddenly invaded by a terrible clarity of vision, the *sang-froid* that comes in the wake of accepting the inevitable. His warning to Dolores Armijo that "if some day you hear that Larra killed himself, don't think he did it for love, but because... everything is impossible" is Buero's attempt to redress the balance, to show Larra as a victim not of his own romanticism, but of the nightmare of Spanish history.

In this way *La detonación* is fired by a clear desire to recuperate Larra as a leading figure in the Spanish tradition of radical protest, to show, by implication, that any attempt to disinherit him from his real political significance is in itself a politically-loaded attitude. On one hand, Larra's liberalism, an ethical and political constant in his thought, clearly characterises him as a direct inheritor of the values of the European Enlightenment which had made a late entry into Spain during the reign of Carlos III (1759–88), the so-called "reformers' king". In this way, *La detonación*, in common with *Un soñador para un pueblo (A dreamer for a people)*, 1958, and *El sueño de la razón (The sleep of reason)*, 1970, which deal with Carlos III's pugnacious minister, Esquilache, and Goya respectively, marks Buero's celebration of those enlightened values which have sought throughout history to protect Spain from its own darker nature.

But on the other hand, Buero is too consummate a playwright to present Larra as a simple embodiment of certain political attitudes. Although he is certainly impatient with the charge that Larra's claim to be considered an important commentator on Spanish affairs has been seriously undermined by rampant romanticism, he certainly does not seek to blur the various internal contradictions and tensions which conformed Larra's

difficult personality and which make of him such a fascinating object of study, dramatic or otherwise.[9] At the end of the play, Larra becomes aware that he too has been wearing a mask, as has in fact been hinted throughout by constant reference to the various *noms de plume* which he has used during his career and which cannot simply be explained away by reference to censorship. It is certainly true that Buero highlights what might be considered elements of specifically left-wing ideology in Larra's political make-up, especially in his concept of the role of the proletariate and his passionate defence of their periodic outbursts of political violence, and in his analysis of the shortcomings of the redistribution of land carried out in the wake of Mendizabal's historic legislation confiscating the assets and properties of the Church. In doing so, Buero is concerned to stress both the modernity of Larra's political analysis and the pedigree of the radical tradition, but he does not hesitate either to show that Larra's leftist defence of popular sovreignty co-exists uneasily with a more elitist strand of thought. Whilst rejecting Mesonero's view of the "rabble" as being both morally and politically objectionable, he is still capable of describing his servant Pedro as being a typical product of ignorance whose needs and responses rarely transcend those of an animal.

It may well be, as the writer Francisco Umbral has suggested in a characteristically provocative study, that the essence of Larra's romanticism lies in the embracing of these apparently irreconcilable contradictions.[10] Even so, the pessimism which leads to Larra's suicide is not a version of the organic style of despair that burgeoned from romantic roots to flower throughout the nineteenth-century. In Buero Vallejo's view, at least, Larra's suicide is the result of the discovery that the hollowness of the world and the hypocritical sham of its ways are duplicated wholly within the private world of men and women, even among those whom he had considered his most intimate friends. This is what he means when he says to Dolores, just before she takes her final leave of him, that "Perhaps it's still too soon. We can't be real men and women. Not yet. Maybe one day...". Moreover, after the crucial conversation with Pedro which occupies a significant portion of the Second Part, his own sense of integrity has led him to the inescapable conclusion that the liberal class, whose stamp he bears and whose emotional and intellectual sufferings and frustrations he has embraced, is completely out of touch with the reality of the existence of the vast majority of ordinary Spaniards. All of his life, perhaps from an undeniably paternalistic standpoint, he has sought to speak for those denied a voice. Now he has learnt that he is part of the problem (a suspicion which, as we see from the dream in which he participates in the firing squad, he has long harboured.)

It may well be, if we decide to look for autobiographical elements in the play, that Buero is here casting a critical eye on the limitations of the role that any writer can play in the unfolding of any historical process. Be that as it may, it is to Pedro's final speech, which comes as a sort of epilogue to the young writer's delirium – in fact, it takes place over thirty-five years after the death of Larra – to which we must turn our attention in order to understand the important lessons of this suicide. Couched in these terms, the scene might sound drily didactic. Nothing could be farther from the truth. The whole suicide scene intensifies in a quickening, exquisitely choreographed, rhythm of bitter remembrance as Buero attributes blame for Larra's death in the most graphic and dramatic way possible, reaching its inevitable climax immediately before the forceful final speech of Pedro. In short, it is a remarkable dramatic tour-de-force which is designed not solely to move the spectator, but also to clarify the sources of hope and despair which have formed the basic poles of Larra's experience throughout the play.

Pedro is an extremely enigmatic figure. At times he has acted as the voice of Larra's growing popular consciousness, at others he has been part and parcel of both the intense sufferings and violent reactions of the ordinary people, and at others he has been nothing more than Larra's personal servant. This confusion of roles is entirely appropriate to the dream-like nature of Larra's recreation of his past. But the scene in which the writer asks his servant to speak to him "as if I were your son" is of special significance because it is here that Larra undergoes a sort of re-birth through his sudden initiation into a world of experience hitherto closed to him. Therefore, it is quite plausible that his remembering of things past should be coloured by the perceptions of a conversation which marks a key moment in his intellectual and emotional development. If Larra's actual father was responsible for bringing up his son in the ways of bourgeois liberalism, then Pedro is the catalyst which brings home to the writer the real nature of life for the dispossessed. Miguel de Unamuno, the writer and philosopher who died in 1936 just as the Civil War was flaring, another significant contributor to the radical Spanish tradition and a wholehearted admirer of Larra's work, would have had little problem in seeing Pedro as the voice of what he called the "eternal people". Very briefly, by this he meant the continuing presence of the ordinary people of the country underneath the surface of an official and frequently hostile history, just like the sunless depths of the sea moving silently under the waves.

Through Pedro, Larra has been afforded an unusual insight into those depths. But he has been unable to assimilate the lesson of "unending

endurance" which the metaphor suggests and which Pedro, especially after his horrific ordeal at the hands of General Cabrera, certainly embodies. In his dual role at the end of the play, as both *vox populi* and that part of Larra's conscience which had convinced him of the bad faith of the liberal bourgeoisie, Pedro's words, spoken directly to the audience, are clearly geared towards the galvanising of a popular consciousness. The final scenic image of the work is a very powerful one, both in terms of its staging and in its range of meanings. Pedro's call to the ordinary people of Spain to re-awaken to their historical and political potential is, in part, a way of redeeming Larra's suicide. This is reinforced by the re-appearance of the figure of the writer, standing with the gun pressed eternally to his forehead, as a particularly powerful reminder of the terrible consequences of this young man's confrontation with the most negative forces of Spanish history. Taken together, Pedro's words and the "pale statue" of the suicide, provide a final and fitting image of the need to awaken from the nightmare of national history.

Most serious historical drama is, of course, as much a comment on the times in which the play was actually written as on the times in which it is set. Much of the real skill of the historical dramatist, therefore, lies in locating a moment in history which can be seen as embodying important lessons for a contemporary audience. In the broadest of terms, the era in which Larra's life unfolded and the period in which Buero actually wrote and performed *La detonación* can be held to be two turning points in modern Spanish history. During the twenty-seven years of Larra's short life, between 1809 and 1837, and especially in the so-called "ominous decade" of 1823 to 1833, Spain wavered between brutal oppression and frustrated liberal attempts, set against a backdrop of virtual civil war, to modernise a country which was already becoming an anachronism in Europe. The parallel with 1977 is not difficult to establish. Just as the writers in the café in the play are engaged in a constant debate between the commitment to new freedoms and a yearning nostalgia for authoritarian discipline and absolutism, so Spain in 1977 was in the melting-pot of democracy and dictatorship.

Written, then, in the year in which Spain held its first free elections since 1936, *La detonación* is, first and foremost, a play which warns that the quality of the country's future is directly dependent upon the democratic quality of its structures and institutions. More importantly, it reminds its audience that, in the final analysis, both moral sovreignty and political power are vested in the people, and that any attempt to inhibit the path towards democratic reform is ultimately doomed to failure. Within the framework of this broad-based parallel, Buero presents a skilful

analysis of specific aspects of the period of transition to which the Spanish people suddenly awoke on the death of Franco. As one must expect, given the political convictions of Buero himself, this analysis is very much geared towards the Spanish left. On one level, the dramatist is sounding a warning through the suicide of Larra that the traditional Spanish right is still very much a force to be reckoned with. Father Froilán's nostalgia for hardline authoritarianism, expressed as "Life was better under Fernando Vll", is an immediately recognisable version of the slogan "Life was better under Franco" which became -and perhaps still is – a rallying call for those dissatisfied with Spain's rapid transition towards full democracy. The venom which Father Froilán displays in his last speech was Buero's way of reminding his audience that the forces ranged against democratic Spain must be taken seriously, no matter how outmoded or superficially comic they might appear. History was to prove him right when Father Froilán's brand of nostalgia and dissatisfaction boiled over into the attempted coup d'état of 1981, (shortly after Buero had sounded a similar warning in his *Jueces en la noche (Judges in the night)* in 1979).

On another level, we can see in *La detonación* an important echo of the warning, given as early in 1962 in the masterly *El concierto de San Ovidio (The concert at Saint Ovide)*, that liberty is not an ultimate value in itself but is simply the starting point, the base from which other values may flourish. Obviously, this is not to be taken as a cut and dried rejection of liberalism. But its limitations are certainly exposed, especially through the figures of the two most apparently liberal Prime Ministers who appear in the play, Mendizábal and Istúriz. Their attempts to regenerate the nation are shown to be limited to the injection of life into the stagnant economy, whilst they ignore the injustices which are still deeply ingrained in the life of the common people. In 1977, therefore, Buero was clearly calling for the creation of a system which could be both effective and just. The extent to which that call has been listened to is still very much under debate in the democratic Spain which is now shaping itself for the twenty-first century.

Finally, in the confused swirl of events of 1977, when the shadow of the past continued to loom large and the future still seemed distant and vulnerable, Buero is counselling the Spanish left to be both patient and resilient. This can be understood in two ways. Firstly, the dramatist is underlining the need not to lose heart, as did Larra, in the face of disappointment and deceit. In similar circumstances, one hundred and forty years earlier, this young writer had blown out his brains in despair, convinced that any qualitative change in human affairs was impossible. When Pedro confirms to the audience that Larra "died because he was

impatient", he is subtly urging the Spanish left not to commit political, indeed historical, suicide. It was impatience, not romanticism, which was the principal defect of the young writer, the tragic flaw which caused this hero to succomb in his unequal struggle with the forces of inertia and dissimulation that were ranged against him. In a sense, Buero had already foreseen the wave of disillusion which would follow in the wake of freedom, and his own unease as to the moral rectitude of the new politicians who would emerge from the shadows of exile and clandestine opposition to take the reins of the new Spain is reflected in Larra's disenchantment with apparently radical leaders like Mendizábal and Istúriz. Secondly, in the face of an entrenched and still powerful right-wing, the dramatist is echoing Larra's warning to Espronceda not to destabilise an already delicate situation by acting in an unnecessarily provocative manner. In this case, patience can be equated to prudence, a necessary virtue which, in the event, was in great part responsible for Spain's remarkably smooth transition from dictatorship to democracy. In this way the play sounds a double warning. On one hand, it is a message to the Spanish left that betrayal is always on the cards and that only great coherence of resolve and moral organisation can prevent an historical suicide. On the other hand, it is a call to the Spanish people to protect their real interests amidst all the confusion of change, to remind them that social justice is not necessarily synonymous with freedom.

La detonación, then, is the fruit of Buero Vallejo's considered analysis of the most recent turning point in Spanish history, a play which both highlights the possible pitfalls and dangers that still remain to be negotiated, and which emphasises a hope central to all of Buero's theatre, namely that change and growth are ever-present possibilities in human life. But it is also a play which transcends its immediate Spanish context. The characters, who in themselves form a rich pageant of Madrid life in the first third of the nineteenth-century, also represent divergent, at times conflicting, attitudes to the major forces which determine the personal and political quality of life in any society. The constant flux of freedom and oppression, the dynamic backdrop against which the nightmare vision of Larra's life is projected, is a reminder to any audience that neither is an immutable reality, and that the never-ending struggle for one and the defiance of the other are two sides of the same coin, the very difficult business of being human in an inhuman world.

David Johnston
Madrid/Glasgow, March/April 1989.

NOTES
TO THE INTRODUCTION

1. Ricardo Doménech, *El teatro de Buero Vallejo,* Madrid, 1973, p.62.

2. The full text of Buero's *"Obligada precisión acerca del 'imposibilismo'"* can be found in *Primer Acto,* no.15, 1960, pp.1–6.

3. See Buero's important article *"De mi teatro",* in *Romanistisches Jahrbuch,* no.30, 1979, pp.217–227.

4. See the interview with José Luis Vicente Mosquete, published in *Antonio Buero Vallejo. Premio Miguel de Cervantes [1986],* p.53. This is the official catalogue to the exhibition organised by the Spanish Ministry of Culture in recognition of the award of the Cervantes Prize to Buero in 1986.

5. D. Marín Molina, Introduction to *Larra, Artículos Escogidos,* London, 1958, p.32.

6. For one critic, Larra represents the spirit of eighteenth-century France transferred into Spain. See José R. Lomba y Pedraja, *Mariano José de Larra. Cuatro estudios que le abordan o le bordean,* Madrid, 1936.

7. For a general treatment of this innovative aspect of Buero's theatre, see Victor Dixon, "The 'immersion-effect' in the plays of Antonio Buero Vallejo", in *Drama and Mimesis,* Cambridge, 1980, pp.113–137.

8. Juan Luis Alborg, *Historia de la Literatura Española,* vol.4, Madrid, 1980, p.216.

9. Especially interesting is Paul Ilie's "Larra's Nightmare", *Revista Hispánica Moderna,* XXXVIII, 1974–5, pp.153–66.

10. Francisco Umbral, *Larra. Anatomía de un dandy,* Madrid, 1965, pp.27–8.

THE SHOT

(*La detonación*)

This play received its première on the 20th September, 1977, in the
Teatro Bellas Artes, Madrid.

Mariano José de Larra - the only known portrait
Museo Romántico, Madrid (Photo, courtesy José Luis Antigüedad)

Cast List

Mariano José de Larra (27 years old)

Pedro (his servant, 39 years old)

Don Mariano de Larra (50 years old)
Brigadier Nogueras (45 years old)

Don Homobono (45 years old)

Calomarde (52 years old)
Cea Bermúdez (50 years old)
Martínez de la Rosa (50 years old)
Mendizábal (50 years old)
Istúriz (52 years old)
Calatrava (56 years old)

Royalist Volunteer #1
Militiaman #1
[Assailant #1]

Royalist Volunteer #2
Militiaman #2
[Assailant #2]

Mesonero Romanos (34 years old)

Ventura de la Vega (29 years old)

Bretón de los Herreros (40 years old)

Clemente Díaz (25 years old)

Carnerero (45 years old)
Borrego (40 years old)

Arriaza (57 years old)

Grimaldi (40 years old)

Father Froilán (50 years old)

Pepita Wetoret (20 years old)
Dolores Armijo (26 years old)

Pipí (waiter, 30 years old)

José María Cambronero (34 years old)
General Cabrera (35 years old)

Father Gallego (60 years old)

José de Espronceda (28 years old)

Juanín (14 years old)

María Griñó (60 years old)

[Priest of the Order of Mercy]

[Dominican Priest]

[Jesuit Priest]

[Assailant # 3]

[Assailant # 4]

[Captain Cristino]

Voices of Adelita, Pepita's mother
and María Manuela

Grouped characters were played by the same actor in the 1977 production. Those characters in square brackets were suppressed in that production in response to the pressures of running time imposed by the twice-nightly performance system which Madrid theatres still insist upon using.

Right and left correspond to those of the audience.

All of Larra's speeches which appear between inverted commas are taken from his original writings. Several other speeches, similarly indicated but attributed to other characters, are also taken from original sources.

The Spanish text of *La detonación* reproduced here has been completely revised and checked by Antonio Buero Vallejo expressly for this edition.

EL DECORADO

Un gabinete, un café, la antecámara de un ministro, su despacho, el rincón de otra sala, la calle, las afueras y el campo, son los lugares que en esta fantasía se suscitan esquemáticamente, a veces de modo simultáneo. Su disposición respectiva puede variar mucho según el espacio disponible. Si imaginamos un escenario habitual, pero de gran anchura, el decorado podría ser como el que a continuación se describe.

La escena se dividiría en tres zonas principales. La más amplia, casi central, si bien un tanto corrida hacia la izquierda, sugiere el gabinete del piso que ocupó Mariano José de Larra en la Calle de Santa Clara, número 3. Tal vez elevado su suelo por un peldaño, su perímetro avanza en gran parte hacia el proscenio, aunque dejando sitio suficiente para el cruce de personajes. La disposición de esta salita es simple: en el primer término derecho, un fino velador sobre el que brilla el plateado servicio de café y chocolate. Junto a él, dos sillas forradas de seda. La pared del fondo carece de esquinas y se pierde, tanto en los laterales como en la altura. En su centro hay una chimenea cuya repisa sostiene dos candelabros, dos floreros de cristal cuajados de claveles, un reloj, un apagavelas y un frasquito de esencia. Encima cuelga el espejo o *tremor* corriente en los interiores burgueses de la época. A la derecha de la chimenea, doble puerta de cristales esmerilados, y a la izquierda, el menudo bufete de caoba donde el escritor tiene sus papeles. En el centro de su cuerpo superior descansa un estuche de madera amarilla y a la derecha de éste, un quinqué. Algo sesgado y ante este escritorio, el sillón de badana verde. No hay paredes laterales en el gabinete. Las sustituyen en parte dos gradas algo oblicuas que avanzan hasta la mitad de la estancia. Entre ellas y la pared del fondo, dos huecos laterales. Estas dos escaleras conducen a la parte superior de las otras dos zonas del escenario: dos bloques más retrasados que el borde anterior del suelo del gabinete, cuyos muros frontales, no obstante hallarse separados por éste, pertenecen al mismo lugar. Trátase de aquel destartalado Café del Príncipe al que el humor romántico llamó *El Parnasillo*. El bloque de la izquierda no es muy elevado: quizá su altura no alcance a la de un hombre en pie. Por la izquierda se pierde en el lateral; su derecha la dibuja oblicuamente la escalera que, desde el gabinete, conduce a su parte superior. Adosados a este muro frontal, dos quinqués de petróleo, y, delante, dos o tres toscas mesitas pintadas de chocolate, con sillas de Vitoria a su alrededor. A lo

THE SET

A study, a café, a minister's anteroom and office, the corner of another room, a street, the city outskirts and open country, form the areas of action in which this fantasy takes place. They are presented schematically, at times simultaneously. The relationship between these areas may vary considerably depending on the scenic space available. If we imagine a stage of normal depth, but perhaps of greater breadth, the   set might well resemble the one described as follows.

The stage is divided into three main areas. The largest of these, occupying more or less stage-centre, although perhaps lying slightly to the left, suggests the study of Larra's apartment at no.3 Calle de Santa Clara, Madrid.[1] The floor here is perhaps one step high, its edge jutting out towards the apron of the stage, although sufficient space must be left to enable characters to cross freely. The lay-out of this room is simple: in the foreground, to the right, an elegant occasional table upon which shines a silver coffee and chocolate service. Beside this, two silk-covered chairs. The back wall is totally flat and stretches into the darkness, both upwards and across. In the centre of the wall there is a fireplace upon whose mantlepiece rest two candelabra, two crystal vases filled with carnations, a clock, a candle-snuffer and a small bottle of essence. Above it hangs a mirror, the so-called *shimmer* then fashionable in the salons of the bourgeoisie. To the right-hand side of the fireplace, a double frosted-glass door, and to the left, the slim mahogany bureau in which the writer keeps his papers. Resting upon this, in the centre, is a yellow wooden box, and to the right of this, an oil lamp. At an angle to, and in front of, this writing desk sits a green leather armchair. The study has no side walls. In their place there are two angled sets of steps which stretch almost into the centre of the room. Two gaps are formed at the side between the back wall and these stairs, which lead to the two other principal areas of action. These are made up of two rostra which lie behind the front line of the study and whose facing walls, although separated by the room itself, are clearly those of just one location - the rather rundown Café del Príncipe, dubbed *Little Parnassus* by the Romantic wits of the day.[2] The left-hand rostrum is not particularly high, perhaps reaching slightly less than head height. On the left it stretches into darkness; its right-hand side is obliquely delimited by the stairs which lead from the study to its upper level. Two oil lamps rest against this facing wall, in front of which sit two or three small but rough tables of a chocolate brown colour, surrounded by

alto del bloque se puede acceder también por gradas invisibles. En su breve superficie, dos sillas de estilo, y junto a su borde posterior, un piano con su taburete. No hay paredes; en el fondo y a cierta distancia síguese viendo el muro del saloncito de Larra. El bloque de la derecha, más elevado y complejo, tiene asimismo su muro frontal oblicuamente cortado por las gradas que conducen a sus alturas, y en él se divisa otro quinqué idéntico a los de la izquierda. Delante, otro par de mesitas achocolatadas con sus correspondientes sillas. Este bloque es más ancho que el izquierdo, pues a su derecha forma un saliente que se acerca al proscenio cobijando en parte las mesitas, y en cuya cara frontal se abre la no muy limpia puerta vidriera del café, con su ventilador de hojalata. Sobre este primer cuerpo del bloque álzase otro más estrecho y de menguada altura. Aparte de su acceso oculto, se llega a él por una corta escalerilla, que sube oblicuamente a su izquierda casi como una continuación de la grada derecha del gabinete central. Un breve espacio entre ambas permite bordear el primer cuerpo y llegar hasta el saliente, sobre el cual hay sitio suficiente para una pequeña mesa de trabajo colmada de manuscritos y papeles y una silla; ambos muebles de perfil al proscenio. La ornamentación del alto zócalo del segundo cuerpo sugiere suntuosidad oficial. Lujosamente alfombrada, su superficie superior parece pertenecer a un saloncito de recibo. Cerca del borde anterior hay un sillón y al fondo un sofá pequeño, ambos de costosa talla. En el gran muro del fondo que abarca la escena se percibe durante casi toda la acción una misma transparencia.

PARTE PRIMERA

(Oscuridad. Amortiguados por la distancia, sordos cañonazos y crepitar de fusilería que adquieren intensidad. El quinqué del bufete y la chimenea se encienden solos lentamente. La vaga silueta de un criado prende las velas de los candelabros y desaparece después por el hueco posterior del lado derecho. La luz general se eleva en el gabinete; el resto de la escena permanece oscuro. Continúan los disparos. En el centro del aposento y con los ojos fijos en la puerta, un joven bajo y delgado, de levita azul con cuello de terciopelo negro. Cuando se vuelve hacia el frente, destellan el dorado tisú de su chaleco y el albor de su cuello de nipis sobre el negro corbatón. En su mano izquierda brilla la piedra de una sortija. Atrozmente pálido y ojeroso, el rostro de este mozo de

small wooden seats. On top of the rostrum, which can also be reached by means of an invisible staircase, are two elegant chairs and, near the back edge, a piano and stool. There are no walls; some way behind the rostrum can be seen the continuation of the wall of Larra's room. The facing wall of the right-hand rostrum, which is both higher and more complex than the left-hand one, is also cut diagonally by the stairway which leads to its upper level. An oil lamp, identical to those on the left, rests against it. In front sit another couple of chocolate brown tables with their corresponding chairs. This rostrum is wider than the other one because its right-hand side juts out towards the proscenium, partly enclosing the tables as it does so. The somewhat less than scrupulously clean glass door into the café, with its tin ventilator, is situated in the front wall of this projection. On top of this first section of the rostrum stands another, narrower and of reduced height. It is reached, apart from via a hidden access, by means of a short stairway which rises diagonally to its left-hand side as though a continuation of the steps rising from the ground floor of the study. A small gap between both stairways enables the first section to be skirted, thereby giving access to the extension. The extension must be spacious enough to hold a small desk, piled high with manuscripts and papers, and a chair; both items of furniture are side-on to the proscenium. The ornamental cornice of the second section suggests the opulence of officialdom. Luxuriously carpeted, its upper surface appears to be that of a small reception room. Near its front edge is an armchair and, towards the rear, a small settee, both exquisitely carved. The huge back wall which closes off the entire stage bears a single motif projected during virtually the whole action.

FIRST PART

(*Darkness. Muffled by distance, dull cannon shot and the crackle of gunfire which grow in intensity. The oil lamp on top of the bureau and the fire in the study slowly begin to glow of their own accord. The shadowy figure of a servant lights the candles in the candelabra before disappearing through the gap on the right. The general lighting in the study grows; the rest of the stage remains in darkness. The shooting continues. In the centre of the room, his eyes fixed on the door, stands a young man, short, slim, wearing a blue frock coat with a black velvet collar. As he turns to the front the gold material of his waistcoat and the whiteness of his stiff collar glisten against his black cravat. A ring set with a precious stone gleams on his hand. The face of this young man,*

veintiocho años aún no cumplidos es el del desdichado que responde al
nombre de *MARIANO JOSÉ DE LARRA;* una curiosa fisonomía de
rasgos aniñados, tersas mejillas y gruesos labios todavía no trabajados por
la madurez, alta frente y ojos penetrantes sin la menor arruga en los que
se agazapa, sin embargo, el enigmático cansancio de un anciano.   La
mosca bajo el labio se une a la sedosa y endrina barbita de collarín; el
breve pero grueso bigote, que no llega a unirse con la barba, resalta la
sensualidad de la boca.   El aparente desaliño romántico de su negra
cabellera está muy estudiado: ayudados por el cosmético para evitar la
expansión lateral de la melena que otros escritores ostentan, los mechones
de las sienes avanzan bien pegados y el gran tupé, minuciosamente vuelto
hacia arriba, intenta acaso ayudar a la apariencia de una estatura mayor
de la que su dueño posee realmente.   Por un momento, LARRA humilla la
cabeza y cierra los párpados.   El ruido de las descargas se amortigua.   En
el muro del fondo se transparenta poco a poco el inmenso firmamento
negro y estrellado que acompañará todo el delirio del suicida, aunque, en
ocasiones, otras luces lo hagan palidecer.   La atormentada cabeza se
yergue con resolución y el lejano fragor bélico cesa bruscamente.   Silencio
total.   El escritor gira y se acerca a la chimenea.   Toma el apagavelas de
metal y, una tras otra, mata las luces de los candelabros.   Deja el
apagador y mira la caja amarilla.   Saca una llavecita de su chaleco
mientras se aproxima al bufete y la introduce en la diminuta cerradura
plateada del estuche.   Algo nota de repente y retira aprisa la llavecita
mirando hacia la puerta.   Abrese ésta muy despacio y entra PEDRO: un
criado que no llega a los cuarenta años, pero cuyo recio semblante
aldeano, ajado por las arrugas, parece más viejo.   Su atuendo, discreto y
sobrio, es propio de un sirviente de confianza.   Al reparar en la actitud
de su señor le observa un instante y cierra despacio la puerta sin dejar de
mirarlo.)

LARRA.   ¿Qué quieres?
PEDRO.   (*Habla con extraña lentitud.*)   A...de...il...ta...de...sea...
dar...le...las...bue...nas...no...ches...
LARRA.   ¿Por qué hablas tan despacio?
PEDRO.   Per...do...ne...Es...el...se...ñor...quien...ha...bla...
muy...de...pri...sa...
LARRA.   Te he dicho que acompañes a las señoras hasta el portal.
PEDRO.   Es...que...A...de...li...ta...   (*Se oye la voz de una niña*

not yet turned twenty-eight, is dreadfully pale and his eyes are darkly ringed. This is the face of the unhappy being who answers to the name MARIANO JOSÉ DE LARRA. It is a face which combines in a curious way certain immature, almost childlike features -smooth cheeks and full lips not yet hardened by age, a high forehead and penetrating eyes, all without a single wrinkle- with the enigmatic weariness of an old man. The tiny tuft of hair under his lip joins the silky black narrow beard which runs along the line of his jaw; the short but thick moustache, which is separate from the beard, emphasises the sensuality of the mouth. The romantic disarray of his black hair has been carefully contrived: he has used various cosmetics to prevent his hair from thickening into the mane favoured by other writers and to plaster down two quiffs to either side of his forehead. The large wave at the front of his hair is carefully turned upwards, intending perhaps to lend its wearer greater height than he in fact possesses. For an instant LARRA bows his head and closes his eyes. The sound of shooting grows muffled. Onto the back wall is gradually projected the vast black star-studded sky which is continually present throughout the suicide's delirium,[3] although occasionally other lighting states may cause it to fade. He raises his troubled head resolutely, and the distant tumult of war suddenly ceases. Total silence. The writer turns round and walks to the fireplace. He lifts the candle-snuffer and, one by one, extinguishes the lights in the candelabra. He puts down the snuffer and looks at the yellow box. He goes over to the bureau, taking a small key from his waistcoat as he does so, and inserts it into the box's tiny silver-plated lock. He suddenly becomes aware of something and quickly withdraws the key, looking towards the door. It opens slowly and PEDRO enters: a servant who has not yet reached forty, but whose strong country face, heavily lined, makes him seem older. His discreet and sober dress is proper to that of a confidential servant. Upon noticing his master's stance he pauses for a second to observe him, then slowly shuts the door, watching him constantly.)

LARRA: What is it?
PEDRO (*Speaking in an unnaturally slow way.*): A...de...li...ta ... wo...uld... like... to... say... go...od... night..., sir...
LARRA: Why are you speaking so slowly?
PEDRO: For...give... me,... but... it... is... you,... sir,... who... are... spea...king... ve...ry... fast.
LARRA: I asked you to see the ladies to the door.
PEDRO: It'...s... just... that... A...de...li...ta...(*The voice of a girl*

de cuatro o cinco años trás de la puerta.)

ADELITA. (*Su voz.*) Pa...pá...¿pue...do...dar...te...un...be...so...?

LARRA. (*Sombrío.*) ¿Por qué habla como tú?

PEDRO. (*Sorprendido.*) ¿Co...mo...yo?

LARRA. (*Desvía la vista.*) Dile a Adelita que estoy muy cansado. (*PEDRO lo mira, perplejo, y abre despacio la puerta, que vuelve a cerrarse tras su lenta salida. LARRA cierra los ojos, se pasa la mano por la frente y se acerca al estuche. Lo abre y saca de él una pistola de dos cañones, que examina. Se oye su voz, aunque él no despega los labios.*)

LARRA. (*Su voz.*) No fallará. Unos instantes... y la paz. No otra cosa: este mundo es demasiado horrible para atribuírselo a un Autor bondadoso. Veintisiete años... como un siglo. Tengo bastante. (*Levanta un poco la pistola.*) Demasiado pesados... Me aplastan. ¿Será porque ya soy un moribundo? El que va a morir lo recuerda todo en un momento. Eso dicen... (*Se adelanta hacia el frente.*) El criado hablaba despacio. También Adelita. Era yo quien hablaba aprisa. Mi mente ha entrado ya en la carrera final. (*La voz baja su tono.*) ¡Y no quiero, me niego a recordar! (*Durante estas palabras el quinqué se apaga solo y la luz que ilumina a LARRA se reduce hasta dejar visible solamente la palidez de yeso de su cara. Los oscuros cristales de la puerta se iluminan con un lento destello.*)

ADELITA. (*Su voz, sobre la extraña claridad.*) Pa...pá...¿pue... do...en...trar...? (*Los cristales vuelven a oscurecerse.*)

LARRA. (*Su voz.*) Perdóname tú.

ADELITA. (*Su voz.*) Pa...pá... (*La puerta se aclara y oscurece de nuevo.*)

LARRA. (*Su voz.*) ¿Es mi voz? ¿No llamaba yo así, en mi soledad infantil del internado de Burdeos?

ADELITA. (*Su voz, sobre el efecto luminoso que se repite.*) Pa... pá...

LARRA. (*Su voz atribulada, al mismo tiempo.*) Pa...pá... (*Una irreal claridad creció en el gabinete. Entre la escalera izquierda y el muro del fondo se proyecta un foco de fría luz. Por el hueco entra una figura enmascarada. LARRA deja la pistola sobre el velador y habla con su boca.*)

LARRA. Pa...pá... (*Se vuelve hacia la figura que se acerca: un hombre maduro, de levita gris y alto sombrero de copa, que se descubre en silencio. La media careta que lleva muestra cejas altivas, ojos de fuego.*)

D. MARIANO. ¿Quieres dejarnos?

of about four or five years of age is heard from behind the door.)
ADELITA (*Off.*): Pa...pa..., can...I...kiss...you...go...od...ni...ght?
LARRA (*Sombrely.*): Why is she speaking like you?
PEDRO (*With surprise.*): Like... me...?
LARRA (*Looking away.*): Tell Adelita I'm very tired. (*PEDRO looks at him, perplexed, and then slowly leaves the room, opening and closing the door slowly as he does so. LARRA closes his eyes, passes his hand over his brow and goes to the box. He opens it and takes out a double-barrelled pistol, which he examines closely. His voice is heard, although his lips do not actually move.*)
LARRA (*Voice off.*): There will be no mistake. A few seconds... and then peace. Peace and nothing else. This world is too full of horror to be the work of any benign Creator. Twenty-seven years... like a century. Enough to have lived. (*He raises the pistol slightly.*) They weigh so heavy... Crushing me down. Perhaps it's because I'm about to die. Your whole life flashes past in an instant. That's what they say... (*He walks forward.*) My servant was speaking slowly. So was Adelita. But it was really me who was speaking fast. My mind is galloping towards the final moment. (*In a lower tone.*) And I don't want to! I refuse to remember! (*In the course of this speech the lamp goes out on its own and the light falling on LARRA dims to the extent that only the chalky pallor of his face can be seen. The dark glass panels in the door slowly begin to gleam.*)
ADELITA (*Voice off, above the strange glow.*): Pa...pa..., may... I... come... in...? (*The glass panels grow dark again.*).
LARRA (*Voice off.*): I'm so sorry, my little one.
ADELITA (*Voice off.*): Pa...pa... (*The door lights up and then grows dark again.*)
LARRA (*Voice off.*): Is that my voice? Didn't I use to call out like that, small and lonely, when they sent me to school in Bordeaux?[4]
ADELITA (*Voice off, as the same lighting effect is repeated.*): Pa...pa...
LARRA (*Voice off, simultaneously, sounding distressed.*): Pa...pa... (*An unreal quality of light grows in the study. A single cold light is projected between the left-hand staircase and the back wall. A masked figure appears through the gap. LARRA puts the pistol down upon the occasional table and speaks.*)
LARRA: Pa...pa. (*He turns towards the approaching figure: an older man in a grey frock coat and tall top hat, which he takes off in silence. The half-mask he is wearing reveals arched eyebrows and burning eyes.*)
D. MARIANO: So you've made up your mind to leave us?

LARRA. Sí.

D. MARIANO. Sólo cuentas dieciséis años. Sigues bajo mi potestad y has de continuar tus estudios.

LARRA. (*Con suavidad.*) En Valencia tal vez, o de nuevo en Madrid, si usted me autoriza.

D. MARIANO. (*Suspira.*) Los azares de la política nos han obligado a tenerte lejos mucho tiempo. Ahora que podemos, permanezcamos juntos. Aquí, en Valladolid, la Universidad es buena.

LARRA. Yo quiero irme.

D. MARIANO. ¡Tu madre no para de llorar!

LARRA. Se le pasará. No es ninguna tragedia. Todos los hijos se alejan de sus padres tarde o temprano.

D. MARIANO. Si de algo puede servirte el consejo de este médico no demasiado tonto que es tu padre, no te enfrentes aún con el mundo. Lo desconoces.

LARRA. Por eso me voy. Debo conocerlo si quiero escribir de él. Y arrancar las caretas.

D. MARIANO. ¿Qué caretas?

LARRA. Todos llevan alguna.

D. MARIANO. También tú la necesitarás. Este es un mal mundo.

LARRA. Aunque los demás crean vérmela, intentaré no llevarla. (*Ríe.*) Mi careta será mi risa. Pero no ocultará nada al que sepa leer.

D. MARIANO. (*Melancólico.*) Un escritor satírico... La pasión adolescente por la verdad... (*Se aleja unos pasos.*)

LARRA. La pasión por la verdad, *tout court*.

D. MARIANO. No hables mucho en francés, Mariano José.

LARRA. (*Con ironía.*) No hay peligro. Se ha vuelto distinguido.

(*Entretanto los dos niveles del bloque de la derecha se iluminan suavemente. En el sillón de arriba se halla sentado el Excelentísimo Señor Don Francisco Tadeo CALOMARDE: un cincuentón de recargado uniforme ministerial. En su semblante, media máscara que recuerda el ojo sagaz y la olfateadora nariz del zorro. A ambos lados de la escalerilla que conduce a su sitial, dos Voluntarios Realistas con la bayoneta calada hacen guardia, inmóviles. CALOMARDE lee unos decretos mientras, sentado a la mesa del nivel inferior, DON HOMOBONO tacha con su gran pluma de ave líneas y líneas de un manuscrito. Sobre su levita oscura y un tanto raída lleva manguitos de*

LARRA: Yes.

D. MARIANO: You are sixteen years of age. Still under my authority. And you will continue with your studies.

LARRA (*Gently.*): In Valencia perhaps, or back in Madrid, if that's acceptable to you.

D. MARIANO (*Sighing.*): The fortunes of politics forced us to send you away for a long time. Now that we are able to, we should stay together. There is a perfectly good university here, in Valladolid.

LARRA: I want to go away.

D. MARIANO: Your mother has done nothing but cry.

LARRA: She'll get over it. It's hardly a tragedy. All children leave their parents sooner or later.

D. MARIANO: If you'll accept a piece of advice from your father, from this old doctor, who's not exactly a fool, you won't challenge the world just yet. You have no idea of its ways.

LARRA: That's why I'm going. I've got to know the world if I am to write about it. To pull off the masks.

D. MARIANO: What masks?

LARRA: Everyone wears some sort of mask.

D. MARIANO: You'll need one as well. It's a false and dangerous world.

LARRA: Even though other people may imagine they see mine, I'll try to do without. (*He laughs.*) My laughter will be my mask. But for those who have eyes to see, it won't hide anything.

D. MARIANO (*Gloomily.*): A writer of satire... the adolescent's passion for truth... (*He moves several steps away.*)

LARRA: Passion for truth, *tout court.*

D. MARIANO: Try not to speak too much French, Mariano José.

LARRA (*Ironically.*): There's little danger of that. It's become fashionable.

(*Meanwhile, light begins to fall on both levels of the right-hand rostrum. In the large chair on the upper level is seated His Excellency Don Francisco Tadeo CALOMARDE: a man of about fifty years of age, dressed in ornate ministerial attire.[5] On his face a half-mask which suggests the cunning eye and alert snout of a fox. Two motionless Royalist Volunteers, bayonets fixed, stand guard on either side of the little stairway which leads up to his ceremonial seat. CALOMARDE is reading decrees whilst, seated at the table on the lower level, DON HOMOBONO is crossing out line after line of a manuscript with a large quill pen. He is wearing work-sleeves on top of his dark, rather threadbare, frock coat: the half-mask covering his face gives him the*)

*trabajo; la media máscara que cubre su rostro le asemeja a una lechuza.
DON MARIANO sigue hablando.)*

D. MARIANO. Cierto. Desde que Luis XVIII nos impuso al rey felón... Yo serví al rey José. O sea, a su hermano Napoleón, que nos parecía la encarnación de la libertad. Y lo era en cierto modo... Pero fue barrido... y la libre Francia apoya ahora a nuestro tirano... Fui afrancesado cuando soñaba, como tú, en quimeras. Y tuve que huir con José Bonaparte, y no habría podido regresar sin el amparo del infante don Francisco de Paula. *(Se acerca a su hijo.)* Y a ti ya te llaman liberal y afrancesado, por ser hijo mío. Un descuido, una palabra imprudente y te desterrarán. Vivimos bajo el terror de las Comisiones Militares, los Voluntarios Realistas, las Juntas de la Fe... Y fusilan por nada: por haber callado cuando otros daban vivas al rey absoluto, mientras se premia y se honra a los delatores. En España ya no hay más que cobardes y verdugos: otros cobardes. Pues bien, te aconsejo la cobardía. En la poltrona de Gracia y Justicia se ha sentado un monstruo, o quizá un enfermo. Y ese enfermo es quien manda, oprime y mata...

D. HOMOBONO. *(Se levanta y se cuadra.)* Excelentísimo señor...

CALOMARDE. ¿Don Homobono?

D. HOMOBONO. *(Tocando con su dedo lo que leía.)* En este albañal creo encontrar una alusión de mal gusto a vuestra excelencia, aunque muy velada.

CALOMARDE. ¿Cuánto se lo he de repetir? Si algo le ofrece duda, no dude en tachar.

D. HOMOBONO. Yo sólo quiero servir a vuestra excelencia con mi mayor celo... por el bien de España.

CALOMARDE. *(Seco.)* Lo sé. Vuelva a su tarea.

(DON HOMOBONO se inclina, se sienta y tacha con voluptuosidad. LARRA ha permanecido pensativo, con la cabeza baja. La luz abandona el bloque izquierdo.)

D. MARIANO. Bajo su mano está la censura. ¿Y tú quieres ser un escritor satírico? ¡Te lo tacharán todo! Y será lo mejor que pueda sucederte.

LARRA. Yo voy a intentarlo.

D. MARIANO. *(Reprime su contrariedad.)* Después de terminar tus estudios... ¿No? *(Breve silencio.)* No, claro. Conozco esa obstinación silenciosa. Has resuelto abandonarlos, vivir a salto de mata y burlar a

appearance of a watching owl, ready to pounce. DON MARIANO continues speaking.)

D. MARIANO: Yes. Ever since Louis XVIII set that scoundrel on the throne of Spain... I served King Joseph. Or rather his brother Napoleon, who seemed to us to be freedom itself. And in a sense he was. But then he was swept aside and now France, for all her much-vaunted love of freedom, stands behind the tyrant of Spain. I grew to love France in the days when I too dreamed impossible dreams, just like you. And I had to flee along with Joseph Bonaparte, and would never have been able to return had it not been for the protection of the Infante don Francisco de Paula. (*He draws closer to his son.*) They're already calling you a liberal and a French sympathizer just because you're my son. Step out of line or speak out of turn just once and you'll be forced to leave the country. We live in terrible times, with the Military Commissions, the Royalist Volunteers, the Councils of Faith... People are shot at the drop of a hat: for just standing in silence whilst others round about make a show of cheering on the tyrant who masquerades as king; and then they simply reward the informers. In Spain there are only cowards and executioners left: cowards themselves. So take my advice, choose cowardice. The throne has fallen to a man who's a monster, or perhaps he's just sick. But that sick man gives orders, squeezes and kills...[6]

D. HOMOBONO (*Rising and standing to attention.*): Excellency...

CALOMARDE: Don Homobono?

D. HOMOBONO (*Running his finger over the page he is reading.*): I believe I have located an unpleasant allusion to Your Excellency in this trash, albeit a heavily disguised one.

CALOMARDE: How many times must I tell you? When in doubt, cross it out.

D. HOMOBONO: My sole desire is to serve Your Excellency with the utmost zeal... for the greater glory of Spain.

CALOMARDE (*Drily.*): I know. Go back to your work.

(*D. HOMOBONO bows, sits down and continues erasing with delectation. LARRA has remained pensive, his head bowed. The light fades on the left-hand rostrum.*)

D. MARIANO: He has the full weight of censorship behind him. And you want to be a satirist? They'll cut every last word. That is if you're lucky.

LARRA: I intend to try anyway.

D. MARIANO (*Controlling his anger.*): When you've finished your studies... Agreed? (*Short silence.*) No, of course not. I recognise that silent obstinacy. You've already decided to abandon them, to live off your wits

Calomarde... hasta que él te destruya.

LARRA. Ese ministro desaparecerá un día, papá. Y también el rey. Entretanto el país va de miseria en miseria. Los escritores deben denunciarlas. Yo no seré un títere; no escribiré futesas.

D. MARIANO. ¡Irás a la cárcel!

LARRA. Acaso. Pero quizá se pueda hablar... sin hablar.

D. MARIANO. (*Escéptico.*) ¿A medias palabras?

LARRA. También son poderosas. Y se usaron siempre, porque siempre hubo mordazas.

D. MARIANO. (*Después de un momento.*) No permitiré que te arrojes a los leones. Te prohíbo que salgas de Valladolid.

LARRA. (*Suspira. Da unos pasos. Se vuelve hacia su padre.*) ¿Cree que tiene el derecho de prohibírmelo?

D. MARIANO. (*Irritado.*) ¿Cómo?

LARRA. Seamos humildes los dos, se lo ruego. Los hijos somos imperfectos... y también los padres. (*Lo mira fijamente.*) ¿Está seguro de que puede mantener su autoridad sobre mí? (*El padre vacila, lo mira durante una larga pausa. Al fin se despoja con suavidad de la máscara y muestra su semblante marchito, su mortecina mirada.*)

D. MARIANO. (*Su voz tiembla.*) Si te quieres ir por mi culpa, te pido perdón. Sé que conoces... mi flaqueza. Pero ya he abandonado a esa mujer.

LARRA. (*Con tenura.*) No es una flaqueza. Es un impulso natural.

D. MARIANO. También es natural... que tú te hayas prendado de ella. (*LARRA desvía la vista.*) Te lleva años y ha jugado contigo. Hasta que, un día, descubres que esa doncella angelical era... demasiado amiga de tu padre. El día entero te pasaste llorando.

LARRA. Calle, por favor.

D. MARIANO. (*Va a su lado.*) Comprendo cuánto sufres. Tu padre es, como todos, un pobre hombre sujeto a sus pasiones. Y estoy muy pesaroso de haber ofendido a tu madre. Tú estás en lo cierto: nada debo prohibirte. Pero no te vayas. Yo he roto ya con esa loca.

LARRA. Si me quedo, no podré olvidarla.

D. MARIANO. Siempre tienes razón...

LARRA. Yo le comprendo. Sé que en casi todos los matrimonios sucede lo mismo. También por eso quiero irme: para buscar, lejos de esa embustera..., el amor. Y mi afecto hacia usted es aún mayor: más humano.

D. MARIANO. ¿De veras?

and to trick your way round Calomarde... until he destroys you.

LARRA: That particular minister won't last for ever. Neither will the King. Meanwhile the country sinks deeper into misery. It's up to writers to denounce that misery. I refuse to be a puppet; I won't write about trifles.

D. MARIANO: You'll end up in prison!

LARRA: Perhaps. But it might be possible to speak out... without speaking.

D. MARIANO (*Sceptically.*): With half words?

LARRA: They're equally powerful. And they've always been used because writers have always been gagged.

D. MARIANO (*Pausing for a moment.*): I won't let you throw yourself to the lions. I forbid you to leave Valladolid.

LARRA (*He sighs and moves a few steps. Turning towards his father.*): Do you really think you have the right to forbid me?

D. MARIANO (*Annoyed.*): What?

LARRA: Let's be humble for a moment, I beg you. Children have their faults... as do their parents. (*He looks at him pointedly.*) Are you sure that you have the right to continue exercising your authority over me? (*His father hesitates, staring at him in silence. Finally he gently removes his mask and reveals his withered face, his jaded gaze.*)

D. MARIANO (*In a trembling voice.*): If you want to leave because of me, then I beg you to forgive me. I know that you are aware of... my weakness. But it's over now, I've left her.

LARRA (*Tenderly.*): It's not a weakness. It's a natural impulse.

D. MARIANO: It was natural as well that you... should grow fond of her. (*LARRA looks away.*) Just a few years older, she played with you. Until one day you discovered that that beautiful angel was... more than just your father's friend. And you cried all day long.[7]

LARRA: Please, don't

D. MARIANO (*Going over to his side.*): I realise just how much you've suffered. Your father is just like everyone else, a poor man tied to his passions. And I regret so much having hurt your mother. You're quite right: I shouldn't forbid you anything. But don't go. I've finished with that mad woman.

LARRA: If I stay, I'll never be able to forget her.

D. MARIANO: You're right, once again.

LARRA: I understand you. I know that the same thing happens in nearly every marriage. That's another reason for wanting to go: to get away from that little cheat and look for... real love. But my affection for you is all the greater: more human.

D. MARIANO: Is that really so?

LARRA. (*Ríe, conmovido.*) Abrace al hijo petulante que quiere amar y triunfar. (*El padre le oprime contra su pecho.*)

D. MARIANO. Ten cuidado... (*Se sobrepone y se separa.*)

LARRA. Lo tendré.

D. MARIANO. (*Con un hondo suspiro.*) Adiós, hijo mío.

LARRA. Que sea muy feliz. (*Sin ponerse la máscara, el padre se cubre y da unos pasos hacia el hueco de donde surgió.*) Papá... (*El padre se vuelve.*) Ya ve que no es imposible.

D. MARIANO. ¿El qué?

LARRA. (*Cariñoso.*) Conseguir que caigan las caretas. (*DON MARIANO sonríe avergonzado y sale por el hueco izquierdo al tiempo que, por el derecho, reaparece PEDRO sosteniendo un frac, sombrero y capa. Dejando en una silla lo demás, se acerca con el frac a LARRA.*)

PEDRO. ¿De frac, señor?

LARRA. (*Mirando hacia donde salió su padre.*) De frac. (*Empieza a despojarse de la levita. Súbitamente irritado se vuelve.*) ¿Por qué tú?

PEDRO. 1826. Usted está en Madrid.

LARRA. (*Mientras abandona la levita y el criado le pone el frac.*) ¡Antes de casarme no tuve criado!

PEDRO. (*Impasible.*) ¿La capa?

LARRA. Sí. (*Se la deja poner. PEDRO le tiende el sombrero y lo toma.*)

PEDRO. (*Va a recoger la levita.*) ¿Bastón?

LARRA. No. (*Lo mira.*) ¡Vete!

PEDRO. Ya me fui con las señoras.

LARRA. (*Colérico.*) ¿Pues qué haces aquí? (*PEDRO se encoge de hombros. Su señor deja de mirarlo y baja la voz.*) ¿He muerto ya?

PEDRO. (*A media voz.*) Casi. (*LARRA se abstrae y reflexiona. La luz volvió a iluminar el bloque derecho. Desde su sillón, habla CALOMARDE. Sumiso y atento, le escucha DON HOMOBONO.*)

CALOMARDE. Su majestad el rey don Fernando...

D. HOMOBONO. Que Dios guarde...

CALOMARDE. Suele decir que él es el tapón de la botella de cerveza.

D. HOMOBONO. Sabias palabras, excelencia.

LARRA (*He laughs, moved.*): Embrace your petulant son who seeks love and fame. (*His father holds him to his breast.*)

D. MARIANO: Be careful... (*He reasserts control of himself and moves away.*)

LARRA: I will be.

D. MARIANO (*Sighing deeply.*): Goodbye, my son.

LARRA: I wish you every happiness. (*Without replacing his mask, his father puts on his frock coat and walks towards the gap from which he appeared.*) Papa... (*His father turns round.*) You see... it's not impossible.

D. MARIANO: What isn't?

LARRA (*Affectionately.*): To get rid of the masks. (*DON MARIANO smiles embarrassedly and exits through the left-hand gap at the same time as, from the one on the right-hand side, PEDRO reappears carrying an evening jacket, hat and cape. He approaches LARRA with the evening jacket, having left the other items on a chair.*)

PEDRO: Dress coat, sir?

LARRA (*Looking at the gap through which his father has disappeared.*): Dress coat. (*He begins to remove his frock coat. Suddenly irritated, he spins round.*) Why you?

PEDRO: 1826. You're in Madrid.[8]

LARRA (*As he takes off his frock coat and his servant helps him on with his evening jacket.*): But I didn't have a servant until I got married!

PEDRO (*Impassively.*): Your cloak?

LARRA: Yes. (*He allows his servant to place it round his shoulders, and then takes the hat which PEDRO holds out to him.*)

PEDRO (*Moving to pick up the frock coat.*): Walking-stick?

LARRA: No. (*He looks at him.*) Just go!

PEDRO: I left at the same time as the ladies.

LARRA (*Angrily.*): Then what are you doing here? (*PEDRO shrugs his shoulders. His master looks away and lowers his voice.*) Am I dead already?

PEDRO (*In a half voice*): Almost. (*LARRA loses himself in thought. The light, once again, picks out the right-hand rostrum. CALOMARDE speaks from his chair. DON HOMOBONO hangs meekly upon his every word.*)

CALOMARDE: His Majesty King Fernando...

D. HOMOBONO: God save the King...

CALOMARDE: Is wont to compare himself to the stopper in a bottle of beer.

D. HOMOBONO: Words of wisdom, Excellency.

CALOMARDE.   Pero ¿usted cree que el tapón regio está bien apretado?

D. HOMOBONO.   (*Cauto.*) ¿Vuestra excelencia no lo cree?

CALOMARDE.   El rey es demasiado bondadoso.   Contemporiza.

D. HOMOBONO.   ¿A pesar de las ejecuciones y los destierros?

CALOMARDE.   ¡Bah! Bien pocos.

D. HOMOBONO.   Entonces, el tapón...

CALOMARDE.   No saltará.   ¡Porque el tapón soy yo! Aún hemos de ver restauradas en nuestra gloriosa España las virtudes que la hicieron grande: la devoción de todos a nuestra Santa Iglesia, de grado o por fuerza; la saludable ignorancia de tanto filosofismo extranjero; el acatamiento al trono absoluto; las hogueras de la Inquisición para todos los masones...

D. HOMOBONO.   ¡Eso sería el Paraíso en la tierra!

CALOMARDE.   Sí... (*Baja la voz.*) Pero quizá con otro rey lleno de santa intransigencia.   Porque su majestad ya no tiene buena salud.   Y si... muriese..., tendríamos otro rey... digno de los altares.

D. HOMOBONO.   (*Tímido.*)   Su hermano don Carlos María Isidro... (*Corto silencio.*)

CALOMARDE.   Que el Cielo nos conserve a don Fernando.

D. HOMOBONO.   ¡Hágase la voluntad divina!

CALOMARDE.   Amén.   Puede ya dejar su tarea, don Homobono.

D. HOMOBONO.   Yo había pensado examinar todavía el periódico de Carnerero...

CALOMARDE.   Otra debilidad del rey.   Si por mí fuera, tampoco se publicaría.   Aunque ese papelucho no es peligroso.   Y alguna espita hay que ponerle al barril para que no estalle.   Porque una cosa es el tapón de la botella y otra, la espita del barril.

D. HOMOBONO.   Admirable sabiduría, excelencia.   (*La luz les abandona.*)

(*Entretanto ha aparecido por la izquierda del primer término don Ramón de MESONERO ROMANOS.   Cuenta treinta y cuatro años y tal vez aparenta algunos más.   Cabello oscuro no muy abundante, leve tendencia a la obesidad, boca sumida y sonriente bajo su media máscara de hombre campechano, donde los ojos miopes apenas son dos puntitos negros protegidos por las diminutas y gruesas gafas.   Viste levita oscura y*)

CALOMARDE: But are you convinced that the royal stopper is sufficiently secure?

D. HOMOBONO (*Guardedly.*): Your Excellency is not?

CALOMARDE: The King is too gentle by nature. He is a peace-maker.

D. HOMOBONO: What about all those he has had executed or exiled?

CALOMARDE: Bah! Precious few.

D. HOMOBONO: Then, the stopper...

CALOMARDE: Will not blow. Because I am the stopper. We have yet to recover in our glorious Spain those virtues which once made her great: the devotion of all and sundry to our Holy Mother Church, willingly or otherwise; a healthy ignorance of foreign idea-mongering; respect for the absolute powers of the throne; the fires of the Inquisition for all freemasons...

D. HOMOBONO: Heaven on earth!

CALOMARDE: Indeed... (*He lowers his voice.*) But perhaps with another king, more unrelenting in his faith. His Majesty is no longer in the best of health. Were he... to die... we would have another king... a saintly man indeed, worthy of our church.

D. HOMOBONO (*Hesitantly.*): His brother don Carlos María Isidro...[9] (*A short silence.*)

CALOMARDE: God bless King Fernando.

D. HOMOBONO: May His will be done.

CALOMARDE: Amen. You may stop work now, don Homobono.

D. HOMOBONO: I thought that I would inspect the newsheet that Carnerero...

CALOMARDE: Another of the King's weaknesses. If it were up to me, it wouldn't be published either. Although as those rags go, it's not particularly dangerous. And if we want to keep the barrel from blowing, we must have some sort of safety valve. It's one thing to put a stopper in a bottle, but quite another to cork a barrel.

D. HOMOBONO: Admirable wisdom, Excellency. (*The light around them fades.*)

(*Meanwhile, don Ramón de MESONERO ROMANOS has appeared downstage from the left.[10] He is thirty-four years old, although he may look older. His hair is dark but thinning, his body already starting to run to fat. His sunken mouth smiles under a half-mask whose features suggest frankness, and his weak eyes are barely more than two black dots behind the thick lenses of his small round glasses. He wears a dark frock coat and a top hat, although not a particularly tall one. He carries a*

chistera no muy alta. En sus manos, el bastón de puño de hueso. Se ha detenido en el lateral y espera, risueño. LARRA levanta la vista, se cubre y se emboza en la capa.)

PEDRO. Señor... (*LARRA lo mira. El criado señala a la puerta del fondo, donde el lento resplandor aparece y se extingue.*) La niña llama.

LARRA. (*Desabrido.*) No oigo nada. (*Avanza, baja el escalón y se acerca a MESONERO. Viva luz los envuelve; el gabinete queda en penumbra. PEDRO desaparece con la levita por uno de los huecos del fondo.*) Mi señor don Ramón de Mesonero Romanos...

MESONERO. (*Amaga un abrazo.*) Cuánta solemnidad, Larra... ¿Es por los años que le llevo?

LARRA. Es respeto y admiración.

MESONERO. No exagere. Ni yo ni nadie escribe aquí apenas... ¿Le presento hoy en el café?

LARRA. Cuando usted mande. (*Dan unos pasos hacia la derecha.*)

MESONERO. ¿Abandonó sus estudios?

LARRA. Pues...

MESONERO. Mal hecho. Yo tengo un buen pasar gracias a mis negocios. Pero usted, ¿de qué va a vivir? De la literatura no es fácil.

LARRA. Vivo de un empleíllo que me ha buscado mi padre.

MESONERO. Menos mal. Vamos al Café del Príncipe. (*Nuevos pasos hacia la derecha.*)

LARRA. ¿«El Parnasillo»?

MESONERO. Así lo ha bautizado la hueste romántica, que va acorralando a las viejas glorias. (*Ríe.*) Yo soy ecléctico: me siento con los mozos y con los maduros. (*Confidencial.*) Haga lo mismo: los maduros tienen en sus manos la poca prensa que nos dejan.

LARRA. (*Risueño.*) Y los jóvenes, sus ilusiones y sus desprecios.

MESONERO. Y los bolsillos vacíos. Pero el dueño no se atreve a echarlos porque el café estaba muerto sin ellos. Incluso ha ideado para ellos el medio sorbete a dos reales de vellón... Van mozos de mérito allí. Espronceda, por ejemplo. ¡Qué tronera! Escribe poemas desaforados, pero buenos. Huyó a Lisboa hace poco.

LARRA. ¿Huyó?

MESONERO. ¡Con diecisiete añitos! Así es él. A los catorce

bone-handled stick. He has stopped at the side and waits cheerfully. LARRA looks up, puts on his hat and wraps himself in his cape.)

PEDRO: Sir... *(LARRA looks at him. The servant indicates the door at the back of the room. The light grows slowly behind its glass panels and then goes out.)* The little girl... she's calling you.

LARRA *(Harshly.)*: I hear nothing. *(He walks forward, goes down the step and approaches MESONERO. They are both brightly lit: the study is left in shadow. PEDRO takes the frock coat and disappears through one of the gaps at the rear.)* Don Ramón de Mesonero Romanos, sir...

MESONERO *(Makes to embrace him)*: So formal, my dear Larra... Perhaps because I am older than you?

LARRA: A sign of my respect and admiration.

MESONERO: Oh, come now. Neither I nor anybody else can really write here. Shall I introduce you in the café today?

LARRA: Whenever you wish. *(They take several steps towards the right.)*

MESONERO: Have you abandoned your studies?

LARRA: Well...

MESONERO: A bad thing. I lead a pleasant enough life thanks to my business interests. But how will you earn your living? Not from literature, I fear.

LARRA: I have a modest position, arranged by my father... I manage with that.

MESONERO: Just as well. Let's go to the Café del Príncipe. *(Once more they walk towards the right.)*

LARRA: "Little Parnassus"?

MESONERO: As it has been dubbed by the romantic hordes who resolutely cling to the old glories. *(He laughs.)* I remain eclectic: I sit with young and old alike. *(Confidential.)* You should follow suit: the very little press permitted to us at all is controlled by our older friends.

LARRA *(Cheerfully.)*: Whilst the young have their dreams and their disdain.

MESONERO: And holes burning in their pockets. But the owner doesn't dare throw them out because the café was simply dead without them. He even invented a cheaper half-sorbet for them... There's a lot of talent there. Espronceda, for example.[11] He's a wild one. He writes outrageous poems, but they're good. He had to flee to Lisbon not so long ago.

LARRA: To flee?

MESONERO: When he was just seventeen. But that's his style. He

presenció la ejecución de Riego y organizó una sociedad secreta con otros mozalbetes: «Los Numantinos». ¡Para vengar a Riego y a todos los liberales ejecutados! Figúrese. Chiquilladas. No sé qué demonios pensarían poder hacer... Pero el pastel se destapó y a Espronceda le cayeron encima cinco años de reclusión en un convento de Guadalajara.

LARRA.   ¿A los catorce?

MESONERO.   La justicia de nuestro amado monarca es muy severa... Por fortuna, a las pocas semanas le dieron los frailes certificado de haber cumplido su condena..., porque tampoco ellos le aguantaban. Alguna otra gatada habrá hecho, cuando huye. A otros sí los va a conocer usted. A Ventura de la Vega... (*Se ilumina la figura del nombrado, sentada a la izquierda del Parnasillo: patillas y melena enmarcan media máscara notablemente aniñada.*) También perteneció a «Los Numantinos» y estuvo a punto de ser atrapado. Algo se olerían de todos modos, porque un día los Voluntarios Realistas le armaron la encerrona y le raparon la cabeza.

LARRA.   ¿Será posible?

MESONERO.   A los apostólicos les irritan las melenas; las consideran subversivas. El peinado de usted es discreto, como el mío. Sea discreto siempre, amigo Larra... Vega sueña con representar sus comedias, que no son nada malas. Don Manuel Bretón de los Herreros ha representado ya tres con muy feliz suceso y ha prometido echarle una mano. Si lo hará o no, nadie lo sabe. (*Sentada junto a VEGA se ilumina la figura de BRETÓN. Careta sardónica, de pocos amigos. En ella, el párpado cerrado del ojo izquierdo que le falta.*) A mí me lleva ocho o diez años. Se sienta con los jóvenes, pero su corazón está con los otros. El segundo Moratín, le llaman, o se llama él quizá. No tanto, claro. Debido a un lance de su mocedad perdió un ojo, y tiene malas pulgas. Una letrilla circula que le va pintiparada. Óigala:

> «Una víbora picó
> a Manuel Bretón el tuerto.
> ¿Murió Bretón? Nor por cierto.
> La víbora reventó.»

LARRA.   (*Riendo.*) ¿La compuso usted?

was only fourteen when he witnessed the execution of Riego, and organised a secret society with a band of lads: "The Numantinos". To avenge Riego and all other executed liberals.[12] Imagine. Juvenile nonsense. The devil knows what they thought they could achieve. But the cat got out of the bag and Espronceda was sentenced to five years' detention in a Guadalajara convent.

LARRA: When he was fourteen?

MESONERO: The justice of our beloved King is severe... Fortunately, he had only been there a few weeks when the monks gave him a certificate confirming that he had served his time... apparently they couldn't stand him either. He must have been responsible for some new frolic to have had to take flight. But you will meet some others. Ventura de la Vega...[13] (*This character is illuminated, sitting at the left-hand side of the café: his long sideburns and mane of hair frame a half mask whose features are markedly childish.*) He was in "The Numantinos" as well, and came within a whisker of being caught. They must have sniffed him out anyway, because one day the Royalist Volunteers got hold of him and shaved his head bare.

LARRA: In God's name, why?

MESONERO: The stalwarts of the church find long hair offensive; they consider it subversive. You wear yours discreetly, as do I. Always be discreet, Larra, my friend... Vega dreams that one day his plays, which aren't at all bad, will be performed. Don Manuel Bretón de los Herreros has already had three of his pieces played with great success, and has promised to lend him a hand. Whether he will or not, though, is anyone's guess (*The figure of BRETÓN, seated beside VEGA, is illuminated. A sardonic mask, that of a man with few friends. His left eye is missing, and the lid is closed.*) He's eight, maybe even ten years older than me. He sits with the younger ones, but his heart is with the others. The second Moratín they call him. Or perhaps that's what he calls himself. He's not, needless to say. He lost an eye in some sort of mishap as a boy, and he has the devil of a temper. There's a little ballad going the rounds which describes him to perfection. Listen:

> A serpent bold
> bit one-eyed Manuel.
> Then Bretón's dead?
> No. But I'm told
> the serpent's none too well.

LARRA (*Laughing.*): Is it yours?

MESONERO. ¿Qué dice?... Yo me llevo bien con todos, hasta con él. A usted le noto, en cambio, ganas de pelea. Pues no le faltarán enemigos. Clemente Díaz, pongo por caso... (*Luz a la izquierda sobre DÍAZ: un tipo flaco, muy joven, con melenas. Media careta de bilioso color, de nariz ganchuda y granulosa.*) Para él nada hay bueno salvo lo suyo, que nadie conoce. ¡Y tantos otros alborotadores! «El Estudiante», que así dice firmarse, aunque no se ha visto dónde; Gil y Zárate, López Pelegrín, Estébanez, Pezuela... Toda una tropa de insolentes ante los mayores en años. Pero entre estos se sienta Carnerero, a quien usted debe conocer ineludiblemente. (*Surge su figura iluminada a la derecha. Cabello ya gris, corpulento, aire afable, media careta inocentísima, cuidado y costoso atavío.*)

LARRA. ¿Quién es?

MESONERO. ¡Grave ignorancia! «El Correo Literario y Mercantil» es de don José María. Un tipo muy curioso.

LARRA. ¿Por qué?

MESONERO. (*Baja la voz.*) Con José Bonaparte, redactor literario de «La Gaceta». Tuvo que emigrar, claro, y regresó más liberal que nunca, para trabajar en «El Patriota Español». Pero viéndolas venir: sólo un poquitín antes de que los cien mil hijos de San Luis nos encajasen en el trono a nuestro amado rey absoluto...

LARRA. (*Con zumba.*) Que Dios guarde...

MESONERO. (*Lo mira y sigue.*) ... se declaró arrepentido de sus errores y furibundo apostólico. Incluso representó una cosita... muy oportuna... acerca de la entrada en Madrid de su majestad, titulada «La Noticia Feliz». En fin: tan bien se las ha sabido arreglar, que ha terminado por obtener el privilegio real de ser el único editor autorizado. Cultive a Carnerero: no hay otra puerta. Sacará pronto «Cartas Españolas», la única revista permitida.

LARRA. Lo pensaré.

MESONERO. No hay nada que pensar... Con él se sienta el poeta Arriaza. Supongo que lo admira... (*Durante estas palabras se hace visible la figura de ARRIAZA. Delgado, elegante, Media máscara arrugada y tristona. Cabellera discreta, entre rubia y gris.*)

LARRA. Lo respeto.

MESONERO. (*Lo mira un momento.*) Muy bien. Hay que ser respetuosos. Lista, Quintana, Juan Nicasio Gallego, también son respetables. Se quiera o no, han sido nuestros maestros. Algunos, todavía

MESONERO: Oh, please! I get on well with everyone, even him. You, however, are clearly spoiling for a fight. Well, you'll have no shortage of enemies. Take Clemente Díaz, for example...[14] (*Light from the left falls on Díaz: thin, very young, with long hair. He wears a half mask of a bilious colour, the nose hooked and granulous.*) As far as he's concerned, the only worthwhile stuff is his own, which nobody has ever seen. And there are many more firebrands like him. He claims that he signs his work "The Student", although no one is quite sure where it appears; Gil y Zárate, López Pelegrín, Estébanez, Pezuela... A whole troop of insolent young pups with not a jot of respect for their elders. But Carnerero sits with the older ones, and you really must meet him.[15] (*Light picks out the figure of CARNERERO on the right. Hair already grey, corpulent, an air of affability, his half mask exudes innocence, carefully and expensively dressed.*)

LARRA: Who is he?

MESONERO: Fearful ignorance! He is "The Mercantile and Literary Post". A particularly curious sort.

LARRA: Why?

MESONERO (*Lowering his voice.*): Under Bonaparte, he was the literary editor of the "Gazette". He had to leave the country, naturally, and returned more of a liberal than ever to work in "The Spanish Patriot". But he saw what was coming: just before the hundred thousand sons of St. Louis deposited our dearly beloved sovreign on the throne...

LARRA (*Facetiously.*): God save the King...

MESONERO (*He looks at him and continues.*): ...he publicly admitted the error of his ways and declared himself a fervent Catholic. He even presented a piece - "Joyful Tidings" - about His Majesty's entry into Madrid. Not much of a piece, but very opportune. In conclusion: he's done so well for himself that he's now, by royal concession, our only authorised editor. You must cultivate Carnerero: there's no other way. He is about to bring out "Spanish Letters", the only journal that has official approval.

LARRA: I'll think it over.

MESONERO: There's nothing to think over... The poet Arriaza sits with him.[16] I assume you admire him... (*As he speaks, the figure of ARRIAZA is lit. Slim, elegant. His half mask is wrinkled and melancholic. The style of his hair is discreet, somewhere between fair and grey.*)

LARRA: I respect him.

MESONERO (*He looks at him for a moment.*): Good. We must be respectful. Lista, Quintana, Juan Nicasio Gallego, all worthy of our respect. Whether we like it or not, they have all been our past masters.

en el destierro...

LARRA. Lo cual es aún más respetable.

MESONERO. Claro: yo lo respeto todo. Le conviene conocer también a don Juan Grimaldi. Vino con los cien mil hijos de...

LARRA. (*Le corta, burlón.*) De eso, sí.

MESONERO. De San Luis, sí. Es francés. De él es la famosísima «Pata de Cabra»... y del otro francés que la escribió antes. Muy liberal en el fondo...

LARRA. Se comprende. Todo absolutista en la superficie debe ser liberal en el fondo si quiere un mañana rentable.

MESONERO. (*Ríe.*) No está mal... Pero cultive a Grimaldi. Es el director del Teatro del Príncipe. (*A la derecha la luz sacó de la penumbra a GRIMALDI. Media edad, máscara de hombre suave y amanerado.*) Sacerdotes y militares tampoco faltan. El padre Froilán... (*Ríe. Se ilumina a la derecha la figura del padre. Calvo, hosco. Careta cejijunta y casi verdosa.*) Seguro que es censor, aunque lo disimula. Nunca se sabe si habla o gruñe... Y el servicial camarero Pipí, que así le llamamos en recuerdo del de «La Comedia Nueva».

LARRA. Bien pudiera ser confesor real ese Padre Froilán.

MESONERO. ¿Por qué?

LARRA. Es tocayo del que fue capellán de Carlos el Hechizado.

MESONERO. Usted sabe mucho...

LARRA. Ese café parece un cumplido resumen de España.

MESONERO. Del avispero de España. ¡Evite picaduras! ¿Usted quiere ser escritor satírico?

LARRA. Eso pretendo.

MESONERO. O sea de costumbres, como yo.

LARRA. No exactamente...

MESONERO. ¿No exactamente? (*Le pone una mano en el hombro.*) Si yo fuese, digamos, Bretón, le animaría a escribir las sátiras más hirientes. Ningún modo mejor de anularlo. En vez de eso, le aconsejo que sea mi rival. Costumbrismo. Haga reír, pero no enfade. (*LARRA se abstrae. Su voz, en el ambiente.*)

LARRA. (*Su voz.*) «Déjate, pues, ya de habladurías, que te han de costar la vida, o la lengua; imítame a mí (...) y escribe sólo (...) de las cosas que natural y diariamente en las Batuecas acontecen...»

Some of them even in exile...

LARRA: Even more worthy of respect in that case.

MESONERO: Of course: I respect everything. You should meet don Juan Grimaldi as well. He came with the hundred thousand sons of...[17]

LARRA (*Interrupting him, mockingly.*): Of yonder, yes.

MESONERO: Of St. Louis, yes. He's French. The famous "The Cloven Hoof" came from his pen... just as it did from the pen of the other Frenchman who wrote it first. Very liberal deep down.

LARRA: That's understandable. Everyone who's an absolutist on the surface must be a liberal deep down, if he wants to stay afloat.

MESONERO (*Laughing.*): That's not bad... But cultivate Grimaldi. He's the director of the Príncipe Theatre (*On the right-hand side a light has focused on GRIMALDI. Middle aged, his mask suggests both polish and affectation.*) There are soldiers and priests a-plenty as well. Father Froilán... (*He laughs. On the right a light shines on the priest. Bald, sullen. A heavily frowning mask, almost of a greenish hue.*) He's almost certainly a censor, although he pretends not to be. You can never tell whether he's speaking or grunting... And our obliging waiter Pipí -we took his name from "The New Comedy".

LARRA: That Father Froilán could well be one of the King's confessors.

MESONERO: Why?

LARRA: He has the same name as the former chaplain of Charles the Bewitched.

MESONERO: You're well informed.

LARRA: It's seems as if the café contains the whole of Spain in miniature.

MESONERO: The hornets' nest of Spain. Take care not to be stung. You mean to write satires?

LARRA: I intend to try, at least.

MESONERO: That is, you'll write about social customs, as I do.

LARRA: Not exactly...

MESONERO: Not exactly? (*He puts a hand on his shoulder.*) If I were Bretón, for sake of argument, I would encourage you to write the most biting of satires. No better way of getting rid of you. Instead, I advise you to be my rival. A mirror of social customs. Make your reader laugh, but don't provoke him. (*LARRA loses himself in thought. His voice is heard in the air.*)

LARRA (*Voice off.*): "And so, enough of babblings which will cost you your life, or your tongue; do as I do [...] and write only [...] of the things that transpire daily in the distant land of the Batuecas...[18]"

MESONERO. (*Confidencial.*) Tampoco se le ocurra meterse en conspiraciones. En los cafés se cuenta todo y, por consiguiente, la policía también se entera. Aquí nadie sabe conspirar... Apártese de la política. El más triste secreto a voces es que los liberales no existen.

LARRA. ¿Cómo ha dicho?

MESONERO. Todos son absolutistas, y lo demuestran cuando llegan al poder. Créame: no hay esperanzas. Refúgiese en el cuadro de costumbres. Es el mejor consejo que puedo darle. (*Corto silencio.*) ¿Vamos?

LARRA. Le agradezco de corazón sus advertencias. Palabras son de un verdadero amigo. Pero ¿me ha hablado con entera sinceridad?

MESONERO. ¿Lo duda?

LARRA. Le responderé sinceramente, porque también quiero ser su amigo.

MESONERO. ¿A dónde va usted a parar?

LARRA. A la hipótesis de que su escepticismo de los hombres y de la política no es tal escepticismo, sino otra cosa.

MESONERO. ¿Qué otra cosa?

LARRA. Don Ramón, yo le suplico que me hable sin máscara.

MESONERO. ¡No he podido ser más franco!

LARRA. Pues yo – perdóneme – lo dudo. Y me atrevo a decirle que, en mi opinión, su escepticismo es el disfraz que encubre... su temor.

MESONERO. (*Con voz insegura.*) Usted se equivoca... (*Sofocado, se quita el sombrero.*) Y me ofende...

LARRA. No. Yo le respeto y no quiero que me engañe, porque mi mayor deseo es seguir respetándole.

MESONERO. (*Va a quitarse la careta; no se decide y baja la mano.*) No hable así a todos. Se granjeará enemigos.

LARRA. Escribiré así para todos, pero sólo hablaré así a un verdadero amigo.

MESONERO. (*Titubea. Se despoja lentamente de la máscara y muestra su semblante cansado, triste y medroso.*) Demasiados ahorcados, fusilados, desterrados... Y no pocos escritores entre ellos. (*La luz cambia levemente.*) En 1831 cuelgan al librero Millar, y en Granada a la pobre Marianita Pineda. (*A la izquierda del Parnasillo VEGA y DÍAZ reciben con ademanes consternados estas noticias. Los de la derecha dan cabezazos que entrañan corroboración y hasta alegría. El PADRE FROILÁN llega hasta frotarse las manos.*)

MESONERO (*Confidentially.*): Don't get involved in any conspiracies. No confidence is sacred in cafés, word will always reach the police. Nobody here knows how to conspire. Keep well clear of politics. It's an open secret, I fear, that the liberals no longer exist.

LARRA: What did you say?

MESONERO: They are all absolutists, it's as clear as day when they assume power. Believe me: there's no possible hope. Take sanctuary in the mirror of social customs. It's the best advice I can give you. (*Brief silence.*) Shall we go?

LARRA: I thank you with all my heart for your warnings. They are the words of a true friend. But have you been entirely frank with me?

MESONERO: Do you doubt it?

LARRA: I will answer you truthfully, because I too wish to count myself your friend.

MESONERO: What are you insinuating?

LARRA: The possibility that your sceptical view of men and politics isn't really scepticism as such, but something quite different.

MESONERO: Like what?

LARRA: Don Ramón, I beg you to speak with me freely and not from behind a mask.

MESONERO: I could not have been any more frank.

LARRA: Forgive me, but I doubt that. Indeed, I would go so far to say that, in my opinion, your scepticism is a cloak for... your fear.

MESONERO (*In uncertain tones.*): You are mistaken. (*Disconcerted, he removes his hat.*) And you offend me...

LARRA: No. I have every respect for you and I do not want you to try to deceive me, because my greatest desire is to be able to continue respecting you.

MESONERO (*He makes as if to remove his mask, but cannot make up his mind and lowers his hand*): You must not speak like this to everyone. You will make many enemies.

LARRA: I will write like this for everyone, but I will only speak this way to a true friend.

MESONERO (*He hesitates, then slowly removes his mask, revealing a face which is weary, sad and full of fear.*): Too many people have been hung, shot, exiled... many writers among them. (*The lighting changes slightly.*[19]) In 1831 they hang Millar, the publisher, and, in Granada, poor little Mariana Pineda.[20] (*On the left-hand side of the café VEGA and DÍAZ receive this news with gestures of alarm. Those on the right nod their heads in a way which suggests approval, indeed glee. FATHER FROILAN even rubs his hands together.*)

LARRA. (*Confuso.*) ¿Cómo?

MESONERO. En el mismo año ejecutan a Valdés, a Chapalangarra, ¡a tantos ilusos convencidos de que aquí había leones cuando sólo había ovejas! (*Continúan en el Parnasillo los correspondientes ademanes y gestos.*)

LARRA. (*Turbado.*) Don Ramón, escuche...

MESONERO. Y a Torrijos, con sus cincuenta y dos compañeros, los atraen a una sucia trampa y los fusilan en una playa... (*Descarga de fusilería. Gemidos. En el Parnasillo, horror y satisfacción disimulada.*)

LARRA. ¡Mesonero! (*Tiros de gracia que apagan los gemidos. En el café los acusan con su macabra pantomima. MESONERO está inmóvil, abstraído.*) ¡Estamos en 1828! (*Los del Parnasillo van reasumiendo despacio su anterior inmovilidad.*)

MESONERO. (*Enigmático, mira a LARRA.*) Nada he dicho que no me haya oído en alguna ocasión.

LARRA. ¡No en ésta!

MESONERO. ¿Y cuál es ésta? (*Silencio. LARRA mira a la penumbra de su salita, donde, tras los cristales de la puerta, surge y se apaga de nuevo el silencioso fulgor. La luz vuelve a su anterior estado. MESONERO habla con humilde naturalidad.*) Esta es la ocasión en que yo le pregunto: ¿no tenemos el derecho de vivir lo más tranquilos que podamos, aunque sea cerrando los ojos ante la ignominia? (*En voz muy baja.*) ¿No me va a perdonar mi miedo? Todos no podemos ser héroes, Larra.

LARRA. Acepte mi gratitud.

MESONERO. (*Suspira.*) Ya sabe mi secreto. ¿Cuándo sabré yo el suyo?

LARRA. No lo tengo. Intentaré denunciar esa ignominia en que vivimos. Por nuestro pobre pueblo, que sólo conoce el hambre y que nos sostiene a todos.

MESONERO. (*Vuelve a ajustarse la careta mientras habla.*) Tampoco se fíe de él. Sus estallidos son terribles. Mata, roba...

LARRA. A ellos les matan y les roban más.

MESONERO. (*Se cubre.*) ¿Va usted a defender a la canalla?

LARRA. (*Sonriente.*) Se me antoja que ya no es tan sincero como hace un momento. No importa. Yo le agradeceré siempre ese momento.

MESONERO. (*Grave.*) Olvídelo. ¿Vamos al Parnasillo?

LARRA. Perdóneme. Hoy no.

MESONERO. ¿Ahora sale con ésas?

LARRA (*Confused.*): What?

MESONERO: The same year, Valdés is executed, along with Chapalangarra and so many other fools convinced that they could fight like lions in a country of sheep! (*The corresponding gestures and facial expressions continue in the café.*)

LARRA (*Disturbed.*): Don Ramón, listen...

MESONERO: And then they lure Torrijos, with fifty-two of his men, into a filthy ambush and shoot them down on a beach... (*A burst of gunfire. Cries of pain. In the café, horror and concealed satisfaction.*)

LARRA: Mesonero! (*Single shots which silence the cries. The characters in the café react to them with their macabre pantomime. MESONERO is standing stock still, lost in thought.*) This is 1828! (*In the café they slowly resume their former stillness.*)

MESONERO (*Enigmatically, looking at LARRA.*): I didn't say anything that you haven't heard me say at some time.

LARRA: But not this time!

MESONERO: And which time is this? (*Silence. LARRA looks towards the shadows of his room. Once again the light glows silently behind the glass in the door, and then goes out. The lighting returns to its former state. MESONERO speaks in natural, modest tones.*) This is the time when I ask you: do we not have the right to live in peace, even though it means blinding ourselves to shame and injustice? (*In very muted tones.*) Not everyone can be a hero, Larra.

LARRA: I'm grateful to you.

MESONERO (*Sighing.*): Now you know my secret. When will I know yours?

LARRA: I have no secret. But I will try to denounce the injustice in which we live. For the ordinary people of this country, who know only hunger and who sustain the likes of us.

MESONERO (*Putting his mask back in place as he speaks.*): Don't place too much trust in the people. They can flare up in the most terrible way... killing, stealing...

LARRA: No more than they are killed and stolen from.

MESONERO (*Putting on his hat.*): So you'll defend the rabble.

LARRA (*Smiling.*): I have the impression that your sincerity of a moment ago has evaporated. No matter. I shall always be grateful to you for it.

MESONERO (*Gravely.*): Please forget it. Shall we go to Little Parnassus?

LARRA: Forgive me. Not today.

MESONERO: You surprise me.

LARRA. Y... cuando vayamos... no me presente todavía al señor Carnerero.

MESONERO. (*Estupefacto.*) ¿Ésa es la habilidad que quiere desplegar?

LARRA. (*Sonríe.*) Ésa no. Otra.

MESONERO. (*Esboza un frío gesto de incomprensión.*) ¿De cierto no quiere acompañarme?

LARRA. Otro día. Y muy agradecido.

MESONERO. Como quiera. Quede con Dios. (*Se inclinan. MESONERO sale por la derecha. LARRA se vuelve hacia el Parnasillo y contempla un instante a los hombres inmóviles. La luz los abandona bruscamente, al tiempo que LARRA sube a su gabinete. Junto al velador toca levemente, sin mirarla, la pistola. Luego se desprende de capa y sombrero, dejándolos en el sillón. La luz crece. PEDRO reaparece por el hueco derecho, que se tiñe de lívido resplandor. LARRA no se vuelve, pero se envara: nota perfectamente la presencia ilusoria.*)

PEDRO. ¿No tenía ya un criado a fines del año 28?

LARRA. No. Y tú no estás aquí.

PEDRO. Estoy fuera. Como tu hija, pero más lejos.

LARRA. (*Se vuelve.*) ¿Me tuteas?

PEDRO. (*Con un gesto de ignorancia.*) Tú sabrás. (*Cruza y recoge la capa y el sombrero.*)

LARRA. (*No ha dejado de observarlo.*) ¿Que yo sabré?

PEDRO. (*Se vuelve hacia su señor.*) ¿No es éste tu último drama? (*Va a irse.*)

LARRA. ¡Mi único drama fue el «Macías»!

PEDRO. (*Se detiene. Tono trivial.*) Pues éste será el segundo.

LARRA. ¿Cuál?

PEDRO. Tú evocas, pero también imaginas. Ahora dialogas tu último drama... muy aprisa. Se agota el tiempo.

LARRA. ¿Y tú eres un personaje?

PEDRO. Y tú otro. El principal, quizá.

LARRA. ¿Quizá?

PEDRO. ¿No me estás dando demasiado papel?

LARRA. Cierra esa boca.

PEDRO. No puedo.

LARRA. Nunca son tan vívidas las imaginaciones.

PEDRO. (*Retirándose.*) Excepto si hay una pistola cerca. (*LARRA*

LARRA: And... when we do go... please don't introduce me, just yet, to Señor Carnerero

MESONERO (*In amazement.*): Is that the way you intend to conduct your affairs.

LARRA (*Smiling.*): No. In quite another way.

MESONERO (*His face etching into an expression of cold incomprehension.*): You're sure you won't come with me?

LARRA: Another time. And thank you.

MESONERO: As you wish. Goodbye to you. (*They bow. MESONERO exits stage right. LARRA turns towards Little Parnassus and briefly contemplates the motionless men grouped there. They are suddenly plunged into darkness at the same time as LARRA goes up to his study. He stops beside the occasional table and lightly touches the pistol, without looking at it. Then he removes his hat and cape, putting them down on the armchair. The light grows. PEDRO reappears through the right-hand gap, which is tinged with a deathly light. Although LARRA does not turn round, he stiffens: he is fully aware of the unreal presence.*)

PEDRO: Did you not have a servant towards the end of '28?

LARRA: No. And you're not here.

PEDRO: I'm outside, Mariano. Like your daughter, but farther away.

LARRA (*Turning round.*): So, we're on first-name terms now?[21]

PEDRO (*As though totally unaware.*): You would know. (*He crosses over to pick up the hat and cape.*)

LARRA (*Watching him constantly.*): I would know?

PEDRO (*Turning towards his master.*) Isn't this your final drama? (*He makes to leave.*)

LARRA: My only drama was "Macías"![22]

PEDRO (*Stopping. In a trivial tone.*): Then this must be the second one.

LARRA: Which one?

PEDRO: You're recreating, but you're also inventing. And now you're talking you way through your final drama... as quickly as you can. Time is running out.

LARRA: So you're a character?

PEDRO: As are you. Perhaps the main one.

LARRA: Perhaps?

PEDRO: Don't you think you're giving me too big a part?

LARRA: Shut up.

PEDRO: How can I?

LARRA: Mere imaginings could never be so vivid.

PEDRO (*Withdrawing.*): Except when there's a pistol at hand.

lo mira, desazonado. PEDRO sale por el hueco izquierdo. Tocada suavemente en un piano y apenas perceptible comienza a oírse, hacia su final, la más famosa cavatina de «El Barbero de Sevilla», de Rossini. En la penumbra del bloque izquierdo se divisa vagamente a la ejecutante: una señorita sentada de espaldas que subraya con almibarados contoneos la melodía que arranca del teclado. En el rostro del escritor asoma la emoción y, cuando mira hacia la borrosa presencia, el piano ha llegado a sus tonos normales. La luz del hueco se extinguió y la del gabinete se ha amortiguado mucho, pero otras luces empiezan a bañar a CALOMARDE y a DON HOMOBONO. Cuando rompen a hablar, LARRA les escucha con gesto burlón, y, durante el diálogo de ambos, su atención se reparte entre los dos bloques.)

CALOMARDE. (*Examina un papel.*) ¿Quién es ese Larra a quien se le ha autorizado la publicación de unos cuadernos?

D. HOMOBONO. (*Se levanta.*) Un chicuelo, excelencia. Algo descarado, eso sí. Se ha atrevido a visitarme.

CALOMARDE. ¿Y lo ha recibido?

D. HOMOBONO. Presentó sus manuscritos a don Manuel Abad según lo preceptuado. Pero después he tenido que recibirlo.

CALOMARDE. ¿Por qué?

D. HOMOBONO. Traía una recomendación del comisario de Cruzada.

CALOMARDE. (*Con un mohín de contrariedad.*) ¡El padre Varela!

D. HOMOBONO. El señor duque de Frías también lo protege.

CALOMARDE. ¡Buenos valedores! Por lo menos habrá usted repasado escrupulosamente sus textos...

D. HOMOBONO. Nada grave, excelencia. Escribe que no va a meterse en honduras; que no quiere que le rompan la cabeza.

CALOMARDE. ¿Qué edad tiene?

D. HOMOBONO. Diecinueve años. Pero se expresa con gran prudencia.

CALOMARDE. Peor. Juventud y prudencia juntas son temibles. (*Reflexiona.*) Vigile bien sus próximos cuadernos. (*Mira el papel.*) ¿Los llama... «El duende satírico del día»?

D. HOMOBONO. Puro énfasis. Se inclina más bien hacia las escenas de costumbres, como el señor Mesonero.

CALOMARDE. Bien. Pero vigile.

D. HOMOBONO. ¡Descuide vuestra excelencia! (*Se sienta y continúa su trabajo. La luz los abandona y crece sobre la señorita ejecutante. LARRA la mira y comienza a subir las gradas de la izquierda. El gabinete se oscurece. La señorita termina de tocar con un*

(LARRA looks at him anxiously. PEDRO exits through the left-hand gap. A piano begins to play, barely audibly, the final part of the most popular cavatina from Rossini's "Barber of Seville". In the shadow of the left-hand rostrum can be made out the form of the pianist. Sitting with her back to the audience is a young lady who, as she plays, underlines the melody with gentle swaying movements. LARRA's face fills with emotion. By the time he turns to look at the shadowy presence, the piano has reached normal volume. The light in the gap has been extinguished and the level of lighting in the study has decreased. New light begins to fall on CALOMARDE and DON HOMOBONO. When they break into speech, LARRA follows their conversation with a scornful expression, but his attention is torn between the two rostra.)

CALOMARDE *(Examining a document.)*: Who is this Larra who has been granted permission to publish these journals?

D. HOMOBONO *(Rising.)*: A mere youth, Excellency. Although he isn't lacking a certain temerity. He made bold to visit me

CALOMARDE: Did you receive him?

D. HOMOBONO: He presented his manuscripts to don Manuel Abad in accordance with regulations. But then I had to see him.

CALOMARDE: Why?

D. HOMOBONO: He brought a letter of recommendation from the Commissioner of the Crusade.

CALOMARDE *(With a gesture of annoyance.)*: Father Varela!

D. HOMOBONO: He has the patronage of the Duke of Frías as well.

CALOMARDE: He comes well sponsored. You'll have gone through his texts with a fine toothcomb at least...

D. HOMOBONO: Nothing of note, Excellency. He writes that he's not going to tackle anything too big; that he values his hide.

CALOMARDE: How old is he?

D. HOMOBONO: Nineteen. But he expresses himself with great prudence.

CALOMARDE: All the worse. Prudence and youth are formidable allies. *(Thoughtfully.)* Pay close attention to his next journals. *(Looking at the document.)* He calls them "The Satirical Sprite of the Day"?[23]

D. HOMOBONO: Merely to create interest. He seems rather more inclined towards the description of social customs, like Señor Mesonero.

CALOMARDE: Good. But watch him.

D. HOMOBONO: Indeed, Your Excellency! *(He sits down and continues with his work. They are left in darkness as the light grows on the young lady at the piano. LARRA watches her and begins to climb the steps on the left. The study grows dark. The young lady ends her*

50]

afectado ademán. Amables aplausos de gente invisible. LARRA, ya arriba, aplaude también. Se levanta ella muy complacida, se vuelve y corresponde a los aplausos con sus genuflexiones. Es PEPITA WETORET: una criatura muy joven y linda, de dorados cabellos. Su media máscara, de ingenua muñequita.)

PEPITA. *(Al auditorio invisible.)* ¡Oh, por favor!... *(Sin dejar de aplaudir, LARRA da un paso hacia ella. Cesan los de la sala.)*

LARRA. Pepita..., ¡bravísimo! *(Le besa la mano.)*

PEPITA. ¡Adulador! Eso es de «El Barbero».

LARRA. ¿Nos sentamos?

PEPITA. Como si fuéramos sólo amigos. Mamá nos mira.

LARRA. Sabe que nos queremos.

PEPITA. No te ve con buenos ojos.

LARRA. Ya me verá. *(Se sientan en las dos sillas. Él le toma una mano.)*

PEPITA. *(La retira vivamente.)* ¡Cuidado!

LARRA. *(Risueño.)* En efecto, no nos pierde de vista.

PEPITA. ¿Lo ves?

LARRA. ¿Y si cortásemos el nudo gordiano? Nos levantamos, nos acercamos y le digo: señora, tengo el honor de pedirle la mano de su hija.

PEPITA. *(Sofocada.)* ¿Estás loco?

LARRA. ¿No te atreves?

PEPITA. Eso lo tienen que hacer tus papás...

LARRA. *(Calla un momento.)* Se resisten. Piensan que no debo casarme sin ingresos seguros.

PEPITA. ¡Mariano! Es de mal gusto hablar de esas mezquindades.

(LARRA la mira con cierta tristeza y se abstrae. Ella se abanica y saluda aquí y allá muy remilgada. El foco que ilumina a la pareja deja fuera a PEPITA y se concentra sobre el escritor. Los dos lados del Parnasillo se iluminan entretanto. VEGA está leyendo un folleto. Entre sus amigos, CARNERERO aparece sin máscara y muestra un rostro esquinado y torvo. Todos rehúyen su mirada.)

VEGA. *(A media voz.)* Escuchen esto: «...Y así doy licencia al señor Carnerero para que pueda (...) disputar conmigo, y no se la doy para rebuznar, porque ésa ya la tiene de Dios.»

BRETÓN. *(Con avinagrada sonrisa.)* Lo hemos leído. Y los otros veintinueve insultos que le dedica: los he contado.

VEGA. «El duende» se ha excedido, pero hay que admitir que es diestro esgrimidor... Vean la cara de Carnerero. Parece otra.

performance with a studied flourish. Polite applause from an invisible audience. LARRA, having reached the top, also applauds. She stands up, clearly pleased, turns round and acknowledges the applause by curtseying. She is PEPITA WETORET: a delightful young creature with golden hair. Her half mask is that of an innocent little doll.)

PEPITA *(To the invisible audience.)*: Oh, please!... *(Still applauding, LARRA takes a step towards her. The invisible audience falls silent.)*

LARRA: Pepita, bravo! Bravo! *(He kisses her hand.)*

PEPITA: Flatterer. It's from "The Barber".

LARRA: Shall we sit down?

PEPITA: As if we were just friends. Mama is watching us.

LARRA: She knows we're in love.

PEPITA: She doesn't think very highly of you.

LARRA: She will. *(They sit down on the two chairs. He takes her hand.)*

PEPITA *(Rapidly snatching it away.)*: Be careful!

LARRA *(Happily.)*: Indeed... she hasn't taken her eyes off us.

PEPITA: You see what I mean?

LARRA: And what if we just cut the Gordian knot? We get up, we go over and I say to her: Señora, I have the honour to ask you for the hand of your daughter.

PEPITA *(Flustered.)*: Have you gone completely mad?

LARRA: You wouldn't dare?

PEPITA: It's up to your mama and papa to do that...

LARRA *(Silent for a moment.)* They refuse. They think I shouldn't marry until I have a steady income.

PEPITA: Mariano! It's in very poor taste to talk of such nasty trifles.

(LARRA looks at her sadly and loses himself in thought. She fans herself, daintly acknowledging acquaintances in her invisible audience. The spotlight on the couple now excludes PEPITA and focuses on the writer. Meanwhile both sides of Little Parnassus are lit up. VEGA is reading a pamphlet. Surrounded by his friends, CARNERERO appears without a mask, revealing a face that is angular and grim. They all avoid meeting his eye.)

VEGA *(In veiled tones.)*: Listen to this: "... and so I give Señor Carnerero leave to engage me in debate, but not to bray like an ass, because for that he has leave from God."

BRETÓN *(With a sour smile.)*: We've read it. And the other twenty-nine insults he sends his way: I counted them.

VEGA: "The Sprite" has gone too far, but you have to admire his wit... razor-sharp. Carnerero's wearing a different face today.

DÍAZ. La injuria es una facilidad.

VEGA. No cuando se razona como él lo hace. Además, «El Correo» le injurió antes: le llamó «bestia», «borrico», «cloaca», y afirmó que su «Oda a la Exposición» era malísima.

DÍAZ. Y lo era.

BRETÓN. Usted parece olvidar que también yo escribo en «El Correo».

VEGA. A usted le elogia en su respuesta.

BRETÓN. ¡Ja! ¿Y las alusiones indirectas?

VEGA. No veo ninguna.

BRETÓN. Pues las hay, y contra mí.

VEGA. Imaginaciones suyas.

BRETÓN. O miopía de usted. Ese lechuguino quiere llamar la atención difamando a los demás, como hacen tantos cuando empiezan. Ya se le bajarán los humos.

DÍAZ. Fácil es disparar flechas contra Carnerero. ¿Por qué no se las lanza al Gobierno?

VEGA. No le dejarían.

DÍAZ. Entonces que se calle, como hacemos otros. Todavía está por ver que le prohíban algún artículo. (*Óyese en el aire la voz de LARRA.*)

LARRA. (*Su voz.*) «Un (...) mozalbete con cara de literato, es decir, de envidia...»

VEGA. Por lo menos lo que publica nos ha hecho reír a todos.

BRETÓN. Será a usted.

VEGA. ¡Y se vende!

DÍAZ. Se vocea.

VEGA. (*De buen talante.*) ¿Los dos contra mí? Corriente. Se aplaza el juicio hasta que lo traiga Mesonero. Entonces verán qué tal persona es.

BRETÓN. (*Ríe.*) O no lo veremos. Me han dicho que, de tan bajito que es, ni se le ve.

VEGA. ¡Vamos, Bretón! (*Pero ríe también, y DÍAZ con ellos. Hablan los del otro lado.*)

CARNERERO. Será imperceptible, pero sus artículos no lo son.

GRIMALDI. Se le liman los dientes.

CARNERERO. ¿De qué modo?

GRIMALDI. Echándole algún hueso.

ARRIAZA. Un mosquito no puede picar a una columna del país.

GRIMALDI. *Bien sûr!*

P. FROILÁN. Ese mocoso... (*Y sigue rezongando palabras*

DÍAZ: Insult is the lowest form of wit.

VEGA: Not when it's as reasoned as his. Besides, "The Post" insulted him first: it called him "brutish", "an ass", and "a mind like a sewer", and described his "Ode to the Exhibition" as appalling.[24]

DÍAZ: As indeed it was.

BRETÓN: You seem to forget that I too publish in the "Post".

VEGA: He praises you in his reply.

BRETÓN: Ha! With that innuendo?

VEGA: I don't see any.

BRETÓN: Well, there is, and directed at me.

VEGA: I think you're imagining it.

BRETÓN: Or perhaps you are too blind to see it. The young milksop wants to attract attention by slandering the rest of us, just like so many other novices. He'll soon be taken down a peg or two.

DÍAZ: It's not difficult to shoot barbs at Carnerero. Why doesn't he fire them at the government?

VEGA: They wouldn't let him.

DÍAZ: Then he should shut up, like the rest of us. As far as I can see he hasn't had any of his articles banned yet. (*The voice of LARRA is heard in the air.*)

LARRA (*Voice off.*): "A (...) sturdy lad with the look of a man of letters, that is, of envy..."

VEGA: At least what he's published has made us all laugh.

BRETÓN: It might have made you laugh.

VEGA: And it sells well.

DÍAZ: It's being well-publicised.

VEGA (*Good-naturedly.*): Two against one? As usual. We'll suspend judgment until Mesonero brings him. Then we'll see the stature of the man.

BRETÓN (*Laughing.*): Perhaps we won't. I've been told he's so short that you can't see him at all.

VEGA: Come come, Bretón! (*But he laughs as well, as does Díaz. Those on the other side of the café begin to speak.*)

CARNERERO: He may pass unnoticed, but his articles don't.

GRIMALDI: We must take the edge off his teeth.

CARNERERO: How?

GRIMALDI: By throwing him the odd bone.

ARRIAZA: A mosquito cannot sting a man who is a national institution.

GRIMALDI: *Bien sûr!*

F. FROILÁN: Young upstart... (*He continues muttering unintelligible*

inininteligibles, que un perenne gargajo retenido en la garganta hace aún
más rasposas, ante la inútil atención de los demás.)

CARNERERO. No es que me vaya a quitar el sueño. Pero su
intención es clara: suplantar a «El Correo».

GRIMALDI. *Oh, là, là!* !Suplantar! (*MESONERO entra por la
puerta de cristales. Reverencias.*)

MESONERO. Felices, señores.

GRIMALDI. Don Ramón, convenza usted al señor Carnerero de que
no es tan fiero el león como lo pintan.

MESONERO. ¿Qué león?

ARRIAZA. «El duende satírico del día».

GRIMALDI. Háganos la merced de sentarse y háblenos de ese
mocito.

MESONERO. Mil gracias. Es el caso...

VEGA. ¡Mesonero! ¡Le estamos esperando!

MESONERO. Ya lo oyen. Si me permiten...

CARNERERO. Vaya, vaya con sus románticos.

MESONERO. Discúlpenme. Ya hablaremos de Larra. No es mal
chico. (*Se inclina y cruza bajo la recelosa mirada de CARNERERO.*)

GRIMALDI. (*Riendo.*) ¡Por cierto! ¿Sabe usted que el padre
Varela me lo ha recomendado vivamente como traductor de comedias?
(*MESONERO saluda en el otro lado y se sienta.*)

CARNERERO. ¿Y le va usted a complacer?

GRIMALDI. Como el pillastre domina mi lengua...

CARNERERO. Y como lo recomienda el padre Varela...

P. FROILÁN. (*Ceñudo.*) ¡Hum!... ¡El padre Varela!...

CARNERERO. ¿Me estaré quedando sin amigos?

GRIMALDI. *Mais non!* ¿Usted no comprende? (*Baja la voz.*) Dos
o tres traduccioncitas... y se volverá manso y bueno.

CARNERERO. (*Sonríe por primera vez.*) Grimaldi, me descubro
ante usted. Pero también yo sé lo que debo hacer. (*Se pone su media
máscara, se levanta y se cubre.*)

P. FROILÁN. ¡Duro!... (*Farfulla.*) ...en la cabeza!

CARNERERO. ¡Señor Bretón!

BRETÓN. Mi señor don José María...

CARNERERO. ¿Me acompaña usted? He de consultarle un asunto.

*words, made even more grating by a permanent frog in his throat. The
others listen uncomprehendingly.*)

CARNERERO: I'm certainly not going to lose any sleep over him.
But he's made his play: he wants to overthrow "The Post".

GRIMALDI: *Oh, là, là!* Overthrow! (*MESONERO comes in through
the glass door. They all bow.*)

MESONERO: Greetings, gentlemen.

GRIMALDI: Don Ramón, please assure Señor Carnerero that the lion
isn't nearly as fierce as he's painted.

MESONERO: What lion?

ARRIAZA: "The Satirical Sprite of the Day".

GRIMALDI: We would be glad if you would sit with us and tell us
about the young man in question.

MESONERO: Thank you, indeed. The fact is...

VEGA: Mesonero! We've been waiting for you!

MESONERO: As you can see. With your permission...

CARNERERO: Go on, go to your romantics.

MESONERO: Excuse me. We'll speak of Larra another time. He's not
a bad sort. (*He bows and crosses the café under CARNERERO's
suspicious gaze.*)

GRIMALDI (*Laughing.*): By the by, did you know that Father Varela
recommended him to me, and in the most glowing terms, as a translator of
plays? (*MESONERO greets the characters on the other side and sits
down.*)

CARNERERO: And will you accede to his recommendation?

GRIMALDI: The rogue does have a perfect command of my native
tongue...

CARNERERO: And, after all, he has been recommended by Father
Varela...

F. FROILÁN (Frowning.): Hmm!... Father Varela!...

CARNERERO: Are all my friends deserting me?

GRIMALDI: *Mais non!* But don't you see? (*Lowering his voice.*) Two
or three little translations... and he'll come round, as good as gold.

CARNERERO (*Smiling for the first time.*): Grimaldi, I take my hat
off to you. But I too know what has to be done. (*He puts on his half
mask, stands up and dons his hat.*)

F. FROILÁN: Hard!... (*Muttering.*) ...in the head!

CARNERERO: Señor Bretón!

BRETÓN: Don José María, sir...

CARNERERO: Will you come with me? There is a matter I should
like to discuss with you.

BRETÓN. (*Se levanta.*) A sus órdenes. (*A sus contertulios.*) Ustedes lo pasen bien. (*Se inclina y se cubre.*)

CARNERERO. (*A todos.*) Dios les guarde, señores. (*BRETÓN se reúne con él y salen cuchicheando por la puerta de cristales, al tiempo que el Parnasillo se oscurece y crece la luz en el bloque izquierdo.*)

PEPITA. (*Molesta.*) ¿Has olvidado que estoy yo aquí?

LARRA. ¿Cómo podría? Nadie me quiere bien sino tú. (*Le toma las manos. Ella mira a todos lados, inquieta.*) Nos casaremos el año que viene. Y si nuestras familias se oponen...

PEPITA. ¿Qué?

LARRA. ¿Te atreverías a cortar el nudo gordiano de otro modo?

PEPITA. ¿Cómo?

LARRA. ¿Te escaparías conmigo? (*Un silencio.*) ¿Vendrías?

PEPITA. (*Baja los ojos.*) Soy tuya. Siempre estaré a tu lado. Y si es menester pasaré contigo privaciones... o te cuidaré con todo mi amor, si te hieren.

LARRA. (*Sorprendido.*) ¿Por qué me van a herir?

PEPITA. Si me raptas, quizá tengas que batirte con mi padrino, o con alguno de esos moscones que me rondan...

LARRA. (*Risueño.*) ¡Novelera!

PEPITA. ¿Tienes pistolas? ¿Eres buen tirador?

LARRA. Pepita, el duelo es una barbaridad.

PEPITA. ¿Tú crees? .

LARRA. ¡Claro!

PEPITA. Será como tú dices. Pero si tienes que luchar por mí... sé que lo harás. Tú no eres un cobarde.

LARRA. Soy tan valeroso que estoy resuelto a luchar también contra ese disparatado código del honor. (*Ríe y le besa la mano.*) Pepita, eres una romántica.

PEPITA. (*Hecha mieles.*) ¡Por tu culpa! ¡Y muy celosa! Tú chicoleas demasiado con las damas en los salones.

LARRA. ¡Meros cumplidos!

PEPITA. (*Puerilmente enfadada.*) ¡No toleraré que me engañes! ¡Tomaré una de tus pistolas...!

LARRA. (*Riendo.*) Y me matarás.

PEPITA. (*Compungida.*) A ti nunca podría, bien mío. Pero a ella...

LARRA. Ella eres tú, amor. No fantasees, que todo se arreglará. Convenceré a nuestras familias. (*Se iluminó el bloque derecho. CARNERERO y BRETÓN han subido por las gradas ocultas al despacho de DON HOMOBONO. El hombrecillo se levanta. Reverencias. El*

BRETÓN (*Rising.*): At your service. (*To those at his table.*) Good day to you. (*He bows and puts on his hat.*)

CARNERERO (*To everyone.*): Goodbye, gentlemen. (*BRETÓN joins him and they pass through the glass door deep in conversation. At the same time the light switches from Little Parnassus to the left-hand rostrum.*)

PEPITA (*Put out.*): Have you forgotten that I'm here?

LARRA: How could I? You're the only person who cares for me. (*He takes her hands. She looks around anxiously.*) We'll get married next year. And if our families are opposed to it...?

PEPITA: What?

LARRA: Would you dare to cut the knot in a different way?

PEPITA: How?

LARRA: By eloping? (*Silence.*) Would you?

PEPITA (*Lowering her gaze.*): I belong to you. I could never leave you. And if it comes to it, I'll share your hardship with you... and I'll look after you, with all my love, if you're wounded.

LARRA (*Surprised.*): Why should I be wounded?

PEPITA: If you snatch me away, you might have to duel with my godfather, or with one of those young fops who are always flitting round me...

LARRA (*Laughingly.*): You read too many novels!

PEPITA: Have you got a pair of pistols? Are you a good shot?

LARRA: Pepita, duels are barbaric.

PEPITA: Do you think so?

LARRA: Of course.

PEPITA: Well, if you say so. But, if you do have to fight for me, I know you will. You're no coward.

LARRA: I'm so brave that I will fight, but against a foolish code of honour. (*He laughs and kisses her hand.*) Pepita, you're a born romantic.

PEPITA (*Completely won over.*): It's your doing! I'm consumed with jealousy. You flirt too much with the other ladies in the salons.

LARRA: Merely passing the time of day.

PEPITA (*Childishly peevish.*): I couldn't stand you being unfaithful! I'd take one of your pistols and...!

LARRA (*Laughing.*): And kill me.

PEPITA (*Ruefully.*): I could never do that, my darling. Her...

LARRA: You are her, my love. Stop daydreaming, everything will work out. I'll win over both of our families. (*The right-hand rostrum lights up. CARNERERO and BRETÓN have walked up the hidden stairs to DON HOMOBONO's office.*[25] *He stands up and they all bow.*

semblante de LARRA se nubla.) Porque estoy empezando a ser célebre...
«El duende satírico del día» se vende como pan. (*DON HOMOBONO y
CARNERERO van hacia la escalerilla. BRETÓN se rezaga. Ellos le
instan a que les acompañe. Él se excusa e indica que esperará donde se
halla.*)

PEPITA.   ¿Sabes que hasta mamá se reía con las burlas de tus
artículos?

LARRA.   ¿Lo ves?   Me los ganaré a todos.   (*Se le nota pendiente de
lo que imagina en el otro bloque.*)

PEPITA.   (*Ríe.*)   ¡Y bastantes enemigos también!   (*El censor mima el
ademán de llamar con los nudillos a la puerta de CALOMARDE.   El
ministro asiente y se levanta.   DON HOMOBONO deja pasar a
CARNERERO y entra tras él.   CALOMARDE tiende su mano y el
periodista se la estrecha rendidamente con las suyas.   Después van a
sentarse al sofá, donde departen muy animados sin que se les oiga.   DON
HOMOBONO permanece de pie.*)

LARRA.   ¡Los venceremos juntos!   (*Se aproximan sus cabezas.   Él
va a besarla.   Se oye la voz de la madre de PEPITA.*)

LA MADRE.   (*Su voz.*)   ¡Pepita!   (*Se separan ellos con presteza.*)
¡Deja ya el palique!   El señor duque de Frías quiere felicitarte por tu
ejecución de la cavatina.

PEPITA.   (*Se levanta.*)   Voy, mamá.   (*LARRA se levanta y le besa la
mano.*)

LARRA.   Ojo con los moscones.   No me obligues a desafíos
innecesarios.

PEPITA.   (*Se suelta.*)   ¡Bobo!   El duque de Frías es muy mayor para
mí.

LARRA.   Y además es nuestro protector.   ¡Bendito sea!   (*PEPITA le
sonríe y desciende del bloque por su parte oculta.   Su enamorado se vuelve
y mira hacia el otro bloque.   CARNERERO está asegurando con
vehemencia al ministro que BRETÓN se halla cerca y puede confirmar lo
que él dice.   El servicial censor se dispone a llamarlo y CALOMARDE le
detiene con un ademán.   Siguen hablando.   LARRA inicia la bajada a su
gabinete.   La luz se va del bloque izquierdo y aumenta en el centro.   El
ministro se levanta prometiendo algo y el periodista se inclina agradecido,
volviendo a estrechar la poderosa mano del prócer.   CARNERERO y el
hombrecillo se reúnen con BRETÓN.   El ministro vuelve a su sillón.   Con
un expresivo abrir de brazos, CARNERERO indica a su cómplice la
satisfactoria solución del asunto.   LARRA se demora en los peldaños y los*

[59

ARRA's face clouds.) I'm starting to become famous... "The Satirical Sprite of the Day" is selling beyond all expectations. (*DON HOMOBONO and CARNERERO move towards the staircase. BRETÓN hangs back. The others urge him to accompany them, but he excuses himself and indicates that he will wait below.*)

PEPITA: Did you know that even Mama laughed at some of the jibes in your articles?

LARRA: You see? I'll win them all over. (*He is clearly hanging upon what he imagines to be taking place on the other rostrum.*)

PEPITA (*Laughing.*): And plenty of enemies in the process. (*The censor mimes the gesture of rapping on CALOMARDE's door. The Minister beckons them in and rises. DON HOMOBONO stands aside for CARNERERO and follows him in. CALOMARDE holds out his hand and the journalist takes it obsequiously between his. They then sit on the sofa, where they converse animatedly without being heard. DON HOMOBONO remains standing.*)

LARRA: Together, we'll beat them all! (*Their heads grow closer together. He is about to kiss her. The voice of PEPITA's mother is heard.*)

MOTHER (*Voice off.*): Pepita! (*They quickly move apart.*) Stop chattering. His Excellency the Duke of Frías wishes to congratulate you for your rendition of the cavatina.

PEPITA (*Standing up.*): Yes, mama. (*Larra also stands and kisses her hand.*)

LARRA: Be wary of the fops. I don't want to have to challenge anyone.

PEPITA (*Disengaging herself.*): Idiot! The Duke of Frías is much too old for me.

LARRA: And anyway, he's our patron. God bless him! (*PEPITA smiles at him and leaves the rostrum via its hidden stairway. LARRA turns round and looks towards the other rostrum. CARNERERO is vehemently assuring the Minister that BRETÓN is nearby and can confirm what he is saying. The ever-obliging censor is about to summon him when CALOMARDE halts him with a gesture. Their conversation continues. LARRA begins to walk down to his study. The light fades on the left-hand rostrum and grows in the centre. The minister stands up promising something and the journalist bows gratefully, once again taking the powerful hand of ministerial authority in his. CARNERERO and the censor return to BRETÓN. The minister goes back to his chair. With an expressive opening of his arms, CARNERERO indicates the satisfactory outcome of the affair to his accomplice. LARRA stops on the steps to*

60]

observa. El funcionario despide con zalemas a los dos visitantes y éstos desciendan por la parte oculta. LARRA termina de bajar. El censor toma asiento y se enfrasca en su trabajo. PEDRO entra repentinamente por el hueco de la derecha y su señor se sobresalta. Con misteriosa sonrisa, el criado va al escritorio, toma papeles y se los pone en la mano a LARRA. El escritor los mira y PEDRO, sonriente y con suavidad, le conduce hacia la derecha. Sube LARRA por la escalera con vaga inquietud.)

LARRA. «Fue al Corregimiento, y de allí pasó después a la censura eclesiástica; por más señas, que fue un excelente padre, y en un momento, esto es, en un par de meses, la despachó; volvió al Corregimiento y fue de allí a la censura política; en una palabra, ello es que en menos de medio año salió prohibida.»

(LARRA termina de subir y se acerca a la mesa. El señor chupatintas parece muy ocupado.)

LARRA. ¡Don Homobono!

D. HOMOBONO. ¿Eh?... ¡Ah! Buenos días. *(Sigue trabajando.)*

LARRA. *(Impaciente.)* Quisiera hablarle del sexto número de mi «Duende satírico». *(El hombrecillo no atiende. El escritor carraspea.)* Me dicen que lo han prohibido. Supongo que será un error... El padre Varela no halla nada reprensible en sus páginas. *(DON HOMOBONO se echa hacia atrás sin levantarse.)*

D. HOMOBONO. Siento en el alma tener que desengañarle... Creo que no habrá sexto número.

LARRA. *(Demudado.)* ¿Por qué?

D. HOMOBONO. Lamento confirmárselo... «El duende» ha sido prohibido.

LARRA. *(Le considera por unos segundos.)* ¿Por usted?

D. HOMOBONO. ¡Dios Santo! Yo siempre defiendo a los escritores jóvenes... *(Se encoge de hombros.)* Pero no sé qué demonios habrá dicho usted...

LARRA. *(Le ofrece los papeles.)* ¿Quiere leer los textos?

D. HOMOBONO. ¿Para qué? Es orden superior.

LARRA. ¿Del Consejo de Castilla?

D. HOMOBONO. De allí será.

LARRA. *(Crispado.)* Apelo contra ella. ¿Me hará el favor de solicitar al señor ministro que me reciba ahora mismo?

D. HOMOBONO. Su excelencia no está...

LARRA. Le esperaré.

observe them. CALOMARDE's clerk courteously takes his leave of the two visitors, and they descend via the hidden stairs. LARRA by now has also reached the bottom level. DON HOMOBONO resumes his seat and immerses himself in his work. PEDRO enters suddenly through the gap on the right, startling his master. Smiling enigmatically, the servant goes to the bureau, takes some papers and presses them into LARRA's hand. He looks at them as PEDRO, still smiling, gently leads him towards the right. LARRA reluctantly climbs the staircase.)

LARRA: "...It went first to the Magistrate's Office, and from there proceeded to ecclesiastical censorship; to be more precise, to a worthy priest who dispatched the whole thing in but a moment, that is, in a couple of months; it returned to the Magistrate, and from there to political censorship; in short, in less than half a year it emerged banned".
(LARRA reaches the top and approaches the table. The pen-pusher is hard at work.)

LARRA: Don Homobono!

D. HOMOBONO: Eh? Ah! Good morning to you. *(He continues working.)*

LARRA *(Impatiently.)*: I would like to speak to you about the sixth issue of my "Satirical Sprite". *(He receives no response and coughs.)* I've been told that it has been banned. I imagine that there has been some mistake... Father Varela has found nothing untoward in its pages. *(DON HOMOBONO leans backwards in his seat.)*

D. HOMOBONO: I am deeply sorry to have to disappoint you. I do not believe that there will be a sixth issue.

LARRA *(Crestfallen.)*: Why?

D. HOMOBONO: It is my sad duty to confirm... that "The Sprite" has been banned.

LARRA *(Gazing at him for several moments.)*: By you?

D. HOMOBONO: Heavens! I always defend young writers... *(He shrugs his shoulders.)* But the very devil knows what you must have said...

LARRA *(Offering him the papers.)*: Would you care to read the texts?

D. HOMOBONO: There would be no point. The ruling has come from above.

LARRA: From the Council of Castille?

D. HOMOBONO: I suppose so.

LARRA *(Inflamed.)*: I'll appeal. Would you please ask the Minister to grant me an interview at once.

D. HOMOBONO: His Excellency is not here...

LARRA: I'll wait.

D. HOMOBONO. Vuelva usted mañana...

LARRA. Ustedes siempre saben decir esas palabras, y yo siempre sé volver. Volveré.

D. HOMOBONO. (*Baja la voz.*) De amigo a amigo: no creo que le conceda audiencia... Ya le he dicho que es orden superior.

LARRA. Pido que se me dé por escrito.

D. HOMOBONO. (*Ríe.*) ¡Señor de Larra, no pida la luna! Ya se nota lo nuevo que es en estos trámites. A mí también me lo han confirmado verbalmente. Pero es inapelable. (*Se levanta y le da afectuosas palmaditas en el hombro. Con agria sonrisa, LARRA lo mira sin moverse.*) Usted siga bien. (*Va a su mesa.*)

LARRA. ¿Tal vez ha visitado a su excelencia el señor Carnerero?

D. HOMOBONO. (*Sorprendido, miente muy mal.*) ...No he reparado.

LARRA. (*Breve risa.*) Luego ha venido. No se atribule por mí; no voy a desanimarme. Usted lo pase bien. (*Se dirige a las gradas. Tras él, DON HOMOBONO acecha sus movimientos. Ante la escalerilla pequeña, el escritor se detiene y mira hacia arriba. Los Voluntarios Realistas lo observan, suspicaces, y cruzan sus fusiles. LARRA baja peldaños y los Voluntarios retornan a su anterior posición. El censor se desentiende del asunto con un desdeñoso movimiento de sus manos y va a sentarse. Se inicia un lejano clamoreo de campanas. LARRA sigue descendiendo. Sonriente, le espera el criado. La luz abandona el bloque.*)

PEDRO. Ea, pues a vivir. ¡Cómo repican las campanas en 1829! E duendecito se casa con su ángel. ¡Pero hay un campanario que no tañe por vosotros! Teresa Mancha, la que va a ser amante de Espronceda, no tiene un cuarto y se une con un tal Gregorio del Bayo. «El casarse pronto y mal»... ¡Qué artículo! Lo escribiste después... y siempre lo supiste.

LARRA. ¡No!

PEDRO. Cuando la cubriste de besos y de caricias la primera noche ya lo sabías. Lo que ignoras es por qué quisiste engañarte. Y yo tampoc lo sé... Son cosas del sentimiento. (*El campaneo arrecia.*) ¡Jesús! Ahor son todas las iglesias de España. Su majestad enviudó y se desposa co María Cristina de Nápoles. ¡Alegría! El marido hará lo que disponga est cuarta reina: ya va para maduro. (*Se ilumina el Parnasillo.*) Indultarár regresarán los desterrados... Poco a poco, eso sí. (*Desanimado, se sien el escritor. PIPÍ, un camarero joven, entra por la izquierda y sir*

D. HOMOBONO: Come back tomorrow.[26]

LARRA: Words that you all know how to say so well, and I always know how to come back. Because I will.

D. HOMOBONO (*Lowering his voice.*): Between ourselves, I don't believe he will see you. I'v already told you, the ruling has come from above.

LARRA: I demand it in writing.

D. HOMOBONO: Señor de Larra, you're asking for the moon. It's quite clear that you are new to this procedure. They've confirmed it verbally to me as well. And there's no appeal. (*He rises and affectionately pats LARRA on the shoulder. LARRA watches him, motionless.*) Good day. (*He returns to his table.*)

LARRA: Perhaps His Excellency has received a visit from Señor Carnerero.

D. HOMOBONO (*Taken by surprise, he lies unconvincingly.*):... Not that I am aware of.

LARRA (*With a short laugh.*): Then he has. Don't concern yourself about me; I won't lose heart. Good day. (*He heads towards the steps. DON HOMBONO watches his every movement. When he reaches the small stairway, the writer stops and looks upwards. The Royalist Volunteers watch him suspiciously, crossing their rifles. LARRA descends the steps and the Volunteers resume their former posture. The censor, with a gesture of disdain, symbolically washes his hands of the whole affair, and goes to sit down. Distant bells begin to peal. LARRA continues descending. His servant is waiting for him, smiling. The light fades on the rostrum.*)

PEDRO: Come on, life's waiting. How the bells ring out in 1829! The little sprite marries his angel. But there's one bell that doesn't sound for the happy couple. Teresa Mancha, later to be Espronceda's mistress, with not a penny to her name, joins in marriage with a certain Gregorio del Bayo. "Marry in haste, repent at leisure"... What an article! You wrote it afterwards... but you always knew it in your heart.[27]

LARRA: No!

PEDRO: And that first night when you covered her with kisses and caresses, you knew it then. What you don't know is why you tried to deceive yourself. Neither do I. Affairs of the heart, I suppose. (*The bells grow louder.*) God! Now it's all the churches of Spain. His Majesty has lost one wife, and now he's marrying María Cristina of Naples. Celebrations! The husband will be a puppet in the hands of this fourth queen: he's too old to argue. (*Little Parnassus lights up.*) Pardons are given, exiles return... In trickles, that's true. (*The writer sits down dejectedly. Pipí the*

botellas. Se llenan los vasos en el café. VEGA se levanta con el suyo en la mano.)

VEGA. ¡Viva la reina Cristina!

TODOS. (*Menos el PADRE FROILÁN.*) ¡Viva! (*Beben.*)

PEDRO. Y la tocata llega hasta diciembre, porque... también casan a Dolores Armijo con el apuesto teniente don José María Cambronero.

LARRA. No los nombres.

PEDRO. No. Es pronto. (*La puerta del café se abre y entra CARNERERO.*)

CARNERERO. ¡Señores, viva la esperanza de España!

TODOS. ¡Viva! (*El campaneo se amortigua y cesa.*)

P. FROILÁN. (*Farfulla.*) ...Reina de pacotilla!

CARNERERO. ¡Albricias, Vega! ¡Albricias, Mesonero! (*Se abraza con ellos.*) ¡Brindemos por sus majestades!

GRIMALDI. (*Que está escanciando.*) ¡Aquí tiene su vaso! (*CARNERERO lo toma y lo alza. Menos el PADRE FROILÁN, todos se levantan.*)

CARNERERO. ¡Por nuestro buen rey y nuestra encantadora soberana!

VEGA. ¡Y por la amnistía! (*Beben. El PADRE FROILÁN se cala su teja y se va murmurando. Risas generales.*) ¡Soplan vientos de libertad! (*Se oscurece el Parnasillo.*)

PEDRO. Y escribes tu lamentable «Oda al Rey». ¡Es tan hermosa la esperanza! Cierto que siguen las ejecuciones.

LARRA. Cállate.

PEDRO. Eres tenaz en esos años, aunque todos te creen un vencido. (*Luz sobre CLEMENTE DÍAZ.*)

DÍAZ. ¿Y ése era un rebelde? (*Luz sobre MESONERO.*)

MESONERO. Déle tiempo al tiempo...

DÍAZ. ¡Pero no a Larra! Ya no es más que un pisaverde. (*Luz sobre CARNERERO.*)

CARNERERO. O muy astuto...

DÍAZ. ¡Abajo Larra! (*Luz sobre BRETÓN.*)

BRETÓN. ¡Abajo! (*Luz sobre VEGA.*)

VEGA. (*Se levanta.*) ¡Eso no lo tolero!

CARNERERO. Calma, señores. (*Con intención.*) ¡Todo se andará! (*Vuelve a entrar, al tiempo, el PADRE FROILÁN, satisfechísimo.*)

P. FROILÁN. ¡Y antes de lo que piensan! (*Ocupa su sitio habitual ante la sorpresa de todos. Se va la luz del Parnasillo. Luz sobre CALOMARDE y su empleado.*)

CALOMARDE. ¿Se casó Larra?

young waiter, enters from the left and hands out bottles. Glasses are filled. VEGA stands up with his in his hand.)

VEGA: Long live Queen Cristina!

ALL (*Except FATHER FROILÁN.*): Queen Cristina! (*They drink.*)

PEDRO: And the fanfares last until December, because... Dolores Armijo is married off to the dashing Lieutenant José María Cambronero.

LARRA: Why mention them?

PEDRO: You're right. It's too soon. (*The door of the café opens and CARNERERO enters.*)

CARNERERO: Gentlemen, long live the new hope of Spain!

ALL: The new hope! (*The bells grow distant and stop.*)

F. FROILÁN (*Muttering.*): ... Queen of sham!

CARNERERO: Good health and happiness to us all, Vega! To us all, Mesonero! (*He embraces them.*) A toast to Their Majesties!

GRIMALDI (*Pouring the wine.*): Take your glass! (*CARNERERO takes it and raises it. With the exception of FATHER FROILÁN, they all stand.*)

CARNERERO: Our good King and our charming Queen!

VEGA: And the amnesty! (*They drink. FATHER FROILÁN dons his broad-brimmed hat and exits muttering. General laughter.*) The winds of freedom are blowing! (*Little Parnassus falls into darkness.*)

PEDRO: And you pen your regrettable "Ode to the King". How beautiful hope is! Of course, the executions continue.

LARRA: Don't go on.

PEDRO: You carry on resolutely in those years, although everyone believes you well beaten. (*Light on CLEMENTE DÍAZ.*)

DÍAZ: And we thought him a rebel? (*Light on MESONERO.*)

MESONERO: Give him enough time...

DÍAZ: There's no time enough for Larra. He's nothing more than a dandy. (*Light on CARNERERO.*)

CARNERERO: Or else very astute...

DÍAZ: Down with Larra! (*Light on BRETÓN.*)

BRETÓN: Down with him! (*Light on VEGA.*)

VEGA (*Rising.*): I won't tolerate that!

CARNERERO: Let us stay calm, gentlemen. (*Pointedly.*) Everything in its own good time. (*At the same time, FATHER FROILÁN returns, clearly very pleased.*)

F. FROILÁN: And sooner than you think! (*He takes up his usual position, much to the surprise of the company. The light fades over the café, and falls instead over CALOMARDE and his clerk.*)

CALOMARDE: Larra has married?

D. HOMOBONO. (*En pie.*) Sí, excelencia.

CALOMARDE. ¿Ella es rica?

D. HOMOBONO. No, excelencia.

CALOMARDE. (*Eleva sus brazos piadosos.*) Una familia cristiana que alimentar. Eso le calmará. (*Vuelven los dos a la penumbra.*)

PEDRO. Y la alimentas. Hay que traducir engendros franceses, guiñar el ojo a Grimaldi y a Carnerero...

LARRA. Son ellos quienes me sonríen.

PEDRO. Porque se han dicho: ya es inofensivo. Y tu hijo Luis Mariano viene al año siguiente... (*Descarga de fusilería.*) Más ejecuciones. Y tú, callado.

LARRA. Pero hablaré. No me han quebrado. (*Lo mira.*) «Mil caminos hay; si el más ancho, si el más recto no está expedito, ¿para qué es el talento? Tome rodeos y cumpla con su alta misión. (*Se levanta lentamente.*) En ninguna época, por desastrada que sea, faltarán materias para el hombre de talento; (*Deja de mirar a PEDRO y se vuelve hacia el oscuro Parnasillo.*) si no las tiene todas a su disposición, tendrá algunas. ¡No se puede decir! ¡No se puede hacer! Miserables efugios, tristes pretextos de nuestra pereza. ¿Son dobles los esfuerzos que se necesitan? ¡Hacerlos!»

PEDRO. Lo escribirás más tarde y tienes razón. Pero no convencerás a los necios.

LARRA. No importa. A Quintana le han dejado volver. Espronceda vendrá pronto. La libertad se acerca. (*Nuevo tañido de campanas. Luz en el bloque derecho. CALOMARDE y su adicto, en pie, escuchan con enorme interés.*)

PEDRO. ¡Otro repique! En este país se oyen por cualquier motivo.

LARRA. ¡Por mi hijo!

PEDRO. Y por un regio infante que nace en octubre. Sólo que... no es varón. Una niña. (*CALOMARDE se sienta, muy preocupado. DON HOMOBONO lo imita.*)

CALOMARDE. ¿Podrá engendrar su majestad un heredero? Está muy enfermo y ha promulgado la Pragmática Sanción: con ella restaura el tradicional derecho de las hembras a reinar y deroga la Ley Sálica de Felipe V, que sólo permite varones en el trono. ¿Alcanza usted las consecuencias?

PEDRO. La guerra.

D. HOMOBONO. Puede que don Carlos se allane ante un derecho tan tradicional...

CALOMARDE. (*Ríe.*) ¿En qué nube está usted? ¡Se están ya

D. HOMOBONO (*Standing.*): Yes, Excellency.

CALOMARDE: Is she rich?

D. HOMOBONO: No, Excellency.

CALOMARDE (*Raising his arms in a gesture of piety.*): A Christian family to feed. That should cool his heels. (*Both return to shadow.*)

PEDRO: And you do feed them. You have to translate French spawn, and to wink at Grimaldi and Carnerero...

LARRA: It's they who smile at me.

PEDRO: Because they've said to themselves: he's harmless now. And your son Luis Mariano arrives the following year... (*Volley of shots.*) More executions. And you remain silent.

LARRA: But I will speak out. They haven't broken me. (*He looks at him.*) "There are a thousand paths; if the widest, the straightest, will not serve, then what is talent for? Take the circuitous route and follow on with your important mission. (*He stands up.*) There has never been a time, no matter how wretched, when the man of talent has lacked resources; (*He looks away from PEDRO and towards the darkened café.*) even when every recourse is not open to him, he still has some. You can't say that! You can't do that! Miserable excuses, sad pretexts for our idleness. We need to redouble our efforts? Then, do it!"

PEDRO: You were to write that afterwards, and with good reason. But you won't convince the fools.

LARRA: It doesn't matter. They've given Quintana permission to return. Espronceda will be back soon. Freedom is at hand. (*A new peal of bells. The right-hand rostrum lights up. CALOMARDE and his henchman stand listening with enormous interest.*)

PEDRO: More bells. In this country they ring out for the slightest reason.

LARRA: For my son!

PEDRO: And for a royal baby born in October. Except... it's not a boy. A girl. (*CALOMARDE sits down, very worried. DON HOMOBONO follows suit.*)

CALOMARDE: Is His Majesty capable of siring an heir? He's very ill and has decreed the Pragmatic Sanction: restoring at a stroke the traditional right of females to reign and abolishing the Salic Law of Philip V, which had stipulated that only men could take the throne. Have you any thought of what this might lead to?[28]

PEDRO: War.

D. HOMOBONO: Perhaps don Carlos will be pacified by the fact that it is indeed a right firmly ground in tradition...

CALOMARDE (*Laughing.*): You're living in the clouds. They're

levantando partidas!

D. HOMOBONO. ¿Carlistas?

CALOMARDE. ¡Claro, don Inocente! (*Se levanta y pasea.*)

D. HOMOBONO. Y... ¿qué debemos pensar los buenos patriotas? (*CALOMARDE se detiene y lo mira en silencio.*) ¡Yo tacharé cuanto haya que tachar!

CALOMARDE. He mandado cerrar todas las Universidades. No eran más que focos de agitación liberal.

D. HOMOBONO. ¡Muy bien hecho! Para servir a Dios sobra tanta ciencia falsa.

CALOMARDE. ¡La funesta manía de pensar!

D. HOMOBONO. ¡El horrendo contagio galicano!

CALOMARDE. Pero hay nubes más negras aún.

D. HOMOBONO. ¡No me asuste!

CALOMARDE. Bien sabe que en París hubo revolución en julio y que ha subido al trono Luis Felipe de Orleans. ¡Un rey... liberal!

D. HOMOBONO. ¡Espantosa mezcla!

CALOMARDE. Y en Portugal se ha instaurado... ¡una Constitución!

D. HOMOBONO. (*Se lleva las manos a la cabeza.*) ¡Una Constitución!

CALOMARDE. Estamos cercados por las dos fronteras, y don Fernando ha tenido que reconocer a Luis Felipe. No había otro modo de que el francés retirase su apoyo a nuestros emigrados.

D. HOMOBONO. Del mal el menos... Pero... me pregunto... si no habrá que pactar.

CALOMARDE. ¿Pactar?

D. HOMOBONO. Tolerar algunos liberales en el interior... Permitir algunos regresos...

CALOMARDE. (*Indignado.*) ¡No, mientras yo esté aquí! (*Confidencial.*) Pero con cautela. Vigilaremos con un ojo los avances del carlismo y tendremos el otro muy atento al auge de la infamia liberal. Entretanto, ¡más dureza! Eso es lo que debemos pensar los patriotas. Chapalangarra quiso entrar con cuatro imbéciles y cuatro fusiles. ¡Se los barre y a él se le prende! Y se le ejecuta. (*Descarga de fusilería.*) ¿Torrijos y sus cincuenta ilusos? ¡Fusiladlos! (*Descarga.*) ¡Y a los conspiradores del interior, sean hombres o mujeres, cuatro tiros! (*Descarga.*)

D. HOMOBONO. (*Estusiasmado.*) ¡Cuatrocientos tiros! (*Descargas ligadas como un huracán que se calma de pronto.*)

LARRA. (*Disgustado.*) Y entretanto yo represento «No más mostrador». Hay que vivir. ¿O tal vez no? (*CALOMARDE toma un*

taking sides already!

D. HOMOBONO: Carlists?

CALOMARDE: Naturally, simpleton. (*He gets up and paces to and fro.*)

D. HOMOBONO: And... what is the correct attitude for those of us who are true patriots? (*CALOMARDE stops and contemplates him in silence.*) You can rely on me to censor as much as may be necessary

CALOMARDE: I've ordered all the universities to be shut. Nothing more than hotbeds of liberal agitation.

D. HOMOBONO: A wise move. God's service has no need of so much false knowledge.

CALOMARDE: The dreary obsession with ideas!

D. HOMOBONO: The repellent French disease!

CALOMARDE: But there are even darker clouds on the horizon.

D. HOMOBONO: You fill me full of dread!

CALOMARDE: As you know there was a revolution in Paris in July and that Louis Phillipe of Orléans is now on the throne. A liberal king!

D. HOMOBONO: Fearful combination!

CALOMARDE: And in Portugal they have instigated a... Constitution!

D. HOMOBONO (*Holding his head in his hands.*): A Constitution!

CALOMARDE: We're hemmed in on both frontiers, and don Fernando has had no choice but to recognise Louis Phillipe. There was no other way to get the Frenchman to stop giving aid to our emigrants.

D. HOMOBONO: The lesser of two evils... But... I wonder... whether we shouldn't compromise.

CALOMARDE: Compromise?

D. HOMOBONO: Tolerate a number of liberals inside the country... Permit some to return...

CALOMARDE (*Indignant.*): Not while I'm here! (*Confidentially.*) Caution above all else. We'll keep one steady eye on the progress of the Carlists, and the other on the growing liberal scourge. Meanwhile, we hold a hard line. That's the right attitude for patriots. Chapalangarra thought he could get in with a handful of idiots and as few guns. He was simply swept aside and arrested. And then executed. (*Volley of shots.*) Torrijos and his fifty fools? Shoot them! (*Another volley.*) And a bullet for every traitor in the country, man and woman alike!

D. HOMOBONO (*Enthusiastically.*): One hundred bullets! (*A crescendo of shots bursts like a hurrican and just as suddenly subsides.*)

LARRA (*Disgusted.*): And meanwhile, I write "An end to counters".[29] Still, you've got to live. Or maybe not. (*CALOMARDE lifts a document*

papel del sofá y vuelve a sentarse.)

D. HOMOBONO. Hablando de cosas más gustosas, excelencia, permítame decirle que la revista de Carnerero es un primor. Erudita, amena, tranquilizadora... ¡Después dirán que somos enemigos de la cultura! (*Se sienta y tacha.*)

LARRA. Sí. Hay que vivir y escribir.

PEDRO. Porque Adelita acaba de nacer. Otra boca.

LARRA. (*Molesto.*) ¡No escribo por eso! Mi sombrero.

PEDRO. Al instante. (*Lo toma y se lo ofrece.*) «El Pobrecito Hablador» está levantando ronchas y a ti te agrada comprobarlo. ¿Cómo lograste el permiso para esa revista?

LARRA. ¿De qué hablas?

PEDRO. Voy de prisa. Estamos en agosto de 1832. ¿Llegamos a la muerte de «El Pobrecito Hablador» o prefieres otros recuerdos?

LARRA. (*Sombrío.*) Yo no prefiero nada. (*Se encaja la chistera, se dirige al fondo y desaparece por el hueco derecho.*)

PEDRO. ¿A qué juegas? ¿A que ya has desaparecido? (*Ríe en silencio.*) Mientras yo esté, tú también estás. (*La luz de la salita se amortigua.*)

D. HOMOBONO. Decididamente no me gusta «El Pobrecito Hablador».

CALOMARDE. (*Que leía con gran inquietud.*) ¡Don Homobono! ¡Es demasiado grave lo que está pasando en el palacio de La Granja para que se me moleste con futesas! Tache lo que le parezca.

D. HOMOBONO. Y tacho. Artículos enteros. Pero sería mejor prohibir esos cuadernos.

CALOMARDE. (*De mala gana y pensando a medias en otra cosa.*) No hay que contrariar al padre Varela.

D. HOMOBONC (*Lee con cuidado un párrafo, al tiempo que la voz de LARRA lo recita en el aire.*)

LARRA. (*Su voz.*) «...Nuestra misión es bien peligrosa: los que pretenden marchar adelante, y la echan de ilustrados, nos llamarán acaso del *orden del apagador*, a que nos gloriamos de no pertenecer, y los contrarios no estarán tampoco muy satisfechos...»

D. HOMOBONO. Yo sí que estoy aviado. Por un lado, tachar, y por el otro, autorizar. No sé cómo me las arreglo. (*Dolido.*) Algo muy serio está pasando.

CALOMARDE (*Colérico.*) ¡Muy serio, sí, señor! ¡El rey se muere! (*Se levanta.*) Y yo me voy ahora mismo a La Granja para evitar lo peor.

rom the sofa and sits down again.)

D. HOMOBONO: Speaking of more agreeable matters, Excellency, llow me to inform you that Carnerero's journal is delightful. Erudite, *r*atifying, soothing... Now let them say that we are opposed to culture! *He sits down and begins to delete.)*

LARRA: Yes. One has to live and write.

PEDRO: Indeed. Adelita has just been born. Another mouth.

LARRA (*Put out.*): That's not why I write. Get me my hat.

PEDRO: At once. (*He lifts it and offers it to him.*) "The Poor Little *B*abbler" is raising a few hackles and you're pleased to hear it. How did *y*ou manage to get permission to publish the journal?

LARRA: What are you talking about?

PEDRO: I'm moving fast. This is August 1832. Shall we go on to the *d*emise of "The Poor Little Babbler" or do you prefer other memories?

LARRA (*Darkly.*): I don't prefer anything. (*He dons his top hat, w*alks towards the back and disappears through the right-hand gap.*)

PEDRO: What do you think you're doing? Why have you *d*isappeared? (*He laughs in silence.*) For as long as I'm here, then you will *b*e too. (*The light in the study begins to fade.*)

D. HOMOBONO: Most decidedly, I don't like "The Poor Little *B*abbler".

CALOMARDE (*Reading anxiously.*): Don Homobono! The situation *i*n the palace at La Granja is too serious for you to worry me with trifles. *C*ross out whatever you think.

D. HOMOBONO: I do. Whole articles. But it would be better to ban *t*hese particular journals.

CALOMARDE (*Reluctantly, only half paying attention.*): We mustn't *g*o against Father Varela.

*(DON HOMOBONO carefully reads a section whilst at the same time the v*oice of LARRA is heard.*)

LARRA (*Voice off.*): "...Our mission is indeed a dangerous one: *t*hose who believe themselves to be forging ahead, and who claim to be *m*en of the enlightment, may well see us as being of the order of the *l*amptrimmer, to which of course we pride ourselves on not belonging, and *t*hose on the other side of the fence will not exactly be pleased either..."

D. HOMOBONO: A fine state of affairs, indeed. One hand deletes *w*hile the other authorises. I don't know how I manage. (*Pained.*) *s*omething very serious is occuring here.

CALOMARDE (*Furious.*): Very serious indeed, sir! The King is *d*ying. (*He stands up.*) And I'm going directly to La Granja to prevent the *w*orst from happening.

D. HOMOBONO. (*Se ha levantado trémulo.*) ¿Qué el rey se muere?

CALOMARDE. ¡Poco he de poder si no consigo... que derogue antes la Pragmática Sanción!

D. HOMOBONO. ¿Contra la voluntad de la reina y de sus adictos?

CALOMARDE. Usted no sabe quién es Calomarde. Siga en su trabajo y dentro de unos días le traeré buenas noticias. (*Desciende por la parte oculta. DON HOMOBONO suspira, se sienta y trabaja. La luz abandona al bloque. El café se ilumina.*)

CARNERERO. ¿Cómo se las ingeniará para ir salvando esa revista?

P. FROILÁN. (*Con su acostumbrada jerigonza.*) ...La mala hierba... brota y brota... desastre. (*Entra BRETÓN por la puerta.*)

BRETÓN. Señores, noticias calentitas y de muy buena fuente. ¡Pipí! Un chocolate con bizcochos.

PIPÍ. (*Su voz.*) ¡Al momento!

CARNERERO. ¡Siéntese y cuente!

BRETÓN. (*Sin sentarse.*) Su majestad...

GRIMALDI. ¿Qué?

DÍAZ. ¿Qué? (*Gran expectación.*)

BRETÓN. Se muere sin remedio. (*Se van levantando todos.*)

TODOS. (*Unos consternados; otros tal vez disimulando su regocijo.*) ¡¡Se muere!!

PIPÍ. (*Entra por la izquierda con el chocolate.*) ¿Se muere?

CARNERERO. No quise decirlo por no inquietarles... Es cierto.

ARRIAZA. ¡Dios mío! Cuando usted lo dice... (*Se van sentando.*)

BRETÓN. No saldrá de ésta. (*Silencio embarazoso. Todos se miran. BRETÓN se sienta en su sitio y la emprende con el chocolate.*)

DÍAZ. Si el rey fallece la reina nos dejará escribir.

VEGA. A no ser que don Carlos ocupe el trono. Ya hay partidas.

CARNERERO. Grupitos que nada lograrán... (*Respira fuerte, se decide.*) ¡La libertad se impone, caballeros!

ARRIAZA. (*Escandalizado.*) ¡Carnerero!

CARNERERO. Don Juan, usted sabe que siempre fui liberal. (*Muy asombrado, PIPÍ se va por la izquierda.*)

GRIMALDI. Yo no tengo que proclamarlo... ¡Soy francés!

DÍAZ. (*Se levanta.*) Adiós, señores míos. Tengo que hacer. (*Va*

D. HOMOBONO (*Who has stood up, quivering.*): What... the King is dying?

CALOMARDE: My only hope is to convince him... to abolish the Pragmatic Sanction!

D. HOMOBONO: Against the wishes of the Queen and her supporters?

CALOMARDE: You don't know what sort of man Calomarde is. Continue with your work and within a few days I shall return with happy news.

(*He descends the hidden stairway. DON HOMOBONO sighs, sits down and sets about his work. The light fades here and grows in the café.*)

CARNERERO: How on earth does he manage to keep his journal afloat?

F. FROILÁN (*In his usual gibberish.*):... Weeds... sprouting and sprouting... disastrous. (*BRETÓN comes through the door.*)

BRETÓN: Gentlemen, the latest news, and from a most reliable source. Pipí! A hot chocolate and some cakes.

PIPI (*Voice off.*): At once!

CARNERERO: Sit down and tell us!

BRETÓN (*Without sitting.*): His Majesty...

GRIMALDI: What?

DÍAZ: What? (*General suspense.*)

BRETÓN: Is dying. They've given up all hope. (*They all stand.*)

ALL (*Some concerned, others perhaps concealing their joy.*): Dying!!

PIPI (*Entering from the left with the chocolate.*): He's dying?

CARNERERO: I kept it to myself to avoid alarming you... It's true.

ARRIAZA: My God! If you say so... (*They begin to sit down again.*)

BRETÓN: He's finished this time. (*An embarrassed silence. They all look at each other. BRETÓN takes his usual seat and attacks his chocolate.*)

DÍAZ: If the King dies, the Queen will allow us to write.

VEGA: Unless don Carlos takes the throne. His supporters have organised.

CARNERERO: Harmless little cliques... (*He takes a deep breath before taking the plunge.*) Freedom has triumphed, gentlemen.

ARRIAZA (*Horrified.*): Carnerero!

CARNERERO: Don Juan, you know I have always been a liberal. (*Very surprised, Pipí exits from the left.*)

GRIMALDI: I have no need to proclaim it... I am French!

DÍAZ (*Standing up.*): Goodbye, gentlemen. I have business to attend to. (*He goes towards the door where he bumps into LARRA, who is*

hacia la salida y en la puerta se tropieza con LARRA, que entra.)

LARRA. Perdón. (*PEDRO se va del gabinete por el fondo.*)

DÍAZ. Perdón. (*Va a salir, pero se detiene al oír a MESONERO.*)

MESONERO. ¡Querido Larra! ¿Sabe ya que el rey agoniza?

LARRA. (*Frío.*) Es muy capaz de salir de ésta. (*BRETÓN lo mira con su torvo y único ojo.*)

CARNERERO. (*Por MESONERO.*) «El Curioso Parlante» no opina así... Ya veremos. (*Se levanta y se encara con LARRA.*) Mi admirado Larra... Creo que debemos olvidar viejas querellas. (*Asombrados, todos escuchan. CARNERERO ofrece su mano. MESONERO se levanta y se acerca, muy contento.*)

GRIMALDI. Larra, ésa es una mano leal. Tómela.

MESONERO. ¡Pelillos a la mar! (*LARRA sonríe, irónico, y estrecha la mano de CARNERERO.*)

GRIMALDI. ¡Bravo!

CARNERERO. (*Prolongando el apretón.*) Me sentiría muy honrado si su firma apareciese en «La Revista Española». Le ofrezco la crítica de teatro. ¿Acepta? (*Breve pausa.*). Pero siéntese con nosotros, se lo ruego. (*Le indica una silla.*)

LARRA. Gracias. (*Se sientan. MESONERO se sienta a su lado.*)

MESONERO. ¡Ah, qué hermoso! ¡Todos amigos!

CARNERERO. (*Riendo.*) ¡Es usted el mismísimo Diantre, *Bachiller!*

LARRA. ¡Sólo un pobrecito hablador!

CARNERERO. A ello me refería. ¿Cómo logra usted que le autoricen las cosas que escribe en esos cuadernos? (*LARRA los mira cauto.*)

ARRIAZA. Habrá que pensar en algún valedor poderoso...

LARRA. El secreto está en probar a decirlas. (*Mira al PADRE FROILÁN.*) No todos los censores son iguales... (*El padre desvía la vista.*)

DÍAZ. (*Cruzado de brazos y recostado en la puerta.*) Sólo apruebar lo que no es peligroso. (*Todos lo miran. LARRA le observa con frialdad.*)

P. FROILÁN. (*De mal talante.*) ¡Y así debe ser... porque... (*Gruñe y gruñe con evidente acritud.*) ...¡Y afortunadamente!

CARNERERO. El padre exagera, amigo Larra.

LARRA. Siento no poder saberlo. Un pícaro catarro me ha tomado el oído. Yo sólo le he entendido «afortunadamente». (*Risas contenidas.*)

CARNERERO. ¿No se conocen? Padre Froilán, permítam presentarle a...

oming in.)

LARRA: Excuse me. (*PEDRO leaves the study by the rear.*)

DÍAZ: Excuse me. (*He is about to leave when he hears MESONERO.*)

MESONERO: My dear Larra! Have you heard the King is on his deathbed?

LARRA (*Coldly.*): He's more than capable of a miraculous recovery.[30] *BRETÓN watches him with his one glaring eye.*)

CARNERERO (*Referring to MESONERO.*): "The Voice of Enquiry" doesn't think that... We shall see. (*He stands up and faces LARRA.*) My esteemed Larra... I think we should lay old differences aside. (*The others listen in amazement. CARNERERO holds out his hand. MESONERO stands up and comes over, clearly very pleased.*)

GRIMALDI: Larra, this is the hand of constancy. Take it.

MESONERO: Let bygones be bygones! (*LARRA smiles ironically, and shakes CARNERERO's hand.*)

GRIMALDI: Bravo!

CARNERERO (*Holding on to LARRA's hand.*): I should be honoured if your name were to appear in "The Spanish Review". The position of theatre critic is yours for the taking. Will you accept? (*Brief silence.*) Sit with us, I beg you. (*He points to a chair.*)

LARRA: Thank you. (*They sit. MESONERO sits at his side.*)

MESONERO: How very pleasant! Friends together!

CARNERERO (*Laughing.*): You're the very deuce, Graduate!

LARRA: Merely a poor little babbler!

CARNERERO: Indeed. How do you manage to get authority to publish the things you write in your journals? (*LARRA looks at him cautiously.*)

ARRIAZA: Presumably, one must assume that there is some powerful guarantor...

LARRA: The secret is in the daring to say them.[31] (*He looks at FATHER FROILÁN.*) Not all censors are alike... (*The priest looks away.*)

DÍAZ (*Arms folded, leaning against the door.*): Only the innocuous gains their approval. (*They all look at him. Larra observes him coldly.*)

F. FROILÁN (*Cantankerously.*): The way it should be... because... *He continues grunting with obvious acerbity.*) ... and just as well!

CARNERERO: The Father is exaggerating, my dear Larra.

LARRA: I'm afraid I have no way of knowing. A nasty cold has left me quite deaf. I could only make out "just as well". (*Muffled laughter.*)

CARNERERO: Have you not met? Father Froilán, allow me to introduce...

P. FROILÁN. (*Se quita entretanto su media máscara y se levanta, muy nervioso e intimidado. Su cara es blanda, borrosa, medrosa. Balbucea.*) Ya dije antes... excúsenme... queden con Dios. (*Se pone torpemente la teja, se precipita a la puerta y sale. Risas generales.*)

CARNERERO. ¿Quién diría que por dentro es de mantequilla?

MESONERO. Aun así, usted ha sido imprudente, *Bachiller*.

LARRA. No lo crea. Ellos también nos temen. Y hoy tiene fuertes motivos para sentirse asustado.

CARNERERO. (*Rie y le palmea en la espalda.*) ¡Este hombre es invencible!

LARRA. (*Con sorna.*) ¿Yo? ¡Pobre de mí!

DÍAZ. Ya llegará quien le cante las cuarenta a su satírico-manía. (*Todos lo miran.*)

LARRA. ¿Habla usted de mí?

DÍAZ. ¿Tampoco a mí me oye?

LARRA. Perfectamente. A Dios gracias, el catarro se me acaba de pasar. (*VEGA rie a hurtadillas.*)

DÍAZ. Pues ya lo sabe. Hay quien cae en la manía de ofender con su sátira a ciudadanos respetables. Y la censura la permite porque carece de importancia pública. (*BRETÓN asiente, risueño.*)

MESONERO. Algo tendrá «El Pobrecito Hablador» cuando se vende tan bien, señor Díaz.

DÍAZ. La gente siempre se huelga con los ataques a personas dignísimas. Bien lo sabe el señor Carnerero.

CARNERERO. Por favor. Ya he dicho que no hay que recordar eso.

LARRA. El muchacho tiene razón, señores. Consideren que debe de ser un poeta en ciernes.

DÍAZ. ¡Oiga, señor mío! Está usted hablando con un poeta y nada más.

LARRA. ¡Si le estoy dando la razón! Un poeta, nada más que en ciernes. «Terrible y triste cosa me parece escribir lo que no ha de ser leído; empero más ardua empresa se me figura a mí, inocente que soy leer lo que no se ha escrito.» (*Carcajadas mal disimuladas.*)

DÍAZ. Lo leerá cuando se pueda publicar. Yo prefiero callarme a firmarme Juan Pérez de Munguía o a escribir a don Andrés Niporesa acerca de las Batuecas y los batuecos, en vez de llamarles España y los españoles.

VEGA. ¡Usted no ha entendido! Larra concede algo para sacar más.

F. FROILÁN (*He has taken off his half mask and stood up, nervously and fearfully. His face is soft, indistinct, timorous. He babbles.*) As I said before... excuse me... God be with you. (*He dons his hat clumsily, rushes towards the door and goes out. General laughter.*)

CARNERERO: Who would have guessed that he's as soft as butter inside.

MESONERO: Even so, you have been rash, Larra.

LARRA: You are mistaken. They fear us as well. And today he has every reason to be afraid.

CARNERERO (*He laughs and slaps him on the back.*): This man is invincible!

LARRA (*Scornfully.*): Am I? Poor me'

DÍAZ: He and his satire-mania will get their come-uppance. (*They all look at him.*)

LARRA: Are you referring to me?

DÍAZ: Can you not hear me either?

LARRA: Perfectly. Thanks be to God, I've just shaken off my cold. (*VEGA laughs to himself.*)

DÍAZ: Then you know. There are those who allow themselves to become obsessed with a mania for insulting decent citizens. And the censorship permits it because it is of no public importance whatsoever. (*BRETÓN cheerfully nods agreement.*)

MESONERO: There must be something to "The Poor Little Babbler" if it sells so well, Señor Díaz.

DÍAZ: People always relish the vilification of men of note. Señor Carnerero knows that full well.

CARNERERO: I beg you. I have said that there is no need to dwell on things past.

LARRA: The young man is right, gentlemen. Let us bear in mind that he must be a fledgling poet.

DÍAZ: My dear sir, pay heed! You are addressing a poet and no less.

LARRA: Yes, indeed. No less than a fledgling poet. "It seems to me a sad and terrible thing to write that which will not be read; nevertheless, an even more arduous task, it strikes me in all my innocence, is that of reading what hasn't been written". (*Ill-concealed guffaws.*)

DÍAZ: You will read it when it can be published. I prefer to remain silent rather than to sign myself Juan Pérez de Munguía, or to write to don Andrés Notevenso about Las Batuecas and its inhabitants, instead of calling them openly Spain and the Spaniards.[32]

VEGA: You've missed the point! Larra gives so that he can take even more.

DÍAZ.   Es su opinión.   Yo a eso le llamo una pluma prostituida. (*Silencio. CARNERERO chasquea la lengua, reprobatorio. LARRA se levanta despacio.*)

ARRIAZA.   Eso en mi tiempo costaba un desafío.

VEGA.   ¡Y en éste! (*Se levanta.*) ¡Crúcele la cara!

LARRA.   ¡No habrá desafío!   Que este joven calle y me desprecie. Cuando crea que puede hablar, ya no tendrá voz.   Y su pluma no se prostituye... porque no tiene pluma.

VEGA.   ¡Muy bien, Larra! (*Y se sienta, sonriente.*)

DÍAZ.   (*Da un paso hacia LARRA. Se sobrepone a su rabia.*) Señor de Carnerero: yo le admiro y le doy las gracias por su magnífica «Revista Española»...

LARRA.   ¡No es adulación, señor de Carnerero!   Ya sabemos que este mozo no adula. (*DÍAZ se vuelve hacia él, enfurecido. LARRA le espera a pie firme. DÍAZ se quita su máscara con mano nerviosa y LARRA sonríe. El poeta en ciernes vuelve hacia CARNERERO su anguloso y pálido semblante, cuajado de granos y espinillas.*)

DÍAZ.   Usted sabrá por qué abre sus puertas al charlatán que le injurió.

CARNERERO.   Porque escribe muy bien.

DÍAZ.   (*Se traga el desdén.*) Adiós, señores. (*Sale por la puerta.*)

GRIMALDI.   Carnerero ha demostrado la grandeza de su ánimo. ¡Brindo por él! (*Bebe. LARRA ha bajado la cabeza.*)

CARNERERO.   Gracias, Grimaldi.   Larra, me habían dicho que es usted un hombre triste, y veo que es cierto.   Pero olvide los desplantes de ese chicuelo.   ¿Sabe por qué ha estado tan impertinente?   Porque le he rechazado artículos.

MESONERO.   ¡Pura envidia!

CARNERERO.   (*Se levanta.*) Hágame la merced de acompañarme a mi casa.   Tengo dispuesto el contrato.   ¿Querrá leerlo?

LARRA.   Sí.

GRIMALDI.   *C'est magnifique!*   Nuevos tiempos, sangre nueva.

CARNERERO.   (*Se cubre.*) ¡Pipí, apunta todo a mi cuenta! (*Le indica a LARRA que pase al centro; suben los dos directamente al gabinete.   El Parnasillo se oscurece.   CARNERERO y LARRA se descubren.*) Considere como suya mi humilde vivienda.

LARRA.   Muchas gracias. (*Una claridad dorada embellece la sala.*)

CARNERERO.   Por favor, tome asiento. (*LARRA lo hace junto a velador.*) Y hágame el honor (*Va al bufete para volver con dos hoja.*)

DÍAZ: That's your opinion. But for me it's a pen which prostitutes itself. (*Silence. CARNERERO clicks his tongue, reprovingly. LARRA slowly gets to his feet.*)

ARRIAZA: In my day that would require a challenge.

VEGA: Today as well. (*Standing up.*) Cross his face for him!

LARRA: There'll be no challenge! Let this young man remain silent and despise me. When he thinks he can speak out, his voice will have gone. And if his pen doesn't prostitute itself... it's because he doesn't have one.

VEGA: Well done, Larra! (*He sits down, smiling.*)

DÍAZ (*He steps towards LARRA, overcoming his frustrated rage.*): Señor de Carnerero: I admire you and am grateful to you for your magnificent "Spanish Review"...

LARRA: This isn't flattery, Señor de Carnerero. We know that this lad isn't capable of such a thing. (*DÍAZ turns towards him furiously. LARRA holds his ground. DÍAZ removes his mask with a nervous hand and LARRA smiles. The fledgling poet turns his pale, angular, acne-covered face towards CARNERERO.*)

DÍAZ: Only you can know why you're opening your doors to the charlatan who insulted you.

CARNERERO: Because he writes well.

DÍAZ (*Swallowing his disdain.*) Goodbye, gentlemen. (*He leaves.*)

GRIMALDI: Carnerero has shown his generosity of spirit. A toast to him! (*He drinks. LARRA has lowered his head.*)

CARNERERO: Thank you, Grimaldi. I had been told, Larra, that you are melancholic by nature, and I see it is true. But do not dwell on the insolence of that youth. Do you know why he was so impertinent? Because I've rejected some of his pieces.

MESONERO: Sheer envy!

CARNERERO (*Standing.*): I would be grateful if you would come home with me. I have prepared a contract. You would like to read it?

LARRA: Yes.

GRIMALDI: *C'est magnifique.* New times, new blood!

CARNERERO (*Putting on his hat.*): Pipí. Put the bill on my account! (*Ushering LARRA to the centre; they both go straight up to the study. Little Parnassus grows dark. CARNERERO and LARRA take off their hats.*) Please consider my humble abode your own.

LARRA: Thank you, indeed. (*A golden light embellishes the room.*)

CARNERERO: Do have a seat. (*LARRA does so, beside the occasional table.*) And be so kind as to (*He goes to the bureau and returns with two handwritten sheets of paper.*) read this agreement. (*He hands*

manuscritas.) de leer este convenio. (*Se las da. LARRA lee.*) Como verá, ya lo he firmado.

LARRA. (*Lo mira hondamente.*) Es más de lo que esperaba.

CARNERERO. (*Sonriente.*) Es menos de lo que merece.

LARRA. ¿Tanto le interesan mis artículos?

CARNERERO. Mi revista necesita plumas valientes y liberales.

LARRA. ¿Para la crítica de teatros?

CARNERERO. Siendo suya será valiente.

LARRA. No le quepa duda. ¿De cierto lo desea?

CARNERERO. En sus crónicas teatrales y en otros artículos, que también se citan en la cláusula sexta. (*LARRA repasa el contrato.*) Preveo que podrá escribir pronto cuanto ha tenido que callar. Y lo quiero para mí.

LARRA. ¿Me da una pluma?

CARNERERO. ¡Gracias! (*Va al escritorio y moja una pluma.*) Siéntese aquí, LARRA. (*Va éste al bufete, se sienta y toma la pluma.*)

LARRA. Debo recordarle que no pienso dejar de publicar «El Pobrecito Hablador»...

CARNERERO. ¡Este papel no se lo impide! (*LARRA firma y le tiende uno de los papeles, guardándose el otro. CARNERERO hace una seña hacia la derecha.*) Brindemos por nuestra revista. (*PEDRO ha entrado con dos copas de champaña servidas en una bandeja. Su señor verdadero lo mira, molesto. El viejo periodista toma las copas y ofrece una.*) Si me hace el obsequio... (*LARRA la toma y CARNERERO alza la suya.*) Por usted, dilecto amigo.

LARRA. Y por la revista. (*Dejan las copas sobre la bandeja después de beber. El criado se retira por la derecha y vuelve al punto sonriente.*)

CARNERERO. Y ahora quisiera rogarle que, en prenda de amistad, me aceptase un modesto presente. Es algo que a usted le falta, lo juraría. Y a un caballero no puede faltarle.

LARRA. ¿A qué se refiere?

CARNERERO. (*Se acerca.*) Creo como usted que el duelo es una costumbre bárbara, pero en nuestra torpe época es difícil a veces rehuirlo. ¿Tiene usted pistolas?

LARRA. Acertó. No las tengo.

CARNERERO. (*Con sutil sonrisa, al criado.*) Trae la caja amarilla. (*PEDRO va al bufete, toma la caja y se la lleva a CARNERERO.*)

LARRA. ¡Pero no las necesito!

CARNERERO. Nunca se sabe. Le ruego que acepte éstas. (*Toma*

hem to him. LARRA reads.) As you will see, I have signed already.

LARRA (*With a searching look.*): It's more than I expected.

CARNERERO (*Smiling.*): It's less than you deserve.

LARRA: My articles interest you so much?

CARNERERO: My journal needs courageous pens, liberal ones.

LARRA: To write theatre criticism?

CARNERERO: Your pen will be courageous.

LARRA: You need not doubt it. But do you really want it to be?

CARNERERO: In your pieces on the theatre and in other articles, specified in clause six. (*LARRA looks once more at the contract.*) I envisage that very soon you'll be able to write everything you've had to suppress. And I want it.

LARRA: Have you got a pen?

CARNERERO: Thank you! (*He goes to the writing desk and dips a quill in ink.*) Sit here, Larra. (*LARRA goes to the bureau, sits down and takes the pen.*)

LARRA: I should remind you that I have no intention of stopping publication of "The Poor Little Babbler".

CARNERERO: There's nothing in the contract to make you. (*LARRA signs and hands back one of the sheets, keeping the other for himself. CARNERERO signals towards the right.*) Let us drink a toast to our journal. (*PEDRO has entered with two glasses of champagne on a tray. His real master looks at him, put out. The old journalist takes the glasses and offers one to LARRA.*) If you would do me the pleasure... (*LARRA takes it and CARNERERO raises his.*) To you, my dear friend.

LARRA: And the journal. (*They put the glasses back down on the tray after drinking. The servant exits on the right and returns immediately, smiling.*)

CARNERERO: And now I woul*d* ask you, as a token oi iriendship, to accept a small gift. It's something which I am positive you do not possess and yet which no gentleman can afford to be without.

LARRA: What is it?

CARNERERO (*Drawing closer.*): I, like you, believe duelling to be a barbaric custom, but in our uncivilized times it can sometimes be difficult to avoid. Do you have a set of pistols?

LARRA: You were quite right. I do not.

CARNERERO (*With a subtle smile, to the servant.*): Bring the yellow box. (*PEDRO goes to the bureau, takes the box and brings it to CARNERERO.*)

LARRA: But I have no need of them!

CARNERERO: One can never tell. I beg you to accept these. (*He

la caja y la abre.) Son excelentes. (*Turbado, el suicida se acerca un tanto al velador y mira con disimulo el arma que en él descansa.*) Le harán falta para las grandes decisiones.

LARRA. (*Se vuelve rápido y lo mira.*) ¿Qué decisiones?

CARNERERO. (*Después de un momento.*) Disparar contra algún ratero, por ejemplo. (*Se miran fijamente. CARNERERO cierra la caja y se la tiende.*) En prueba de gratitud. (*LARRA titubea, se acerca despacio. Toma la caja. CARNERERO sonríe, se pone el sombrero y baja del gabinete para tornar a su oscuro sitio en el café. La luz cambia y las estrellas se divisan mejor. Ensimismado, el escritor le tiende a su criado la caja sin mirarlo. PEDRO la devuelve a su sitio y se retira en silencio, al tiempo que, por la puerta del fondo, entra PEPITA WETORET, enmascarada y con modesto atavío. Absorta en sus pensamientos va a sentarse, lenta, junto al velador y se pone a coser medias que traía en un cestito. La penumbra crece en el aposento y un foco destaca a la mujer. Nota ella algo y mira a su marido.*)

PEPITA. ¡Cuánto has tardado!

LARRA. Me entretuve en el café. (*Le da un beso rutinario y va a su bufete, donde repasa papeles. La luz crece.*)

PEPITA. ¿Has visto a Luisito?

LARRA. Le he dado un beso al entrar. ¿Y Adelita?

PEPITA. Duerme en su cuna. (*Nerviosa, se pincha con la aguja. Gritito.*)

LARRA. Mujer, ten cuidado. (*En un arranque, la esposa se quita la careta y muestra la aspereza de su rostro amargado.*)

PEPITA. ¡Yo necesitaría una doncella! ¡Mira mis manos! Rojas, pinchadas.

LARRA. (*Frío.*) Hago todo lo que puedo, Pepita.

PEPITA. ¡Todo, no! Ahora ganas mucho más y yo sigo sin doncella.

LARRA. Pronto la tendrás.

PEPITA. ¿Y por qué no ahora?

LARRA. No me fío de nuestra buena suerte actual. Pueden volver los malos tiempos.

PEPITA. Lo peor de tus temores es que me los contagias a mí. ¿Por qué no escribes como Mesonero? Estaríamos más tranquilos.

LARRA. Mi deber es decir verdades.

PEPITA. ¡Tu deber es velar por tu familia!

takes the box and opens it.) They are superb. (*Disturbed, the future suicide edges towards the occasional table and discreetly glances at the pistol resting there.*) You will have need of them for your greatest decisions.[33]

LARRA (*Spinning round to look at him.*): What decisions?

CARNERERO (*After a moment.*): Shooting some pickpocket, for example. (*They stare at each other. CARNERERO closes the box and holds it out.*) As a token of gratitude. (*LARRA hesitates, walks over slowly and takes the box. CARNERERO smiles, puts on his hat and returns from the study to his darkened place in the café. There is a change of lighting which causes the stars to shine more noticeably. Lost in his own thoughts, the writer hands the box to his servant without looking at him. PEDRO returns it to its place and withdraws in silence at the same time as PEPITA WETORET, masked and modestly dressed, enters through the door at the rear. Lost in her thoughts she moves slowly towards the occasional table, sits down and starts to sew stockings which she carries in a small basket. The shadow grows in the room, the woman being lit by a spotlight. She becomes suddenly aware of something and looks up at her husband.*)

PEPITA: You've been gone ages!

LARRA: I was held up in the café. (*He kisses her mechanically and goes to the bureau to revise some papers. The light grows.*)

PEPITA: Did you see Luisito?

LARRA: I gave him a kiss on the way in. What about Adelita?

PEPITA: She's sleeping in her cot. (*She is nervous and jabs herself with the needle. She utters a small cry of pain.*)

LARRA: Woman dear, take care. (*In a sudden outburst, his wife takes off her mask and reveals the harshness of an embittered face.*)

PEPITA: I need a maid! Look at my hands! They're red and raw.

LARRA (*Coldly.*): I do what I can, Pepita.

PEPITA: Not everything! You earn a lot more now, and I still haven't got a maid.

LARRA: You will soon.

PEPIT: Why not now?

LARRA: I don't trust our present good fortune. The bad times could return.

PEPITA: The worst thing about your fears is that you infect me with them. Why can't you write like Mesonero? We'd have more peace in our lives.

LARRA: My duty is to write the truth.

PEPITA: Your duty is to look after your family!

LARRA. ¡Y lo cumplo!

PEPITA. ¡No! Yo apenas salgo, y me agoto en la cocina. El piano..., olvidado. Ni siquiera lo tenemos.

LARRA. Tendrás piano, tendrás doncella... (*PEPITA rompe a llorar. Él se acerca y le acaricia el cuello.*) Antes lo comprendías todo mejor.

PEPITA. Tú te diviertes, y yo...

LARRA. No. Te consta que estoy librando una penosa lucha. (*Baja la voz.*) Y que tengo miedo. Pero también esperanzas. Dame un poco más de tiempo. Las circunstancias van a mejorar... Yo peleo por todo eso, pero tú ya no quieres ayudarme.

PEPITA. Pon tú algo de tu parte... Deja de ser el pobrecito hablador. Te van a meter en prisión... Vuélvete divertido, amable... para todos. ¡Hazlo por tus hijos!

LARRA. Tienen más de lo que les llega a muchísimos niños que apenas comen.

PEPITA. ¡Oh! ¡Qué mal gusto! Si no tienen remedio, ¿a qué hablar de esas miserias?

LARRA. Tienen remedio.

PEPITA. Tú no las vas a arreglar...

LARRA. Otros me ayudarán.

PEPITA. (*Con suavidad.*) ¿A destruirte?... ¿No comprendes que hay que reír, gozar de la vida? Mira: en cuanto nos mudáramos y comprases piano, con sólo tener doncella y cocinera podríamos abrir nuestro propio salón.

LARRA. ¡No te has casado con un gomoso, Pepita! (*Va brusco hacia el fondo.*)

PEPITA. (*Se levanta.*) ¡Me he casado con el miedo!

LARRA. Pero muy mal. (*Toma su chistera.*)

PEPITA. (*Casi grita.*) ¿A dónde vas?

LARRA. A tomar el aire.

PEPITA. (*Se acerca a él unos pasos.*) ¿A tomar el aire... con otra mujer? (*Llora un niño. LARRA mira a su esposa sin responder y va hacia la izquierda.*) ¿Quién te manda las esquelitas que te trae Simón? (*LARRA se detiene un segundo y empieza a subir peldaños. PEPITA, pendiente un instante del llanto infantil, corre hacia él.*) ¿Quién es ella?

LARRA. Adiós. (*Sube otros dos escalones.*)

PEPITA. ¡Mariano! (*Él se detiene, pero no se vuelve. Ella suspira, llorosa.*) Voy, Adelita. Voy, hija mía... (*Recoge el cestillo y la máscara. Se va presurosa por el hueco de la izquierda. Entristecido, LARRA se sienta en los escalones.*)

LARRA: And I do!

PEPITA: No! I hardly get out, I do nothing but cook. My piano... forgotten. We don't even have one.

LARRA: You'll have a piano, you'll have a maid... (*PEPITA bursts into tears. He goes over to her and strokes her neck.*) You used to be more understanding.

PEPITA: You enjoy yourself, while I...

LARRA: No. You should know I'm waging a painful war. (*He lowers his voice.*) And I'm frightened. But I have hopes as well. Give me just a little more time. Things will improve... That's what I'm fighting for, and now you turn against me.

PEPITA: You have to give as well... Stop being the poor little babbler. They'll put you in prison... Be fun again, nice... to everyone. For the sake of your children!

LARRA: They have a lot more than many get, the ones who hardly ever get a thing to eat.

PEPITA: Oh! That's in very poor taste! Why mention such depressing things if there's no help for them?

LARRA: There is help.

PEPITA: You can't change them

LARRA: Other people will work with me.

PEPITA (*Gently.*): To destroy you?... Don't you see that life is for laughing, for enjoying? Look: as soon as we move and buy a piano, with nothing more than a maid and a cook we could open our own salon.

LARRA: You didn't marry a dandy, Pepita! (*He moves brusquely to the back.*)

PEPITA: (*Standing up.*): I married fear!

LARRA: It was a serious mistake. (*He takes his top hat.*)

PEPITA (*Almost shouting.*): Where are you going?

LARRA: Out... to get some fresh air.

PEPITA (*Taking a few steps towards him.*): Out... with her. (*A child cries. LARRA looks at his wife without answering and walks to the left.*) The little notes that Simón brings you, who are they from? (*LARRA stops for a moment and then begins to climb the steps. PEPITA, distracted for a second by the crying child, runs after him.*) Who is she?

LARRA: Goodbye. (*He goes up another two steps.*)

PEPITA: Mariano! (*He stops but doesn't turn round. She sighs, close to tears.*) I'm coming, Adelita. I'm coming, my love... (*She lifts the basket and the mask, and hurries out through the left-hand gap. Saddened, LARRA sits on the steps.*)

LARRA: "Everything is positive and rational in the reasonless animal.

LARRA.   «Todo es positivo y racional en el animal privado de la razón.   La hembra no engaña al macho, y viceversa; porque como no hablan, se entienden...» (*Suspira. Cambia de postura. Se descubre. Su voz suena ahora más honda y dolorida.*) «Escribir como escribimos en Madrid es tomar una apuntación, es escribir en un libro de memorias, es realizar un monólogo desesperante y triste para uno solo.   Escribir en Madrid es llorar, es buscar voz sin encontrarla, como en una pesadilla abrumadora y violenta.   Porque no escribe uno siquiera para los suyos. ¿Quiénes son los suyos?   ¿Quién oye aquí?» (*La luz se va yendo del gabinete al tiempo que crece sobre el bloque izquierdo.   Cuando llega a su mayor intensidad aparece en él DOLORES ARMIJO: una arrogante criatura de 26 años, de labios deliciosos y media máscara deslumbradoramente bella, enmarcada por los azulados brillos de su negra cabellera.   Viene leyendo con precaución un billetito, que dobla luego y esconde en su seno.   El raso de su elegante vestido cruje cuando se sienta al piano y comienza a tocar.   LARRA se incorpora y escucha. Curiosamente, DOLORES inicia la famosa cavatina de «El Barbero de Sevilla».   LARRA se levanta y adelanta el pie hacia otro escalón, mirando a DOLORES sin moverse.   DON JOSÉ MARÍA CAMBRONERO, esposo de la dama, se reúne con ella.   Tiene unos 34 años y viste uniforme de capitán de Caballería.   Media máscara de espesas cejas y nariz roma, labios gruesos y sensuales.   DOLORES deja de tocar.*)
CAMBRONERO.   Continúa.   Yo voy al Ministerio.   Tardaré. (*La besa fríamente.*) Adiós. (*Baja por la parte oculta.   Ella reanuda la pieza interrumpida con aire de despecho.   LARRA termina de subir. DOLORES advierte su proximidad, deja de tocar y se vuelve.*)
LARRA. (*Avanza.*) También a usted le gusta esa cavatina... (*Deja su sombrero sobre el piano.*)
DOLORES.   Está de moda.
LARRA.   Las mujeres no pueden cantarla.
DOLORES.   No.   Pero usted me recuerda a ese barberillo.
LARRA.   ¿Fígaro?   Era un despreocupado.
DOLORES.   También el «factotum della città».   Como usted. (*Se levanta.   Él le besa la mano.*)
LARRA.   ¿Tengo esa fama?   Le aseguro que no la merezco. ¿Tardará en regresar su esposo?
DOLORES. (*Suspira.*) Sí. (*LARRA la abraza y besa con pasión.*) ¡Por favor! (*Se desprende, va al lateral y escucha.*)
LARRA. (*Anhelante.*) Dolores... ¿cuándo?
DOLORES. (*Va al primer término y se sienta.*) No sé si debo... ceder.

The female doesn't deceive the male, nor viceversa; not having the power of speech, they enjoy a perfect mutual understanding..." (*He sighs and changes position. He removes his hat. His voice sounds deeper and more pained now.*) "To write as we write in Madrid is like scribbling notes, or composing a book of memoires, it's carrying on a sad, despairing monologue just for oneself. To write in Madrid is to weep, to search in vain for a voice, as though in some stifling, violent nightmare. For one cannot even write for one's own. Who are they? Is there anyone here who listens?" (*The light fades in the study and shines on the left-hand rostrum. When it reaches its full intensity DOLORES ARMIJO appears: 26 years old with an arrogant air, exquisite lips and a half mask of radiant beauty, framed by the bluish gleam of her black hair. She is cautiously reading a note, which she then folds and hides in her cleavage. Her elegant satin dress rustles as she sits at the piano and begins to play. LARRA sits up to listen. Curiously, she begins the same cavatina from "The Barber of Seville". LARRA stands up and moves his foot towards another step, motionlessly contemplating DOLORES. She is joined by DON JOSÉ MARÍA CAMBRONERO, her husband. He is 34 and wears the uniform of a cavalry captain. His half mask reveals bushy eyebrows, an aquiline nose and fleshy, sensual lips. DOLORES stops playing.*)

CAMBRONERO: Don't stop. I'm going to the ministry.³⁴ I shall be quite some time. (*He kisses her coldly.*) Goodbye. (*He descends the hidden stairway. She resumes her playing with an air of disdain. LARRA reaches the top. DOLORES becomes aware of his presence, stops playing and turns round.*)

LARRA (*Walking forward.*): You like that cavatina as well... (*He puts his hat on the piano.*)

DOLORES: It's fashionable.

LARRA: But not to be sung by women.

DOLORES: No. But you remind me of the little barber.

LARRA: Of Figaro? But he didn't have a care in the world.

DOLORES: He was the "factotum della città". Like you. (*She rises, and he kisses her hand.*)

LARRA: Is that my reputation? It's totally undeserved, I assure you. Will your husband be away long?

DOLORES (*Sighing.*): Yes. (*LARRA embraces her and kisses her passionately.*) Please... (*She disengages herself, walks to the side and listens.*)

LARRA (*Fervently.*): Dolores... when?

DOLORES (*She moves to the front and sits down.*): I'm not sure whether I should... give in.

LARRA. Dolores, usted no ama a su marido, y él le es infiel. Tampoco tienen hijos... Yo sí, y no voy a dejar de atenderlos. Desprecie el escándalo; nuestro amor es verdadero. ¿A qué esperar? (*Se inclina y le besa el cuello.*)

DOLORES. (*Se aparta.*) ¡En mi casa no, Mariano! (*Se ilumina una vez más la puerta cristalera del gabinete.*)

ADELITA. (*Su voz.*) ¡Pa...pá! (*Se extingue la claridad. LARRA ha escuchado. Se toca la frente. Mira a DOLORES y se sienta a su lado.*)

LARRA. (*Le toma las manos.*) Vivamos juntos. ¡A la luz del día!

DOLORES. Déme tiempo... Debo pensarlo.

LARRA. Usted me ama, Dolores. (*Le levanta la barbilla y escruta su rostro enmascarado.*) Ese rostro adorable no oculta nada... No me miente. Sea mía.

DOLORES. En secreto. Por ahora, en secreto.

LARRA. (*Trémulo.*) ¿Quiere decir... que accede a una cita? (*DOLORES no responde y baja la cabeza.*) He buscado un lugar muy discreto...

DOLORES. (*Le corta.*) ¡No! (*Él la mira, dolido por su vehemencia.*) Una amiga mía tiene una quinta fuera de puertas... No está en Madrid y me ha dejado la llave. Yo... preferiría... ese sitio.

LARRA. ¡Donde usted diga, Dolores! No puede imaginarse lo feliz que me hace. Yo estaba... tan cansado de mi vida vacía...

DOLORES. ¿Cree que yo no estoy también infinitamente hastiada de mentiras? En los salones, en la Ópera, me sentía, de pronto, muy sola. Y me refugiaba como una colegiala en esos pobres poemitas que a veces intento y que usted ha leído.

LARRA. Son maravillosos.

DOLORES. Usted es maravilloso. Yo vivía triste y despechada hasta que empecé a leer sus cuadernos. ¡Cómo respiré! Al fin, la verdad, la ironía saludable, el latigazo a esta sociedad hipócrita... Y pensé: a este hombre sí podría amarlo.

LARRA. Yo cometí el error de casarme pronto y mal...

DOLORES. Su bellísimo artículo. Lloré por mí misma cuando lo leí.

LARRA. (*Acentúa con gravedad el tuteo que inicia.*) No me equivocaré por segunda vez. Tú eres ya, para siempre, mi verdadera esposa. La mujer capaz de compartir mis ilusiones y mis peligros.

DOLORES. Sé que me necesitas tanto como yo a ti.

LARRA. Entonces...

LARRA: Dolores, you don't love your husband, and he's unfaithful to you. You have no children. I know I do, but I won't just abandon them. What does the scandal matter? We love each other. Why wait? (*He leans forward to kiss her neck.*)

DOLORES (*Pulling away.*): Not here, Mariano! (*Once again the glass door in the study begins to glow.*)

ADELITA (*Voice off.*): Pa...pa! (*The light goes out. LARRA has heard the voice and rubs his brow. He looks at DOLORES and sits at her side.*)

LARRA (*Taking her hands.*): Why don't we   live together... and bring it all out into the open.

DOLORES: Give me time... I must think.

LARRA: You love me, Dolores. (*He lifts her chin and looks into her masked face.*) Your lovely face couldn't hide anything... It couldn't lie. Be mine.

DOLORES: In secret. For the time being, in secret.

LARRA (*His voice trembling.*): You mean... you will meet me? (*DOLORES remains silent and lowers her head.*) I've found a very secluded place...

DOLORES (*Interrupting him.*): No! (*He looks at her, hurt by her vehemence.*) A friend of mine has a house outside the city... On the outskirts of Madrid, and she's given me the key. I... would rather... go there.

LARRA: Wherever you say, Dolores. You can't imagine how happy you make me. I was... so tired of the emptiness in my life...

DOLORES: And don't you think that I am anything if not tired of a life of lies? In the salons, the opera, I felt suddenly so lonely. And I took refuge like a schoolgirl in those silly poems I sometimes try and write, and which you have read.

LARRA: They're wonderful.

DOLORES: It's you who are wonderful. I led a life of sadness and rejection until I began to read your journals. How I breathed! At last, truth, a healthy sense of irony that cuts through the lies we have to live... And I thought: I could love this man.

LARRA: I made the mistake of marrying in haste...

DOLORES: Your exquisite article. I cried for myself when I read it.

LARRA (*His tone becomes more intimate.*): I won't repeat the mistake. You are my real wife now, for ever. The woman who is capable of sharing my dreams and my dangers.

DOLORES: I know that you need me as much as I need you.

LARRA: Then...

DOLORES. (*Después de un momento.*) Quizá me resisto porque... lo deseo demasiado. (*LARRA estampa en sus manos ardorosos besos.*) Basta... Basta, bien mío. (*Se levanta, agitada.*) Espera mis noticias. Te mandaré un billete con el día, la hora y el sitio. (*Le da un beso rápido en la boca, se zafa de los brazos que intentan retenerla y desciende por las gradas ocultas. Emocionado, LARRA toma su sombrero y se vuelve hacia el frente, al tiempo que se ilumina el bloque de la derecha. Abrumado y en pie ante su mesa, DON HOMOBONO se quita los manguitos de trabajo y se los guarda. Levanta un manuscrito, lo repasa..., lo deja melancólicamente. Entretanto los dos VOLUNTARIOS REALISTAS se miran, perplejos. Agachan la cabeza, se cuelgan al hombro sus fusiles y empiezan a bajar peldaños. DON HOMOBONO oye algo y se asoma.*)

D. HOMOBONO. ¿Se van?

VOLUNTARIO 1.° Cumplimos órdenes.

VOLUNTARIO 2.° ¡Dios hará que volvamos!

D. HOMOBONO. ¡Él les oiga! (*LOS VOLUNTARIOS bajan al gabinete.*)

VOLUNTARIO 1.° Discutiremos en el cuartel lo que hay que hacer. (*Van al proscenio y se cuadran. Comienza un jubiloso campaneo lejano.*)

VOLUNTARIO 2.° ¡Somos más de cien mil en todo el país!

VOLUNTARIO 1.° No se saldrán con su gusto. Y ahora, bien derechos. La canalla masónica no debe perdernos el respeto. (*Tuercen a la derecha y salen en formación. DON HOMOBONO mira el cercano sillón vacío, recoge su sombrero y empieza a bajar, preocupado, por la escalera. El escritor lo ha observado todo. Se cubre y comienza a descender a su vez. Se miran. Sombrerazos.*)

D. HOMOBONO. ¡Señor de Larra, cuánto celebro verle! ¿Me consiente que le acompañe?

LARRA. (*Muy serio.*) Será un placer. (*Terminan de bajar. Se oscurecen los dos bloques.*)

D. HOMOBONO. ¿Sabe ya la noticia?

LARRA. ¿La amnistía otorgada por la reina?

D. HOMOBONO. También, por supuesto. ¡Al fin, todos reconciliados! Pero... lo demás... (*El Parnasillo se ilumina despacio.*)

LARRA. ¿Hay algo más? (*Bajan del gabinete.*)

D. HOMOBONO. (*Muy triste.*) Ya lo creo. (*LARRA se dirige a la izquierda; el hombrecillo se aparta hacia la derecha.*)

LARRA. (*Se vuelve.*) ¿Además, qué, don Homobono? (*Se descubre*

DOLORES (*Hesitating.*): Perhaps I resist because... I want it too much. (*LARRA smothers her hands with ardent kisses.*) Not now... not now, my darling. (*She stands up in agitation.*) Wait to hear from me. I'll send you a note with the day, time and place. (*She kisses him rapidly on the mouth, slips away from his arms as he tries to hold her back and descends the hidden stairway. Deeply moved, LARRA takes his hat and turns towards the front, at the same time as the right-hand rostrum is lit. Standing dejectedly in front of his desk, DON HOMOBONO removes his work sleeves and puts them away. He lifts a manuscript, reads over it..., and sadly puts it down. Meanwhile, the two ROYALIST VOLUNTEERS look at each other in confusion. With their heads down, they sling their rifles over their shoulders and begin to go down. DON HOMOBONO hears something and peers out.*)

D. HOMOBONO: You're leaving?

VOLUNTEER #1: Orders.

VOLUNTEER #2: With God's will we'll be back!

D. HOMOBONO: Amen to that! (*The VOLUNTEERS go down to the study.*)

VOLUNTEER #1: We'll discuss what has to be done in barracks. (*They go to the front of the stage and stand to attention. Distant bells begin to peal jubilantly.*)

VOLUNTEER #2: There are more than a hundred thousand of us in the country!

VOLUNTEER #1: They won't have it all their own way. And now, chest out. The masonic scum mustn't lose respect for us. (*They turn to the right and march out. DON HOMOBONO looks at the empty chair nearby, picks up his hat and begins to descend the stairs, a worried man. The writer has watched the whole scene. He puts on his hat and also descends. The two men come face to face, and raise their hats.*)

D. HOMOBONO: Señor de Larra, I am delighted to see you. May I walk with you.

LARRA (*Gravely.*): It would be a pleasure. (*They reach the study. The two rostra grow dark.*)

D. HOMOBONO: Have you heard the news?

LARRA: Of the Queen's amnesty?

D. HOMOBONO: That as well, of course. Everyone reconciled in the end. But... the other news... (*Little Parnassus is slowly lit up.*)

LARRA: Is there something else? (*They go down from the study.*)

D. HOMOBONO (*Sorrowfully.*): Oh, I'm afraid so. (*LARRA walks towards the left; the little censor steps to the right.*)

LARRA (*Turning round.*): What else, don Homobono? (*He takes off

y les hace un guiño a los escritores de la izquierda. DON HOMOBONO se descubre y saluda a los de la derecha con una gran reverencia.)

CARNERERO. ¿Además, qué?

D. HOMOBONO. ¿No lo saben? La bofetada...

TODOS. *(Menos LARRA.)* ¿Qué bofetada?

D. HOMOBONO. *(Se sienta a la mesa de CARNERERO. En la izquierda ríen disimuladamente.)* La infanta doña Carlota, en plena Cámara Real, le ha dado un bofetón...

VEGA. Al excelentísimo señor ministro don Francisco Tadeo Calomarde. *(Risas generales. DON HOMOBONO parece muy corrido.)*

D. HOMOBONO. No es cosa de risa.

CARNERERO. Cierto que no. Calomarde le llevó la mano al rey moribundo para que firmase el restablecimiento de la Ley Sálica...

BRETÓN. Todos sabíamos que era un carliston.

CARNERERO. Pero el rey se repone, la reina Cristina y su hermana doña Carlota se lo afean, se restaura la sucesión femenina al trono...

MESONERO. Y al pobre Calomarde lo echan, después de...

VEGA. *(Da una palmada.)* ¡Plaf! El bofetón. *(Risas.)*

LARRA. ¡Y su excelencia se hunde para siempre en las tinieblas exteriores!

VEGA. Con una frase, eso sí, que pasará a la historia.

CARNERERO. *(Riendo.)* «Señora...»

GRIMALDI. «Manos blancas no ofenden.» ¡El *esprit* francés en su boca, por primera vez!

VEGA. ¡Y última! ¡Mudo para siempre! ¡Autocensurado!

CARNERERO. ¡Viva la libertad, don Homobono! *(Entró por la puerta CLEMENTE DÍAZ. Va a cruzar a la izquierda, pero ve a LARRA y opta por sentarse en la derecha.)*

DÍAZ. Señores...

D. HOMOBONO. *(Se resuelve.)* ¡Pues bien, caballeros, viva la libertad! Yo... me he pasado la vida dulcificando las mutilaciones que ese hombre exigía en los escritos de ustedes. ¡Y ahora lo puedo decir muy alto! *(Risitas.)*

LARRA. *(Se sienta junto a VEGA.)* ¿Le han dejado ya cesante, don Homobono?

D. HOMOBONO. Su excelencia don Francisco Cea Bermúdez aún no ha comparecido en el Ministerio...

VEGA. *(Indignado.)* ¿Espera usted continuar?

D. HOMOBONO. Yo haré... lo que me manden.

ARRIAZA. Pues no se mueva de allí, hombre, y aclare su situación

*his hat and winks at the writers on the left. DON HOMOBONO removes
his also and bows effusively in the direction of those on the right.)*

CARNERERO: What else?

D. HOMOBONO: You don't know? The slap...

ALL (*Except LARRA.*): What slap?

D. HOMOBONO (*Sitting at CARNERERO's table. Those on the left
laugh discreetly.*): Her Highness Princess Carlota, in full parliamentary
session, struck...

VEGA: His Excellency don Francisco Tadeo Calomarde. (*General
laughter. DON HOMOBONO looks abashed.*)

D. HOMOBONO: It's no laughing matter.

CARNERERO: Of course not. It was Calomarde who led the King to
re-instate the Salic Law...

BRETÓN: We all knew he was a Carlist through and through.

CARNERERO: But then the King recovers, Queen Cristina and her
sister Princess Carlota cast it up to him, the right of female succession is
restored...

MESONERO: And poor old Calomarde is given his marching orders,
after...

VEGA (*Clapping.*): Slap! She hits him! (*Laughter.*)

LARRA: And His Excellency falls for ever into outer darkness!

VEGA: But with a phrase that will go down in history.

CARNERERO (*Laughing.*): "Your Highness...,"

GRIMALDI: "Hands so white cause no offence." French *esprit* on his
lips, for the first time.

VEGA: And the last! Silent for ever! He's censored himself!

CARNERERO Long live liberty, don Homobono! (*CLEMENTE
DÍAZ has just come through the door. About to cross to the left, he spots
LARRA and sits instead on the right.*)

DÍAZ: Gentlemen...

D. HOMOBONO (*Taking the plunge.*): Indeed, gentlemen, long live
liberty! I... have spent my life tempering the severity of the mutilations
which that man sought to inflict upon your writings. And now I can
proclaim it aloud. (*Snorts of laughter.*)

LARRA (*He sits down next to VEGA.*): Have you been given a
pension, don Homobono?

D. HOMOBONO: His Excellency don Francisco Cea Bermúdez still
hasn't appeared in the ministry...

VEGA (*Indignant*): But you expect to carry on?

D. HOMOBONO: I will do... as I am ordered.

ARRIAZA: Well, stay put and clarify your situation as quickly as

cuanto antes.

D. HOMOBONO. Sí, señor. Mi situación... a favor de la libertad. Porque yo, señores..., yo... (*Se echa a llorar.*)

GRIMALDI. *Mon Dieu!*

CARNERERO. Sosiéguese...

D. HOMOBONO. Perdonen. Estoy tan confuso... Me vuelvo allá. (*Se levanta.*) Yo espero que... intercedan ustedes por mí. Usted sabe que su Revista, señor de Carnerero...

CARNERERO. (*Le corta.*) No pierda el tiempo y vaya a esperar al nuevo presidente.

D. HOMOBONO. Sí, señor. Siempre a sus órdenes, señores. (*Se cala el sombrero.*)

BRETÓN. Don Homobono, usted no ignorará que estamos al borde de una guerra civil.

D. HOMOBONO. Pero... se asegura que a don Carlos lo van a mandar a Portugal.

BRETÓN. Y desde allí desautorizará la sucesión femenina, y el rey se enfadará como él sabe hacerlo, y le confiscará todos sus bienes. Y estallará la guerra.

D. HOMOBONO. ¡Pero triunfará la causa de la libertad!

BRETÓN. O no.

MESONERO. Nadie sabe cómo termina una guerra...

LARRA. Cierto. Conque habrá de pensarlo bien. O se ofrece usted a Cea Bermúdez...

BRETÓN. O busca a Calomarde y procura consolarlo. (*Silencio. Se oye en el aire la voz de LARRA.*)

LARRA. (*Su voz.*) «Nosotros, que creemos que el interés del hombre suele tener, por desgracia, alguna influencia en su modo de ver las cosas (...) juzgamos que *opinión* es, moralmente, sinónimo de *situación*.»

D. HOMOBONO. (*Confundido y humillado.*) Son ustedes la esperanza de la patria, siempre lo he dicho. Adios, señores. (*Sale aprisa por la puerta.*)

VEGA. ¡Hasta el Valle de Josafat! (*Carcajadas.*)

CARNERERO. ¡Venga a mi lado, queridísimo Larra! Tenemos que hablar. (*LARRA se excusa en su mesa y se levanta. DÍAZ se levanta, herido por el nulo caso que le han hecho y, cuando LARRA se acerca, se aparta hacia la entrada del café. LARRA ocupa el sitio por él abandonado. DÍAZ cruza con la vista baja y se sienta junto a BRETÓN. Socarrón, se acaricia el ilustre tuerto la barbilla y sonríe.*)

GRIMALDI. (*Oprime un brazo de LARRA y le indica a DÍAZ cuando cruza.*) Se le han atragantado las dos respuestas de usted al folletc

possible.

D. HOMOBONO: Yes indeed, sir. My situation... in favour of liberty. Because I, gentlemen... I... (*He breaks down.*)

GRIMALDI: *Mon Dieu!*

CARNERERO: Calm yourself...

D. HOMOBONO: Forgive me. I'm so confused... I'll go back. (*He gets to his feet.*) I hope that... you will intercede on my behalf. You know that your journal, Señor de Carnerero...

CARNERERO (*Interrupting him.*): Don't waste your time here... go and wait for the new minister.

D. HOMOBONO: Indeed, sir. At your service, gentlemen. (*He pulls his hat down on his head.*)

BRETÓN: Don Homobono, you are aware that we are on the brink of civil war.

D. HOMOBONO: But... it's widely reported that don Carlos is to be sent to Portugal.

BRETÓN: And from there he'll quash the right of female succession Then the King will simply fly into one of his furies and confiscate all his properties. And that will mean war.

D. HOMOBONO: But the cause of liberty will triumph.

BRETÓN: Or not.

MESONERO: No one can foretell the outcome of a war...

LARRA: Indeed. Therefore, you must consider your position. Either you offer your services to Cea Bermúdez...

BRETÓN: Or you seek out and console Calomarde. (*Silence. LARRA's voice is heard in the air.*)

LARRA (*Voice off.*): "Those of us who hold that a man's self-interest tends to have a sorry influence on his vision of things (...) conclude that opinion is, in moral terms, a synonym of situation".

D. HOMOBONO (*Confused and humiliated.*): Gentlemen, you represent the hope of the nation, I've always maintained that. Goodbye. (*He leaves quickly.*)

VEGA: Until the Valley of Jehoshaphat! (*Guffaws.*)

CARNERERO: Sit with me, my dear Larra. We must talk. (*LARRA excuses himself at his table and stands up. DÍAZ, aggrieved by the scant attention he has received, also stands up and, when LARRA comes over, moves away towards the door. LARRA occupies the place he has left. Looking at the floor, DÍAZ crosses over and sits beside BRETÓN. The one-eyed writer smiles mockingly as he strokes his chin.*)

GRIMALDI (*Squeezing LARRA's arm and gesturing towards DÍAZ as he passes.*): The two replies you made to his pamphlet attacking you

en que le ha atacado.

LARRA. (*Con aire inocente.*) No se quejará de mi mesura. Incluso le he elogiado algunos tercetos.

CARNERERO. (*Ríe.*) Hasta ese lujo se ha permitido, sí, señor. Grimaldi, dígale de qué hablábamos antes.

GRIMALDI. Comentábamos lo conveniente que sería un nuevo seudónimo suyo en «La Revista Española».

CARNERERO. Y Grimaldi ya ha pensado en uno.

BRETÓN. (*Que no los pierde de vista.*) ¿Otro apodo? (*Los de la izquierda lo miran y atienden también.*)

GRIMALDI. Algo más... francés, si puedo decirlo.

CARNERERO. O italiano. (*Comienza a oírse, muy suave, la cavatina de Rossini tocada al piano.*)

MESONERO. ¿Por qué? Larra es español.

GRIMALDI. ¡Y el que yo sugiero!

VEGA. ¡Pues no entiendo nada!

LARRA. (*Sonríe.*) Yo sí. O mucho me engaño, o usted propone que adopte el de «Fígaro».

ARRIAZA. ¡Asombroso!

LARRA. ¡Si es muy fácil! Francés, por Beaumarchais. Italiano, por Rossini. Y español, por Sevilla.

GRIMALDI. *Incroyable!*

CARNERERO. ¿Le gusta?

MESONERO. Preferiría un pícaro más nuestro.

GRIMALDI. Yo lo creo adecuado. «El factotum de la ciudad»: el rapabarbas que siempre ríe y a todos trae en jaque.

LARRA. (*Piensa en DOLORES.*) Curiosísimo.

CARNERERO. ¿Por qué? (*El sonido del piano se extingue poco a poco.*)

LARRA. (*Lo mira, risueño y sin soltar prenda.*) No se hable más. Seré Fígaro.

GRIMALDI. ¡Bravo! (*Y palmea sobre la mesa, ufano.*)

DÍAZ. O sea, lo de siempre. Fígaro dirá, y nada dirá. (*LARRA lo ha mirado muy atento.*)

VEGA. ¡Claro que dirá! Y más desde hoy, si quitan la censura.

LARRA. No lo dé por seguro, Vega. Pero gracias.

DÍAZ. Pues si no desaparece habrá que enmudecer. Lo contrario es ceder ante ella.

LARRA. (*Sin mirarlo.*) O ella ante nosotros. ¿Quién podrá más?

DÍAZ. ¡Embolismos! Hay que hablar claro o callarse.

have stuck in his gullet.

LARRA (*With an air of innocence.*): He can't complain about my sense of restraint. I even praised several of his tercets.

CARNERERO (*Laughing.*): Indeed, you did make so bold. Grimaldi, apprise Señor de Larra of what we were talking about beforehand.

GRIMALDI: We were commenting on the benefits of a new *nom de plume* for you in "The Spanish Review".

CARNERERO: And Grimaldi has already thought of one.

BRETÓN (*Absorbed in their conversation.*): Another pen name? (*Those on the left watch him, also interested in the conversation.*)

GRIMALDI: Something more... French, if I dare say.

CARNERERO: Or Italian. (*Very softly, a piano begins to play Rossini's cavatina.*)

MESONERO: Why? Larra is Spanish.

GRIMALDI: So is the name I am suggesting.

VEGA: I don't understand any of this.

LARRA (*Smiling.*): I do. Unless I'm greatly mistaken, the name you are proposing I adopt is "Figaro".

ARRIAZA: Incredible!

LARRA: Yes, it's obvious. French, for Beaumarchais, Italian, for Rossini. And Spanish, for Seville.

GRIMALDI: *Incroyable!*

CARNERERO: Does it appeal to you?

MESONERO: I would prefer a rogue who was more one of ours.

GRIMALDI: I find it appropriate. "The factotum of the city": the cut-throat barber who laughs first and then who laughs last.

LARRA (*Thinking about DOLORES.*): Very strange.

CARNERERO: Why? (*The piano gradually falls silent.*)

LARRA (*Looking at him cheerfully and without giving anything away.*): Let there be no more discussion. I shall be "Figaro".

GRIMALDI: Bravo! (*He slaps the table triumphantly.*)

DÍAZ: So, the same old story. Figaro will speak, and say nothing. (*LARRA looks at him sharply.*)

VEGA: Of course he will say things! And even more things if, as from today, censorship disappears.

LARRA: Don't be too sure of that, Vega. But thank you.

DÍAZ: If it stays, then all any of us can do is fall silent. Otherwise we're giving in to it.

LARRA (*Without looking at it.*): Or it to us. Who will prove the stronger?

DÍAZ: Just addled ideas! Either we speak clearly or we say nothing.

LARRA. Usted ya se calla muy bien, señor Díaz. Déjeme a mí decir algo.

VEGA. ¡Larra, no le conteste!

LARRA. «Ni somos santos ni autoridades, que son los únicos que a todo el mundo oyen y a ninguno contestan.» (*BRETÓN ríe para su capote. GRIMALDI, CARNERERO y ARRIAZA ríen abiertamente. VEGA, a carcajadas. MESONERO sonríe.*)

DÍAZ. (*Rojo de ira, se levanta.*) Soy yo quien no se digna contestar.

LARRA. (*Inocentísimo, a los de su mesa.*) ¿Será un santo? ¿O acaso autoridad? (*Arrecian las risas.*)

DÍAZ. Adiós, señores. (*Cruza rápido y sale por la puerta.*)

CARNERERO. Asunto saldado. ¡Viva Fígaro! (*Se oscurece el Parnasillo, menos el foco que cae sobre LARRA. En la penumbra, CARNERERO se despide y sale del café. Otra luz ilumina en el gabinete a PEDRO, que espera con un papel en la mano. LARRA lo advierte, se levanta y pasa directamente a su sala. PEDRO le alarga el billete, que LARRA abre y lee. Su rostro resplandece.*)

LARRA. ¡Mi capa! (*El criado la tenía ya en el brazo y se la pone. Su señor va al bufete y guarda el billete en un cajón.*)

PEDRO. ¿No lo destruyes?

LARRA. Quiero conservarlo. (*Echa la llave.*)

PEDRO. Tú nunca cierras el bufete con llave. Y has roto otros billetes de la misma mano.

LARRA. ¡Cállate! (*Avanza hacia el frente. Se ilumina el bloque derecho.*)

PEDRO. Espera. ¿No sabes lo que sucede en las alturas?

LARRA. No fui testigo.

PEDRO. Lo imaginaste. (*DON HOMOBONO aguarda ante su mesa, muy nervioso. LARRA suspira y vuelve su vista hacia el bloque. Seguido de CARNERERO, DON FRANCISCO CEA BERMÚDEZ sube a su salita por la parte oculta. Es un cincuentón que lleva exactamente el mismo uniforme de CALOMARDE, y en nada se diferencia de su antecesor salvo por su media máscara de obtuso y mofletudo jefecillo. DON HOMOBONO se inclina profundamente.*)

CEA. Van a regresar diez mil emigrados; las Universidades se abrirán de nuevo. Es deseo expreso de su majestad la reina.

LARRA: You are very good at saying nothing, Señor Díaz. Now let me say something.

VEGA: Larra, there's no need to answer him!

LARRA: "We are none of us either saints or divine authority, both of whom are unique in that they can enjoy the privilege of hearing all but yet are not constrained to reply". (*BRETÓN laughs into his cloak. GRIMALDI, CARNERERO and ARRIAZA laugh openly. VEGA guffaws. MESONERO smiles.*)

DÍAZ (*Flushed with anger, he stands up.*): I shall be the one who doesn't deign to reply.

LARRA (*With an innocent air, to those at his table.*): Can he be a saint? Or, indeed, divine? (*The laughter intensifies.*)

DÍAZ: Goodbye, gentlemen. (*He hurries from the café.*)

CARNERERO: That's that. Health to Figaro! (*Little Parnassus grows dark, with the exception of the spotlight on LARRA. In the shadow CARNERERO takes his leave and exits. Another light falls on PEDRO, who is waiting with a slip of paper in his hand. LARRA notices it, stands up and walks directly to his room. PEDRO hands him the note which he opens and reads. His face shines.*)

LARRA: My cape! (*The servant already has it over his arm, and helps him on with it. LARRA goes to the bureau and puts the note into a drawer.*)

PEDRO: Aren't you going to destroy it?

LARRA: I want to keep it. (*He turns the key.*)

PEDRO: You never lock the bureau. And you've torn up notes in the past... written by the same hand.

LARRA: That's enough! (*He walks towards the front. The right-hand rostrum is illuminated.*)

PEDRO: Wait. Don't you know what's going on in the higher echelons?

LARRA: I wasn't there to see it.

PEDRO: But you imagined it. (*DON HOMOBONO is waiting nervously at his table. LARRA sighs and turns to look at the rostrum. Followed by CARNERERO, DON FRANCISCO CEA BERMUDEZ enters the room via the hidden stairway. A man of about fifty who wears exactly the same uniform as CALOMARDE, and whose only feature which distinguishes him from his predecessor is the half mask of a dull, chubby-cheeked little autocrat that he wears. DON HOMOBONO bows deeply.*)

CEA: Ten thousand emigrants will return; the universities will re-open. By the express wish of Her Majesty.

CARNERERO.   Todo el país lo agradecerá, excelencia.

CEA.   Terminaré con las aduanas interiores, las vinculaciones y los mayorazgos.   Habrá libertad para la industria, la contrata y los despidos de los obreros.   El país necesita desperezarse.

CARNERERO.   Pero sin innovaciones peligrosas...

CEA.   ¡Así lo diré en mi manifiesto!   Se requieren medidas administrativas más que políticas.   (*Se sienta, mira a CARNERERO.   Su tono cambia.*)   En cuanto a la prensa, hay que ser cautos, para no perjudicar las reformas.   Autorizaré algún periódico nuevo, más revistas...   La censura será... más comprensiva.   Sé que sus publicaciones no me causarán dificultades.

CARNERERO.   Seré su más leal colaborador, excelencia.   Siempre a sus órdenes.   (*Se inclina respetuosamente y baja por la parte oculta.   DON HOMOBONO vuelve a inclinarse, muy inquieto.   Quizá tose un poquito.   CEA lo mira.*)

D. HOMOBONO.   Excelentísimo señor don Francisco Cea Bermúdez...

CEA.   Diga.

D. HOMOBONO.   He sido siempre un fiel servidor del Estado...   Si vuestra excelencia resolviese que puedo seguir en mi puesto...

CEA.   (*Frío.*)   Don Manuel Abad permanece en el suyo y usted seguirá a sus órdenes.   Tampoco en la Administración convienen innovaciones peligrosas.   Y el señor Carnerero me ha hablado bien de usted.   Trabaje y consulte cuando tenga dudas.

D. HOMOBONO.   (*Que ve el cielo abierto.*)   A...gra...decidísimo, excelencia.   (*Se sienta y se pone con torpe diligencia los manguitos.   La luz se va del bloque.*)

PEDRO.   Ya sabes a qué atenerte.   Acude a tu cita.   (*Señala al frente, donde se oye ruido de cascos y de ruedas.   LARRA baja del gabinete y se acerca, ansioso, a la derecha.   Se ilumina el primer término; el café y sus inmóviles parroquianos siguen en penumbra.   Cesa el ruido.   Discretamente vestida de oscuro y con un velo de crespón que le oculta el rostro, entra DOLORES ARMIJO.   LARRA le besa la mano.*)

DOLORES.   ¡Aprisa!   ¡Que nadie nos vea!

LARRA.   Vamos.   (*Suben al gabinete, oscuro salvo el foco que los ilumina.*)

DOLORES.   Debo volver pronto a casa...   Le he dicho al cochero que espere.

LARRA.   Yo he esperado mucho más, Dolores mía.   ¿Me dejas? (*Aparta su velo.   Aparece la atractiva máscara de DOLORES.   La abraza y besa apasionadamente.*)   ¡Gracias, cielo mío!   ¡Sin ti estaba muerto!   ¡Hoy

CARNERERO: The whole country will be grateful, Your Excellency.

CEA: I'll do away with internal tariffs, perpetuities and rights of land succession. There will be new freedom for industry, to contract and to discharge workers. The country needs to be shaken up.

CARNERERO: But with no dangerous departures...

CEA: That's how I'll put it in my manifesto! It's a question of administrative rather than political measures. (*He sits down and looks at CARNERERO. His tone changes.*) As for the press, we must move with caution so as not to prejudice the reforms. I will authorize the occasional new periodical, more journals... Censorship will be... more understanding. I know that your publications won't cause me any problems.

CARNERERO: I shall be your most loyal collaborator, Excellency. Always at your command. (*He bows respectfully and descends the hidden stairway. DON HOMOBONO anxiously bows again. He may even cough lightly. CEA looks up.*)

D. HOMOBONO: Your Excellency, sir, don Francisco Cea Bermúdez...

CEA: Yes.

D. HOMOBONO: I am the faithful servant of the State... If Your Excellency were to decide that I could continue in my position...

CEA (*Coldly.*): Don Manuel Abad has filled your position and you will take your orders from him. No dangerous departures even in the Administration. And Señor Carnerero has spoken well of you. You may set to work and consult whenever you have any doubts.

D. HOMOBONO (*For whom the sky has opened up.*): I... am... most grateful, Excellency. (*He sits down and with clumsy eagerness puts on his work sleeves. The light fades on the rostrum.*)

PEDRO: You know what's expected of you. Go to your appointment. (*He points frontwards, from where can be heard the sound of hooves and wheels. LARRA goes down from his study and, anxiously, walks over to the right. The foreground is illuminated; the café and its motionless faithful remain in shadow. The noise stops. DOLORES ARMIJO enters, dressed in discreet, dark colours, a veil of knotted silk hiding her face. LARRA kisses her hand.*)

DOLORES: Quickly! Don't let anyone see us!

LARRA: Let's go. (*They go up to the study, which is in darkness except for the spotlight iluminating them.*)

DOLORES: I can't stay long... I told the coachman to wait.

LARRA: I've waited much more, Dolores, my love. May I? (*He lifts her veil to reveal her attractive mask. He embraces her and kisses her passionately.*) Thank you, my darling! Without you I was dead! Today I

revivo!

DOLORES. Ya hay un matrimonio roto y vamos a romper otro...

LARRA. Los dos estaban destruidos. (*Abrazada por el talle la lleva hacia el fondo. A punto de salir por el hueco derecho, el gabinete se ilumina de pronto fuertemente. LARRA se detiene, sorprendido, y se separa de DOLORES, que permanece de espaldas, inmóvil y con la cabeza baja. LARRA mira a PEDRO.*)

PEDRO. No. Tú ya no quieres revivir la más intensa hora de tu vida. Aquella gloria de vuestra carne y - creías - de vuestras almas, te resulta ahora insoportable. (*LARRA baja la cabeza.*) ¡Más que cualquier otro de tus insoportables recuerdos! Ahora no podrías resistir las imágenes de aquella tarde, y aún tienes que llegar al final.

LARRA. ¿Entonces?

PEDRO. Basta el recuerdo sin imágenes. Sal con tu amante de la quinta y revive el infierno que te resta. (*LARRA suspira hondamente. Enlaza de nuevo a DOLORES y vuelve con ella hacia las sillas. La luz se va despacio y, con la misma lentitud, PEDRO sale por la izquierda. LARRA entrega a DOLORES su velo y ella se lo pone, mientras el escritor se pone su capa y su sombrero. Entretanto, la luz crece en el primer término de la escena y CAMBRONERO, de paisano y con bastón, entra por la derecha y aguarda impasible. Los amantes se cogen del brazo y avanzan, muy amartelados. Bajan del gabinete y, al girar, se enfrentan con el marido burlado. DOLORES gime sordamente y retrocede, tirando de LARRA.*)

CAMBRONERO. ¡Quietos! (*DOLORES se refugia tras su amante.*) Aquel coche te espera, Dolores. Vuelve a casa.

LARRA. ¡Señor de Cambronero!

CAMBRONERO. ¡Hablo con mi esposa!

DOLORES. ¡José María, te juro que te equivocas! (*Da unos pasos hacia él.*) El señor de Larra me ha visto sola y se ha brindado a acompañarme. (*Su marido saca entretanto el billete y se lo muestra.*)

CAMBRONERO. Esta es tu letra. (*Ella gana un paso, observa el papel y se lleva las manos al rostro. LARRA se interpone.*)

LARRA. (*Ha reconocido la esquela con asombro y tiende la mano.*) ¡Ese papel es mío!

come back to life!

DOLORES: One marriage is broken already and we're about to destroy another...

LARRA: They were both destroyed long since. (*With his arm round her waist, he leads her towards the back of the room. They are just about to go through the right-hand gap when, suddenly, an intense light bathes the study. LARRA stops in surprise, and moves away from DOLORES. She stands motionless, back to the audience, her head hanging. LARRA looks at PEDRO.*)

PEDRO: No. You no longer have any desire to relive that most intense hour of your life. At this moment you couldn't bear to remember that glory of your bodies and -as you thought- of your souls. (*LARRA lowers his head.*) Of all your unbearable memories, this is the worst! At this time you couldn't endure images of that afternoon, and you still have to get to the end.

LARRA: In that case?

PEDRO: The memory is enough. You don't have to look. Bring your lover out of the house you've been lent and relive the hell waiting for you outside. (*LARRA sighs deeply. He slips his arm round DOLORES once again and returns with her towards the chairs. The light fades slowly as PEDRO, at the same speed, exits on the left. LARRA hands DOLORES her veil, which she puts on as the writer dons his hat and cloak. Meanwhile, the light grows in the foreground and CAMBRONERO, out of uniform and carrying a walking-stick, enters from the right and waits impassively. The pair of lovers walk forward lovingly, arm-in-arm. They come down from the study and, as they turn, they come face to face with the deceived husband. DOLORES moans softly and pulls back, tugging at LARRA.*)

CAMBRONERO: Stay where you are, both of you! (*DOLORES takes refuge behind her lover.*) That coach is waiting for you, Dolores. Go home.

LARRA: Señor de Cambronero!

CAMBRONERO: I'm talking to my wife!

DOLORES: José María, you're mistaken, I swear it! (*She takes several steps towards him.*) Señor de Larra saw me on my own and offered to accompany me. (*Her husband, meanwhile, produces the note and shows it to her.*)

CAMBRONERO: It's in your hand. (*She steps forwards, looks at the sheet of paper and raises her hands to her face. LARRA interposes.*)

LARRA (*Astonished, he has recognized the note and stretches out his hand.*): That paper belongs to me!

CAMBRONERO. Ya no. (*Se lo guarda.*)

LARRA. ¿Cómo ha llegado a usted?

CAMBRONERO. ¡No tiene usted el derecho de preguntármelo! ¡Sube al coche, Dolores!

LARRA. ¡La señora irá conmigo!

DOLORES. ¡No, señor de Larra! Debo obedecer a mi marido. (*A CAMBRONERO.*) He hecho mal, lo reconozco. (*Llora.*) Pero una mujer ofendida necesita confiarle a alguien sus penas... Larra sólo es un amigo generoso y paciente, que escucha... Te lo juro. ¡Larra, júrelo usted también! Es usted hombre de honor y él le creerá.

LARRA. (*Amargo.*) ¡Dolores!

DOLORES. (*A su esposo.*) ¡No te entregues a la cólera, no des pábulo a las habladurías!

CAMBRONERO. ¡Vuelve a casa!

DOLORES. Señor de Larra, confío en su caballerosidad. (*LARRA la está mirando con obsesiva fijeza. Con la cabeza humillada, DOLORES sale por la derecha. A poco, llega el ruido de los cascos que se alejan.*)

CAMBRONERO. Si hubiese venido de uniforme, le habría partido el cráneo con mi sable.

LARRA. (*Se vuelve hacia él.*) ¿Va a retarme?

CAMBRONERO. Espere mis noticias.

LARRA. Le ahorraré gestiones inútiles. Yo no me batiré.

CAMBRONERO. ¿También cobarde? Entonces me daré el gusto de apalearle ahora mismo. (*Empuña su bastón.*) A no ser que me dé su palabra de honor de que mi esposa es inocente...

LARRA. Basta, señor de Cambronero. Usted ha venido en traje civil sabiendo bien lo que hacía. Usted no quiere batirse y yo tampoco. Ahórreme su canto al honor y a otros embustes.

CAMBRONERO. (*Irritado.*) ¿Embustes?

LARRA. Antes de hablar de honor recuerde que tiene una querida.

CAMBRONERO. ¿Y usted? ¿No ha traicionado a su esposa?

LARRA. Me traicionó ella antes.

CAMBRONERO. (*Sardónico.*) ¿Puedo saber con quién?

LARRA. Me refiero a otras traiciones. (*Se aparta y se sienta, sombrío, en el escalón del gabinete. Habla sin mirar a CAMBRONERO.*) Mi matrimonio es como el suyo: una mentira. Más sincero que usted con Dolores, yo voy a separarme de Pepita. La libertad es nuestra única

CAMBRONERO: Not any longer. (*He puts it away*.)

LARRA: How did it come into your possession?

CAMBRONERO: You have no right to ask me that! Dolores, get into the coach.

LARRA: The lady will go with me!

DOLORES: No, Señor de Larra! I must obey my husband. (*To CAMBRONERO*.) I have been indiscreet, I admit. (*She weeps*.) But an affronted wife needs someone with whom she can share her pain... Larra is but a generous and patient friend, someone who listens... I swear it. Larra, you swear it as well! You are a man of honour and he'll believe you.

LARRA (*Bitterly*.): Dolores!

DOLORES: (*To her husband*.): Don't let your anger get the better of you, don't create a scandal!

CAMBRONERO: Go home!

DOLORES: Señor de Larra, you are a gentleman, and I rely upon that. (*LARRA is staring at her obsessively. Her head lowered, DOLORES leaves from the right. Shortly afterwards, the sound of horses' hooves as the coach draws away*.)

CAMBRONERO: If I had come in uniform, I would have split your skull with my sabre.

LARRA (*Turning towards him*.): Are you going to challenge me?

CAMBRONERO: You will be hearing from me.

LARRA: I'll save you the trouble. I will not fight.

CAMBRONERO: A coward as well? In that case I'll have the pleasure of thrashing you now. (*He brandishes his stick*.) Unless I have your word of honour that my wife is innocent.

LARRA: Enough, Señor de Cambronero. You came here in civilian dress knowing full well what you were doing. You have no wish to fight, and neither do I. Please spare me this appeal to honour, and all these other shams.

CAMBRONERO (*Angrily*.): Shams?

LARRA: Before you talk about honour, remember that you have a mistress.

CAMBRONERO: And what about you? Have you not betrayed your wife.

LARRA: She betrayed me first.

CAMBRONERO (*Sardonically*.): May I know with whom?

LARRA: I'm talking about a different kind of betrayal. (*He moves away and sits down on the step into the study. He speaks without looking at CAMBRONERO*.) My marriage is like yours: a lie. But I'm going to leave Pepita, which is being more honest than you are with Dolores.

dignidad. Y el amor, nuestra única verdad. Por una mujer que debió ser la mía, que es la mía, a todo estoy dispuesto. Y usted pretende encadenarla mientras se distrae con mujerzuelas... Pues, lo quiera o no, yo romperé esas cadenas. Y ahora, déjeme solo.

CAMBRONERO. (*Se acerca.*) Tuve otros indicios antes de esa esquela, y callé. Porque es cierto: yo tampoco quiero batirme. (*LARRA lo mira, sorprendido. CAMBRONERO se despoja lentamente de su careta y aparece un semblante triste y desvalido.*) Pero la opinión ajena me es muy cara. Es preciso que subsista la mentira de que mi mujer no me engaña, y también las demás mentiras que sostienen el mundo. Con sus verdades corrosivas usted no lo mejorará. Si no hay duelo es que mi mujer no me engaña: eso es lo que todos deben creer. Por eso no le desafío. Por eso... y porque ella no lo merece. (*LARRA lo mira, iracundo. CAMBRONERO, que parece súbitamente cansado, se sienta no lejos de él.*) Usted no ha sido el primero.

LARRA. (*Colérico.*) ¿Qué dice?

CAMBRONERO. Míreme. (*El escritor observa su cara desengañada, su mirada sin brillo.*) Le estoy diciendo la verdad. Su devota admiradora no ama a Larra, como tampoco a los anteriores. (*LARRA se levanta, descompuesto.*) Una embustera, y usted lo sabe. Usted no ha podido jurarme que nada grave ha sucedido. Pero ella juró.

LARRA. Ella no quería que corriera sangre. Vendrá conmigo cuando pierda ese miedo que todos ustedes le han inculcado. Y entonces la enseñaré a no mentir.

CAMBRONERO. No. Usted y ella no darán mal ejemplo, y los rumores se apaciguarán. La alejaré de Madrid... y también yo me iré. He solicitado la Secretaría del Gobierno de Manila. Me iré, y todos callaremos. (*Se levanta.*) Usted no la volverá a ver y terminará por olvidarla.

LARRA. (*Desvía la vista.*) Nunca.

CAMBRONERO. Peor para usted. Adiós. (*Se cubre y se encamina hacia la derecha.*)

LARRA. ¡Señor de Cambronero!

CAMBRONERO. (*Se vuelve rápido, con la faz crispada.*) ¿No quería la verdad? Ya la tiene. (*Sale y se ilumina el gabinete. Con mantilla y tocado, PEPITA entra por la izquierda del fondo con una maleta en la mano. No lleva máscara. Su marido la divisa y pasa al gabinete.*)

LARRA. (*Deja su sombrero en una grada.*) ¿A dónde vas?

PEPITA. (*Asombrada, deja la maleta en el suelo.*) ¿Has vuelto?

LARRA. Siento contrariarte. Dos caballeros no se matan en las

Freedom is our only dignity. And love, our only truth. I will do anything for a woman who should be mine by rights, who is mine already. You seek to lock her away and all the while you amuse yourself with sluts... Well, whether you like it or not, I'll smash that lock. And now, leave me alone.

CAMBRONERO (*Drawing close.*): I had other indications before that note, and I said nothing. Because it is true. I don't want to fight. (*LARRA looks at him in surprise. CAMBRONERO slowly removes his mask, revealing a sad, vulnerable face.*) But I have a high regard for what others think of me. The lie that my wife is not unfaithful is vital to me, like so many other lies upon which this world rests. And which you, with your corrosive truths, will not make any better. If there is no duel it's because my wife remains faithful to me; that's what everyone must think. For that reason I won't challenge you. For that reason... and because she's not worth it. (*LARRA looks at him in fury. CAMBRONERO, who seems suddenly tired, sits down on a step near LARRA.*) You're not the first.

LARRA (*Furiously.*): What do you mean?

CAMBRONERO: Look at me. (*The writer looks into the listless gaze of shattered illusions.*) I'm telling you the truth. Your devoted admirer doesn't love Larra any more than she loved the others. (*LARRA stands up, devastated.*) She's a cheat, and you know it. You couldn't bring yourself to swear to me that nothing of any significance had happened. But she did.

LARRA: She wanted to avoid bloodshed. She'll come with me when she's lost the fear which you and your kind have drummed into her. And then I'll teach her how not to lie.

CAMBRONERO: No. Neither of you will give any cause for gossip... and the rumours will fade. I'll take her away from Madrid... and I'll leave as well. I've applied for the post of Secretary to the Government in Manila. I'll go away, and none of us will say anything. (*He stands up.*) You won't see her again and eventually you'll forget her.

LARRA (*Looking away.*): I'll never forget her.

CAMBRONERO: All the worse for you. Goodbye. (*He puts on his hat and walks towards the right.*)

LARRA: Señor de Cambronero!

CAMBRONERO (*Spinning round, his face creased in anger.*): Didn't you want the truth? Well, now you have it. (*He leaves and the study is lit up. Wearing a mantilla and comb, and carrying a case, PEPITA enters from the back, on the left. She isn't wearing a mask. Her husband catches sight of her and crosses to the study.*)

LARRA (*Leaving his hat on a step.*): Where are you going?

PEPITA (*In surprise, setting the case on the floor.*): You're back?

LARRA: I'm sorry to disappoint you. Two fine gentlemen are not

108]

afueras. Se envían los padrinos, fijan fecha...

PEPITA. ¿Vas a batirte?

LARRA. No.

PEPITA. (*Hacia la puerta.*) ¡Simón!

LARRA. (*Se acerca a ella.*) Tú has descerrajado mi bufete y le has enviado a Cambronero una esquela de su esposa.

PEPITA. ¡No lo niego! Me has ofendido y no puedo tolerarlo. Me voy con mi madre y me llevo a mis hijos. Adiós. (*Recoge la maleta. Él se interpone.*)

LARRA. Quieres abandonar el domicilio conyugal sólo por vanidad. ¡Por vanidad, un escándalo! El marido es un cobarde que no ha querido batirse: que Madrid lo sepa y te compadezca. ¡Una lástima! Si desapareciese el bribón de Larra, quizá no faltase el galán dispuesto a apreciar tus buenas prendas... Ese tercer hijo que estás gestando ya es suyo.

PEPITA. ¡Nunca he conocido a otro hombre!

LARRA. Aunque así sea.

PEPITA. ¿Estás loco? ¡Déjame pasar!

LARRA. Cuando lo engendraste pensabas en ese príncipe de cuento con el que sueñas, no en mí. Te he faltado, pero tú me faltaste antes, al negarte a compartir mi lucha y mis zozobras. Sólo querías fiestas, juegos, mimos...

PEPITA. (*Se separa hacia el frente.*) ¡No se pueden oír tales infamias!

LARRA. No las oirás más. Porque, en efecto, vamos a separarnos Pero no hoy.

PEPITA. (*Se encara con él.*) ¡Saldré ahora mismo!

LARRA. (*Se acerca.*) Nos separaremos sin novelerías. Estaréis atendidos y veré a los niños cuando me plazca. Así se hará y no de otro modo, aunque ya estés muerta.

PEPITA. ¿Qué dices?

LARRA. (*Ríe.*) Y después de lo que hoy has hecho, sin resurrección posible. Eres... mi difunta. (*Le indica con la cabeza que salga. Ella solloza.*)

PEPITA. ¡Me escatimabas el dinero para derrocharlo con esa perdida!

LARRA. (*Frío.*) Tal vez. No soy perfecto. Pero tú ya había muerto. (*Cruza ella llorando y sale por el hueco de la izquierda llevándose su maleta. PEDRO entra al mismo tiempo por el hueco derecho. El escritor se adelanta hacia el frente.*)

PEDRO. (*Risueño.*) Barba Azul cerró la sala de sus muertas para

uelling to the bitter end outside the city. The seconds are on their way to
ix the date

PEPITA: Are you going to fight?

LARRA: No.

PEPITA (*Towards the door.*): Simón!

LARRA (*Drawing closer to her.*): You unlocked my bureau and sent
he note to Cambronero.

PEPITA: I don't deny it! You have offended me and I can't stand it.
am going to my mother and taking my children with me. Goodbye. (*She
icks up the case. He stands in her way.*)

LARRA: You're leaving the marriage home out of mere vanity. And
ut of vanity, you provoke a scandal. Your husband is a coward for not
ishing to fight... well, let the whole city know so that it feels sorry for
ou. What a shame! And with that no-good Larra out of the way, then it
ouldn't be long before your young gallant showed up, hungry for your
harms. It's his child you're carrying now...

PEPITA: You are the only man I've ever been with!

LARRA: Even so!

PEPITA: You're crazy! Let me pass!

LARRA: When you conceived it, you were dreaming about your
rince charming. I have failed you, but you failed me first when you
efused to share my fight, my heartbreaks. You only wanted parties, games,
o be the constant centre of attraction...

PEPITA (*Moving away towards the front.*): I won't listen to such lies!

LARRA: You won't ever have to again. Yes, we will separate. But
ot today.

PEPITA (*Turning to face him.*): I'll go right now!

LARRA (*Walking towards her.*): We'll separate without dramatizing
he whole affair. I'll make provision for you and the children, and I'll see
hem whenever I want. That is exactly how it'll be done, and you are
ow... my dead wife. (*He nods his head to indicate to her to go. She
bs.*)

PEPITA: You gave me a pittance while you squandered everything on
er!

LARRA (*Coldly.*): Perhaps. I don't claim to be perfect. But you were
lready dead for me. (*She crosses the room weeping and exits with her
ase through the left-hand gap. PEDRO enters simultaneously through the
ight-hand gap. The writer moves forward.*)

PEDRO (*Cheerfully.*): Blue Beard locked the room where he kept the
odies so that his wife would open it and give him the excuse to kill her.
ou locked that writing desk, which you never do, so that your wife would

que su esposa la abriese y poderla matar. Tú has cerrado ese escritorio que nunca cierras para que tu mujer lo abra. Así te has cargado de razón y desde ahora será tu difunta.

LARRA. ¡Quise que lo descubriese para salir de esta situación!

PEDRO. Para que cometiese una sandez, y te has salido con la tuya. Pero te compadezco.

LARRA. ¿Por qué?

PEDRO. Por Dolores. Ahora, sube. (*LARRA suspira y va, a desgana, a los peldaños de la derecha. El bloque se ilumina.*)

LARRA. ¿Para qué?...

PEDRO. Sube. (*El escritor sube despacio mientras su voz suena en el aire.*)

LARRA. (*Su voz.*) «Síntomas alarmantes nos anuncian que el hablador padece de la lengua: fórmasele un frenillo que le hace hablar (...) menos enérgicamente que en su juventud. ¡Pobre Bachiller!» (*Ya arriba, LARRA se acerca al hombrecillo de la pluma.*)

D. HOMOBONO. ¡Don Mariano, siempre es un placer verle! Aunque hoy..., (*Se levanta.*) no tanto.

LARRA. ¿Por qué?

D. HOMOBONO. (*Recoge una carpeta atada con balduque.*) Le he defendido..., hasta arriesgar mi puesto..., sin resultado.

LARRA. El liberal Gobierno de Cea me está prohibiendo muchos artículos. ¿Cuáles han caído ahora?

D. HOMOBONO. (*Baja la vista.*) Todos.

LARRA. ¿Qué?

D. HOMOBONO. (*Le tiende la carpeta.*) Al comienzo verá usted una notita sin firma... Esta publicación se suspende. (*Los ojos del escritor echan chispas, pero se contiene.*)

PEDRO. Y pensaste: me quieren anular. Reducirme a cronista de teatros.

LARRA. (*Muy serio.*) Será entonces que «lo que no se puede decir, no se debe decir.»

D. HOMOBONO. ¡Justo! Y me alegra que usted lo comprenda.

LARRA. ¡Ah, de mi comprensión no tenga duda! «Leyendo en el gran libro (...) de las revoluciones (...) debemos aprender algo en él, y no seguir las mismas huellas de los países demasiado libres, porque vendríamos a parar al mismo estado de prosperidad que aquellas (...) naciones.» Lo sensato es ser siempre ministerial, ¿verdad? «El ministerial anda a paso de reforma» (...)

D. HOMOBONO. ¡Exacto!

open it. In that way you are in the right and she will be your dead wife for ever.

LARRA: I wanted her to discover it so as to force the issue.

PEDRO: So that she would do something stupid, and that's certainly what she did. But it's you I feel for.

LARRA: Why?

PEDRO: Because of Dolores. Now, come up. (*LARRA sighs and moves reluctantly towards the steps on the right. The rostrum is lit up.*)

LARRA: What for?

PEDRO: Come up. (*The writer climbs up slowly at the same time his voice sounds in the air.*)

LARRA (*Voice off.*): "Alarming symptoms suggest that the babbler has developed a disease of the tongue: a defect is making itself felt, preventing him from speaking [...] with the same energy as in his youth. Poor young graduate!"[35] (*At the top of the steps, LARRA directs himself towards the little penpusher.*)

D. HOMOBONO: Don Mariano, it's always a pleasure to see you! Although today... (*He rises.*) ... not so much.

LARRA: Why?

D. HOMOBONO (*Picking up a file secured with red tape.*): I defended you... to the point of putting my own position in jeopardy..., but in vain.

LARRA: The liberal government of Cea is banning many of my articles. Which are the latest victims?

D. HOMOBONO (*Looking down.*): All of them.

LARRA: What?

D. HOMOBONO (*Handing him the file.*): You will find a small unsigned note at the beginning... This publication is hereby suspended. (*The writer's eyes flame with anger, but he restrains himself.*)

PEDRO: And you thought: they're trying to neutralize me. Turn me into nothing more than a theatre critic.

LARRA (*Very gravely.*): So it's a case of "what can't be said shouldn't be said".

D. HOMOBONO: Indeed! I'm so glad you understand.

LARRA: Ah, of my understanding you need have no doubt! "Reading through the great book [...] of revolutions [...] we ought to learn something there, and not follow in the footsteps of countries which are overly free, otherwise we would come to fall into the same state of prosperity as [...] they have". The most sensible thing is to be ministerial, don't you feel? "The ministries are advancing at reform pace" [...]

D. HOMOBONO: Precisely.

LARRA. (...) «Es decir, que más parece que se columpia, sin moverse de un sitio, que no que anda.»

D. HOMOBONO. (*Algo mosqueado.*) ¡Ejém!... Usted bromea.

LARRA. ¿Con un funcionario de Calomarde? ¡Pobre de mí!

D. HOMOBONO. De Cea Bermúdez...

LARRA. Cierto. «Nuestra España, que Dios guarde (de sí misma sobre todo)» vive ahora bajo el paternal gobierno de Cea. ¡Si seré distraído! Y es que al país se le podría decir: «¡Hombre, por usted no pasan días! Por nuestra patria efectivamente no pasan días; bien es verdad que por ella no pasa nada: ella es por el contrario la que suele pasar por todo.» Déme eso. (*DON HOMOBONO le entrega la carpeta.*) Buenas tardes. (*Se aleja.*)

D. HOMOBONO. Créame que lo siento.

LARRA. (*Se vuelve.*) Yo me alegro.

D. HOMOBONO. ¿Se alegra?

LARRA. (*Se acerca.*) «Géneros enteros de la literatura han debido a la tiranía y a la dificultad de expresar los escritores sus sentimientos francamente una importancia que sin eso rara vez hubieran conseguido.» Conque imagínese lo importante que me siento, y no es chanza. Adiós. (*Empieza a bajar peldaños. La luz abandona el bloque. La melancólica voz de LARRA, en el ambiente.*)

LARRA. (*Su voz.*) «...Hecha abstracción de lo que no se debe, de lo que no se quiere, o de lo que no se puede decir, que para nosotros es lo más (...), dejamos el puesto humildemente a quien quiera iluminar la parte del cuadro que nuestro pobre pincel ha dejado oscura.» (*Ya abajo, LARRA tira la carpeta sobre su escritorio y se apoya, desalentado, en el sillón.*)

PEDRO. Habrá que seguir escribiendo en la revista de Carnerero. (*LARRA lo mira.*) Ya te has separado de tu difunta, pero Dolores se ha ido. Apenas puedes verla en Badajoz, porque está muy vigilada, o lo parece... El marido ordena desde Filipinas que la lleven a un convento de Ávila.

LARRA. Eso es más tarde. En el 34.

PEDRO. ¿Todavía no entiendes?

LARRA. Estamos en 1833.

PEDRO. Sí. En el principio de la gran esperanza. Los emigrados regresan... y notas que vienen con sus caretas.

LARRA. Excepto uno.

LARRA: [...] "That is, swinging from side to side, rather than advancing".

D. HOMOBONO (*Rather suspiciously.*): Ehem!...I assume you are jesting.

LARRA: With one of Calomarde's officials? Poor me!

D. HOMOBONO: One of Cea Bermúdez's...

LARRA: Of course. "Our Spain, which it may please God in His mercy to save, especially from itself" is now living under the paternal guidance of Cea. I can't think how I didn't notice sooner! Of course, we could say to the nation as a whole: "My friend, how well you have escaped the ravages of time! Time in our country has stood stock still; indeed, everything has stood stock still: except for our country, which has been moved to tears time and time again". I'll take that. (*DON HOMOBONO hands him the file.*) Good day. (*He starts to leave.*)

D. HOMOBONO: Believe me, I am sorry.

LARRA (*Turning round.*): I'm not. I'm glad.

D. HOMOBONO: Glad?

LARRA (*Walking towards him.*): "Entire bodies of literature are indebted to tyranny, and the difficulties it supposes for writers in the free expression of their feelings, for without it they would rarely have achieved such importance". So, imagine how important I feel. And that's not a jest. Goodbye. (*He begins to descend the stairs. The light fades on the rostrum. The melancholy voice of LARRA sounds in the air.*)

LARRA (*Voice off.*): "... What must not be said, what they prefer not to be said, and what cannot be said, which as far as we are concerned is the most common case, having become elevated to the realm of abstract principle (...), we humbly lay down our brush in favour of the one which can cast light on that part of the picture that ours has left in darkness". (*Having reached the bottom, LARRA tosses the file onto his writing desk and leans, discouraged, against the armchair.*)

PEDRO: No alternative but to keep on writing for Carnerero's journal. (*LARRA looks at him.*) You've left your dead wife, but Dolores has gone too. You hardly have a chance to see her in Badajoz, because she's so closely watched, or so it seems... Her husband in the Phillipines orders her to a convent in Avila.

LARRA: That's later on. In '34.

PEDRO: Haven't you understood yet?

LARRA: This is 1833.

PEDRO: Yes. Just as hope is springing fresh and strong. The emigrants return... and you notice that they too come wearing masks.

LARRA: Except one.

PEDRO. Excepto uno. (*El Parnasillo se ilumina. DÍAZ y e PADRE FROILÁN han vuelto a sus sitios. Todos miran al frente susurran.*)

TODOS. (*Menos el PADRE FROILÁN.*) Se muere... (*Algo má fuerte.*) ¡Se muere!... (*Más fuerte.*) ¡Se muere!

ARRIAZA. (*Amedrentado.*) ¿Se muere?

P. FROILÁN. (*Enérgico.*) ¡No se muere!

CARNERERO. (*Preocupado.*) Se muere.

BRETÓN. (*Despectivo.*) ¡Y no se muere!

GRIMALDI. (*Caviloso.*) Se muere...

VEGA Y MESONERO. (*Con tenaz convicción.*) ¡Se muere!

P. FROILÁN. (*Enfurecido.*) ¡No se muere!

CARNERERO Y ARRIAZA. (*Poniéndole en los hombros sus mano conmiserativas.*) Sí... Sí se muere... (*Repentino silencio. Por la puert. del café entra DON JUAN NICASIO GALLEGO, un sacerdote de sesent años orondo y arrogante, de blanco cabello y media máscara de ojo bajos. Se detiene un instante y todos se levantan, pendientes de él Doblan a muerto. GALLEGO levanta un dedo solemne.*)

GALLEGO. Su majestad el rey don Fernando VII acaba de expirar.

TODOS. (*En un grito unánime donde hay muchos matices.*) ¡H muerto!

CARNERERO. Sea muy bien venido el reverendo Juan Nicasi Gallego, que padeció injusticia por la libertad. (*Abrazan unos al PADRE otros le besan la mano.*)

GALLEGO. No exageremos. Aunque en Madrid me estab. prohibido vivir hasta ahora, yo regresé el 28.

BRETÓN. Padre Gallego...

DÍAZ. Clemente Díaz, poeta, para servirle. (*Va el PADRE de uno a otros, prodigando saludos.*)

ARRIAZA. (*Turbado.*) Un abrazo..., después de estos años.

GALLEGO. Otros muchos han regresado en estos días. ¡La flor nata!

P. FROILÁN. (*Después de gruñir algo.*) ...de toda la Masonería!

GALLEGO. Amados hijos: ¡Viva la libertad!

TODOS. (*Menos el PADRE FROILÁN.*) ¡Viva! (*El cura gruñidor que no ha saludado a su compañero de hábitos, se desliza hacia la puert murmurando algo ininteligible. Sale del café, bajo las risas de l izquierda.*)

BRETÓN. Va a esconderse. (*Risas.*)

GALLEGO. Tengamos caridad... Es penoso que la Iglesia esté dividida. (*Se sienta en la silla abandonada por el PADRE FROILÁN. Se

PEDRO: Except one. (*Little Parnassus is lit up. DÍAZ and FATHER FROILÁN have returned to their places. They are all looking forwards, whispering.*)
ALL: (*Except FATHER FROILÁN.*): He's dying... (*Rather stronger.*) He's dying! (*Stronger still.*) He's dying!
ARRIAZA: (*Cowed.*): He's dying?
F. FROILÁN (*Vigorously.*): He's not dying!
CARNERERO (*Worriedly.*): He's dying.
BRETÓN (*Disparagingly.*): And he's not dying.
GRIMALDI (*Thoughtfully.*): He is dying...
VEGA AND MESONERO (*With firm conviction.*): He's dying!
F. FROILÁN (*Furiously.*): He is not dying!
CARNERERO AND ARRIAZA (*Resting their hands on his shoulders in commiseration.*): Yes... He is dying... (*Sudden silence. Through the café door appears DON JUAN NICASIO GALLEGO, a priest of about sixty years old, pompous and arrogant, white-haired and wearing a half mask whose eyes look downwards. He stops for a second and everyone stands up, watching him intently. A funeral bell tolls. GALLEGO raises a solemn finger.*)
GALLEGO: His Majesty King Fernando VII has just passed away.
ALL (*With a single cry in which various tones are discernible.*): He's dead![36]
CARNERERO: I bid you welcome, Reverend Juan Nicasio Gallego, you who suffered injustice for the sake of freedom. (*Some embrace GALLEGO; others kiss his hand.*)
GALLEGO: Let's not exaggerate. Although I haven't been permitted to live in Madrid until now, I returned in '28.
BRETÓN: Father Gallego...
DÍAZ: Clemente Díaz, poet, at your service. (*The FATHER goes from one to the other, exchanging profuse greetings.*)
ARRIAZA (*Disturbed.*): An embrace... after so many years.
GALLEGO: Many others have returned of late. The very best!
F. FROILÁN (*After grunting something.*): ...of the Masons.
GALLEGO: My beloved sons! Long live liberty!
ALL (*Except FATHER FROILÁN.*): Liberty! (*The grunting priest, who has not greeted his colleague, slips towards the door muttering unintelligibly. He leaves the café accompanied by the laughter of those on the left.*)
BRETÓN: He's off to look for a hole to hide in. (*Laughter.*)
GALLEGO: Let us be charitable... It is painful that the church should be divided. (*He sits down in the seat left vacant by FATHER FROILÁN.*

oscurece el gabinete y un foco cae sobre LARRA y PEDRO, qu
atienden.) Pero como lo está el país... Ahora María Cristina es l
Regente v la infantita Isabel, nuestra reina. Y don Carlos no pued
tolerarlo.

CARNERERO. Hay partidas carlistas hasta en Talavera...

GALLEGO. Que Dios nos ayude. (*Luz en el bloque derecho. CE₄*
se .evanta.)

CEA. ¡Confiscación immediata de todos los bienes del pretendiente
¡Destitúyanse de sus Capitanías Generales a los condes de Casa Eguía y d
España!

D. HOMOBONO. (*Escandalizado.*) Pero, excelencia...

CEA. (*Amargo.*) No hay más remedio. (*Desciende de su podio y s*
va. DON JOSÉ DE ESPRONCEDA entra por la puerta del café
permanece junto a ella. Apuesto, de ojos ardientes, negra melena, bigot
y perilla. Veintiocho años agresivos. No lleva máscara.)

PEDRO. En efecto. Para él ya no lo hay. La Regente tiene qu
apoyarse en los constitucionales si quiere conservar la corona para su hija
¡En los hombres que persiguió su esposo! Hasta los generales piden Corte
Constituyentes, de las que Cea no quiere ni oír hablar. La Regente se v.
forzada a nombrar otro primer ministro y elige con tal tino entre los qu
han vuelto, que a todos os complace.

LARRA. Martínez de la Rosa. 15 de enero de 1834. (*Entra y s₄*
sienta en el podio MARTÍNEZ DE LA ROSA: melena gris, medi₄
máscara de nariz fina, frente noble, chupadas mejillas, uniforme idéntic₄
al de CEA.)

PEDRO. (*Con zumba.*) También tú le prodigas alabanzas. Es u₄
gran dramaturgo y lo admiras. Escribes... (*La voz de LARRA en e*
ámbito.)

LARRA. (*Su voz.*) «¡Un Estatuto Real, la primera piedra que ha d₄
servir al edificio de la regeneración de España y un drama lleno d₄
mérito!» (*Avergonzado, el escritor baja los ojos. MARTÍNEZ DE L₄*
ROSA se levanta. Tembloroso, se levantó el censor.)

D. HOMOBONO. Excelentísimo señor...

MARTÍNEZ. (*Lo mira, severo.*) Sí... Me han hablado de usted..
¡Ya le daré nuevas instrucciones!

D. HOMOBONO. (*Casi conmocionado.*
Se...rán...fi...fidelísimamente cumplidas, excelencia. (*Con un movimiento*
el Ministro le manda sentarse.)

MARTÍNEZ. Los siguientes decretos entrarán en vigor
inmediatamente. Supresión definitiva del Tribunal de la Inquisición...

The study grows dark and a spotlight picks out LARRA and PEDRO who are following the conversation.) Just as the country is... María Cristina has become Regent and the young Princess Isabel, our Queen. And don Carlos won't stand for it.

CARNERERO: There are Carlist factions as far south as Talavera.

GALLEGO: May God be with us. (*Light on the right-hand rostrum. CEA stands up.*)

CEA: Summary confiscation of all of the pretender's properties! The Counts of Casa Eguía and España are to be stripped of their rank of Field Marshal.

D. HOMOBONO (*Horrified.*): But, Excellency...

CEA (*Bitterly.*): There's no alternative. (*He descends from his podium and leaves. DON JOSÉ DE ESPRONCEDA comes in through the door of the café and remains standing there. Handsome, burning eyes, long black hair, moustache and goatee beard. Twenty-eight years old, full of youthful aggression. He doesn't wear a mask.*)

PEDRO: Indeed. There isn't any mask he could wear now. The Regent has to rely on the support of the constitutionalists in order to keep the crown for her daughter. The same men who opposed her husband! Even the generals demand a Constituent Assembly, although Cea won't hear of it. The Regent is forced to nominate a new Prime Minister, and she chooses so astutely among those recently returned to the country that everyone is well satisfied.[37]

LARRA: Martínez de la Rosa. The 15th of January 1834. (*MARTÍNEZ DE LA ROSA enters and sits down on the podium: long grey hair, a half mask whose features are a fine nose, a noble brow, hollow cheeks. He wears a uniform identical to that of CEA.*)

PEDRO (*Facetiously.*): You too are quick to heap praise on him. A great dramatist and you admire him. (*The voice of LARRA sounds in the air.*)

LARRA (*Voice off.*) "A Royal Statute, the first stone laid in the foundation of the regeneration of Spain and a most worthy drama!" (*Embarrassed, the writer looks at the floor. MARTÍNEZ DE LA ROSA stands up. The censor also rises, trembling.*)

D. HOMOBONO: Your Excellency, sir...

MARTÍNEZ (*Looking at him severely.*): Yes... I've been informed of your case... I'll issue you with new instructions shortly!

D. HOMOBONO (*Almost excitedly.*): They... will... be... faithfully complied with, Excellency. (*The minister gestures to him to sit down.*)

MARTÍNEZ: The following decrees are to take effect forthwith. Permanent suppression of the Court of the Inquisition...

TODOS. (*En el Parnasillo, menos ESPRONCEDA. ARRIAZA aprueba, pero con lánguidas cabezadas.*) ¡Bravo!

MARTÍNEZ. Reorganización de la Milicia Urbana...

TODOS. (*Lo mismo.*) ¡Viva!

MARTÍNEZ. Disolución del Voluntariado Realista y apertura d proceso a sus jefes...

TODOS. (*Lo mismo.*) ¡A la cárcel los asesinos!

MARTÍNEZ. Quinta de 25.000 hombres para acabar con l sublevación facciosa.

TODOS. (*Lo mismo.*) ¡Bravo! ¡Magnífico!

MARTÍNEZ. Frente a la Santa Alianza del pasado, la Cuádrup Alianza que los tiempos imponen. Francia, Inglaterra y Portugal firmará ese tratado, que será bastión imbatible ante cualquier intentona de l facción.

TODOS. (*Lo mismo.*) ¡Viva España!

VEGA. ¡Y ahora, la Constitución! (*MARTÍNEZ DE LA ROSA* s sienta.)

DÍAZ. ¡Y las libertades! (*MARTÍNEZ DE LA ROSA permanec impasible.*) ¿O no va a haber Consitución y libertades?

MARTÍNEZ. Habrá un Estatuto Real. En él se recogerán las just. aspiraciones por las que hemos luchado tantos años... (*Calla u momento.*) atemperadas a las exigencias del presente.

GRIMALDI. Entonces, esperemos.

MESONERO. Esperemos.

PEDRO. Con ilusión, ¿por qué no? Un hombre como él no pued defraudar. Y aún no sabéis que le van a llamar «Rosita la pastelera».

LARRA. Defraudó.

PEDRO. Eras muy joven y entusiasta... Pero no tonto. Com tampoco lo era el hombre sin máscara. Ve con él. (*Cruza la penumbra se retira por un hueco del fondo. LARRA va avanzando poco a poc hacia el proscenio.*)

VEGA. ¡Con esa quinta, la guerra será un paseo militar!

GALLEGO. No sé... Hay mucho clero con don Carlos, en el camp y en las ciudades.

ARRIAZA. Y los frailes, todos carlistas.

DÍAZ. ¿Y por qué van a ser carlistas?

ESPRONCEDA. (*Se adelanta.*) Porque no quieren el cierre de s conventos ni la confiscación de sus bienes, medidas ineludibles pa

ALL (*In Little Parnassus, except ESPRONCEDA. ARRIAZA also approves, but shakes his head slowly.*): Bravo!

MARTÍNEZ: Re-organization of the Urban Militia...

ALL (*As before.*): Hurrah!

MARTÍNEZ: Dissolution of the Royalist Volunteer Guard and the initiation of proceedings against its leaders...

ALL (*As before.*): Send the murderers to prison!

MARTÍNEZ: The raising of an army of 25,000 to put down the pretender's rising.

ALL (*As before.*): Bravo! Magnificent!

MARTÍNEZ: In place of the Holy Alliance of the past, a Four-way Alliance, more appropriate to the times in which we live. France, England and Portugal will sign the treaty, an unvincible bastion in the face of any new Carlist insurrection.

ALL (*As before.*): Long live Spain!

VEGA: And now, the Constitution! (*MARTÍNEZ DE LA ROSA sits down.*)

DÍAZ: And our liberties! (*MARTÍNEZ remains impassive.*) Or won't there be a Constitution and liberties?

MARTÍNEZ: There will be a Royal Statute. Therein, we will give expression to those legitimate aspirations for which we have struggled for so many years... (*He falls silent for a moment.*) tailored to the demands of the moment.

GRIMALDI: So, we wait.

MESONERO: We wait.

PEDRO: With hope, and why not? A man like him isn't capable of letting you down. And none of you know yet that he's soon to become known as "Rosie the pastry girl".[38]

LARRA: He let us down.

PEDRO: You were young and eager... But no fool. And neither was the man without the mask. Go with him. (*He crosses through the shadow and exits through a gap at the back. LARRA gradually moves towards the front of the stage.*)

VEGA: With a fresh army like that, the war will be little more than a military two-step.

GALLEGO: I'm not so sure. A lot of the clergy are behind don Carlos, in the country and the cities.

ARRIAZA: And in the monasteries they're Carlists to a man.

DÍAZ: Why should they be?

ESPRONCEDA (*Walking forward.*): Because they don't want their monasteries closed nor their property confiscated, necessary measures both

remediar el peso muerto de nuestra arcaica distribución de la propiedad. Ustedes hablan mucho, pero, ¿comprenden las verdaderas causas que enfrentan a españoles contra españoles? (*LARRA ha pasado al primer término. ESPRONCEDA y él se hallan frente a frente. MESONERO se levanta y se acerca a LARRA para hablarle aparte. El Parnasillo se va oscureciendo y dos focos iluminan a los dos jóvenes escritores.*)

MESONERO. Mírelo. Él siempre sabe más que nadie. Engola la voz. Se siente un personaje de teatro. Pero se le nota la máscara.

LARRA. Yo diría que no la lleva.

MESONERO. Ya lo irá conociendo. (*Y sale, lento, por el lateral izquierdo.*)

ESPRONCEDA. Las causas que enfrentan entre sí a los españoles no son bizantinas cuestiones sucesorias. Son intereses inconfesables. Hablan unos de sus sagradas creencias y de los fueros tradicionales, pero defienden la Ley Sálica, que es francesa, para que don Carlos sea rey. Otros hablan de las libertades... y las quieren para que el dinero se mueva y sus caudales crezcan. Si para ello hay que defender el derecho de las hembras a reinar, que es pura tradición, lo proclamarán con el mayor fervor con tal de que la reina les deje hacer... Los primeros quieren mantener sus rentas no ganadas y los segundos arrebatarles el pastel. Acabarán entendiéndose, y el pueblo seguirá en la miseria. Esta guerra es una farsa: mañana pactarán los ricos de ambos bandos. Y sin embargo hay que apoyar al bando que se dice liberal, porque algún paso sí daremos. He pedido ya mi ingreso en los Guardias de Corps, pero no dejaré de escribir. Fundo una revista con Vega y Ros de Olano: «El Siglo». ¡Se acabaron las medias palabras!

CARNERERO. (*Desde su penumbra.*) ¿Una revista más?

ESPRONCEDA. Señor de Carnerero, el tiempo de los privilegios editoriales ha concluido.

LARRA. (*Da unos pasos hacia él.*) Espronceda... Óigame unas palabras reservadas.

ESPRONCEDA. ¡Larra!

LARRA. Para servirle.

ESPRONCEDA. Leo todos sus artículos. ¡Déme un abrazo! (*Se abrazan.*) Nos necesitamos.

LARRA. (*Lo lleva algo más adelante.*) Desconfíe de este Parnasillo, a donde también concurren ministeriales, censores y policías. Usted viene del destierro y cree que las precauciones se han terminado. Pero no se han terminado.

we are going to shift the dead weight of our archaic system of the istribution of wealth. You all talk a great deal, but do you understand ιe real reasons why Spaniards turn on Spaniards? (*LARRA has moved ιto the foreground. ESPRONCEDA and he are face to face. ΙESONERO stands up and approaches LARRA to speak to him privately. ittle Parnassus grows dark and two spotlights shine on the two young ›riters.*)

MESONERO: Look at him. He always knows more than anyone else. Vith his puffed up voice. He thinks he's a character in some play. But you an see his mask.

LARRA: I would say he isn't wearing one.

MESONERO: You'l¹ soon get to know him better. (*He leaves, slowly, ›rom the left-hand side.*)

ESPRONCEDA: The reasons why Spaniard turns on Spaniard are not ue to labyrinthine questions of succesion. They are concealed interests. ome talk of their sacred beliefs and of traditional charters, but they ιpport the Salic Law, which is French, so that don Carlos can be king.)thers speak of freedoms... and yearn for them so that money can move ιd their personal fortunes grow. And if the price of that is to be the efence of the right of women to reign, a traditional one indeed, then they ‹ill proclaim that right fervently as long as the Queen lets them get on ‹ith it... The first group seeks to protect its unearned incomes, whilst the ‹cond group wants to snatch the cake away from them. They'll both end p with some sort of arrangement, and the people will continue in poverty. ‹his war is a farse: tomorrow the rich on both sides will come to terms. ‹nd even so, we've got to support the so-called liberals, because at least :'s some sort of step forward. I've applied to join the Military Guards, but won't stop writing. Along with Vega and Ros de Olano I'm setting up a ɔurnal: "The Century". Half words are finished.

CARNERERO (*From the shadows.*): Another journal?

ESPRONCEDA: Señor de Carnerero, the time of editorial monopoly ιas ended.

LARRA (*Taking several steps towards him.*): Espronceda... Let me ɔeak to you in private.

ESPRONCEDA: Larra!

LARRA: At your service.

ESPRONCEDA: I read all your articles. Embrace me! (*They ‹mbrace.*) We need each other.

LARRA (*Leading him forward.*): Do not trust this café, it swarms ‹ith functionaries, censors and police. You have just returned from exile ‹nd believe precautions to be a thing of the past. But they are not.

ESPRONCEDA. Amigo Fígaro, Martínez de la Rosa es un viejo luchador. No nos traicionará.

LARRA. Así es, pero... Conozco a mis batuecos. Lo que los dos deseamos ni mentarlo podemos.

ESPRONCEDA. ¿A qué se refiere?

LARRA. A la soberanía popular, que es la única indiscutible, En esta guerra somos todavía defensores de una reina por la gracia de Dios... y hemos de seguir usando las medias palabras.

ESPRONCEDA. (*Irónico.*) Me explico sus cautelas. Ha pasado aquí los peores años.

LARRA. No baje la guardia y proteja a su nueva revista de puñaladas hipócritas.

ESPRONCEDA. (*Superior.*) Acepte un consejo, mi prudente amigo: deje de temer.

LARRA. Escuche, Espronceda. Su amante es una mujer casada. He oído que, desde hace un mes, no sale de su piso. ¿Por qué?

ESPRONCEDA. (*Ceñudo.*) Prefiero no hablar de eso.

LARRA. (*Señala al Parnasillo.*) Aquí todo se comenta. Aseguran que ella se ha ofrecido a un amigo de usted si éste lo mataba.

ESPRONCEDA. ¡Por favor!

LARRA. Luego es cierto. ¿Y por qué cree que nos suceden esas cosas? Ustedes eran felices en el extranjero. Pero aquí, bajo el tremendo peso de la pacatería española, ella enloquece. Y lo abandonará, como a mí la mía.

ESPRONCEDA. ¿A usted?

LARRA. A la nuera del magistrado Cambronero, cuyo marido la desprecia y la engaña, la ha separado de mí la hipocresía batueca.

ESPRONCEDA. (*Después de un momento.*) Pues bien, tanto peor. Riamos y olvidemos. Si es preciso, iré a Navarra a combatir.

LARRA. Esa lucha es más franca que la de aquí. Aquí, le repito: desconfíe de los batuecos.

ESPRONCEDA. Larra, discrepamos. Pero esta mano será siempre la de un amigo. (*Leve cambio de coloración en la luz que los alumbra, y que LARRA advierte con vaga aprensión.*) Y aunque haya tratado cruelmente a esa obrita que Ros de Olano y yo dimos al teatro...

LARRA. ¿De... qué habla?

ESPRONCEDA. Me dolió... Pecó usted de severo. ¡Al fin, crítico Pero no lo hizo por mala fe sino a causa de su temperamento, demasiado

ESPRONCEDA: My friend, Figaro, Martínez de la Rosa is a seasoned campaigner. He won't betray us.

LARRA: Indeed, but... I know Las Batuecas. What we both yearn for, we dare not give voice to.

ESPRONCEDA: Which is?

LARRA: The sovreignty of the people, the only indisputable one. In this war we still defend the cause of a queen by the grace of God... and we must still use half words.

ESPRONCEDA (*Ironically.*): I understand your caution. You've spent the worst years here.

LARRA: Don't lower your guard... and protect your new journal from hypocritical knives.

ESPRONCEDA (*With an air of superiority.*): Accept a piece of advice, my prudent friend. The time for fear has gone.[39]

LARRA: Listen, Espronceda. Your mistress is a married woman. I've heard that she hasn't left her apartment in the last month. Why?

ESPRONCEDA (*Sourly.*): I would rather not discuss that.

LARRA (*Pointing towards the café.*): There's nothing that isn't discussed here. I've heard it said with all confidence that she has offered herself to a friend of yours, if he will kill you.

ESPRONCEDA: Please!

LARRA: Then, it is true. And why do you think these things happen to us? You were both happy abroad. But here, exposed to the full force of Spanish scandal-mongering, she grows disturbed. And she'll leave you, just as mine left me.

ESPRONCEDA: Left you?

LARRA: The daughter-in-law of Cambronero, the magistrate, with a husband who despises her and who deceives her... was taken from me by the hypocrites of these Batuecas.

ESPRONCEDA (*After a moment.*): Then so much the worse. Let's laugh and put it behind us. If necessary, I'll go to Navarra to fight.

LARRA: It's a much more open battle there. But here, I repeat, do not trust the inhabitants of the Batuecas.

ESPRONCEDA: You and I see things differently, Larra. But this hand will always be that of a friend. (*There is a slight change of colour in the lighting, which LARRA notices with a vague apprehension.*) Even though you were harsh in your judgment of that insignificant piece that Ros de Olano and I created for the theatre...[40]

LARRA: What... what are you talking about?

ESPRONCEDA: That was hurtful... You were overly hard. A critic, I suppose. But it wasn't an act of bad faith, rather the sign of a

reflexivo. Hace tiempo que se lo he perdonado.

LARRA. Y eso... ¿no sucedió el año 34?

ESPRONCEDA. Sí. ¿Y qué?

LARRA. Y... ¿no estamos en el 33? (*Corta pausa. ESPRONCEDA responde con una voz fría, metálica.*)

ESPRONCEDA. Y qué.

LARRA. (*Sobrecogido.*) Nada.

ESPRONCEDA. Fígaro, permanezcamos unidos.

LARRA. (*Lo mira con enorme suspicacia.*) Me pregunto si no podría yo hacerle decir a usted... palabras muy distintas... si se me antojara.

ESPRONCEDA. (*Lo mira, inquieto.*) Lo que dice... me desconcierta... Está usted fatigado. (*La luz ha vuelto suavemente a su estado anterior. LARRA lo nota y respira con alivio.*)

LARRA. Los dos estamos fatigados. Y casi anulados.

ESPRONCEDA. ¡Yo no!

LARRA. Sí. Porque somos muy semejantes. Para pelear sin desmayo, necesitamos a otro ser... que nos falta.

ESPRONCEDA. (*Desvía la vista.*) Teresa huyó a Valladolid. Fui a buscarla y la traje conmigo. Está en casa. Pero crispada, rencorosa...

LARRA. (*Con sincera tristeza.*) Las Batuecas.

ESPRONCEDA. (*Suspira y reacciona.*) Hay que seguir, Larra.

LARRA. Unidos.

(*Van al gabinete. ESPRONCEDA sube unos peldaños de la escalera derecha y se reclina en ellos. LARRA se recuesta en la escalera izquierda. Se ilumina entretanto el Parnasillo.*)

VEGA. ¡Fígaro está en lo cierto! El Estatuto Real ha sido una carta otorgada, no una Constitución.

DÍAZ. Y la censura, en su sitio.

GALLEGO. Con alguna otra gente. No olvide que me han conferido el honor de ejercer la de la prensa.

VEGA. Padre Gallego, ninguna censura es soportable. Y no llego a comprender cómo una víctima del absolutismo ha aceptado ese puesto.

GALLEGO. ¡Para favorecerles, amigos míos!

ESPRONCEDA. Tendrá que demostrarlo.

VEGA. A «El Siglo» le están prohibiendo muchos artículos.

GALLEGO. No todo depende de mí, querido Vega.

CARNERERO. Señores, tales naderías en tan horribles momentos...

BRETÓN. ¿Se refiere a la peste?

temperament that is much too given to reflection. I forgave you a long time ago.

LARRA: But did that... not happen in '34.

ESPRONCEDA: Yes. So?

LARRA: But... isn't this '33? (*A brief pause. ESPRONCEDA replies in a cold, metallic voice.*)

ESPRONCEDA: So?

LARRA (*Startled.*): Nothing.

ESPRONCEDA: Figaro, we must remain united, you and I.

LARRA (*Regarding him with enormous suspicion.*): I wonder if I couldn't make you utter... very different words... if I wanted to.

ESPRONCEDA (*Looking at him anxiously.*): What you say... perturbs me... You are tired. (*The lighting has returned smoothly to its previous state. LARRA notices it and sighs with relief.*)

LARRA: We're both tired. And virtually invalidated.

ESPRONCEDA: Not me!

LARRA: Yes. Because we're so alike. To fight without caving in, we both need somebody else... and neither of us has her.

ESPRONCEDA (*Looking away.*): Teresa fled to Valladolid. I went after her and brought her back. She's at home... but agitated... resentful.

LARRA (*With genuine sadness.*): The Batuecas.

ESPRONCEDA (*He sighs and shakes himself.*): We must carry on, Larra.

LARRA: Together.

(*They go to the study. ESPRONCEDA climbs some of the steps on the right and leans against them. LARRA reclines against the left-hand staircase. Meanwhile, light grows in Little Parnassus.*)

VEGA: Figaro is quite right! The Royal Statute is a royal charter, not a Constitution.

DÍAZ: And with censorship as firmly entrenched as ever.

GALLEGO: But new people wield the pen. May I remind you I have been honoured with the responsibility of censoring the press.

VEGA: Father Gallego, no censorship is acceptable. And I fail to understand how a victim of absolutism could accept such a position.

GALLEGO: To work on your behalf, my friends.

ESPRONCEDA: You'll have to prove that.

VEGA: "The Century" has had a great many articles banned recently.

GALLEGO: Not everything is in my hands, my dear Vega.

CARNERERO: Gentlemen, to talk of trifles at such a distressing time as this.

BRETÓN: You mean the plague?

CARNERERO. (*Asiente.*) Ya hay muertos en todos los barrios.

GALLEGO. Es peligroso abandonarse al pánico. Dicen que sólo es una epidemia catarral.

BRETÓN. Cabal. Un catarro llamado cólera morbo asiático.

DÍAZ. (*A BRETÓN.*) Entonces, ¿nos engaña el Gobierno?

LARRA. ¡Nada de eso! Dice que «lo que hay no es cólera, sino una enfermedad *reinante* y *sospechosa*; tanto que esas malditas sospechas han llevado a muchos al cementerio, en fuerza sin duda de cavilosos.» (*VEGA saca un folleto y se pone a leer.*)

GRIMALDI. Pues nuestro pobre Mesonero ha caído enfermo, y quizá se nos muera.

CARNERERO. Y la sanidad, sin tomar medidas. (*Saca un periódico y se sume en su lectura. Luz súbita en el bloque de la derecha. MARTÍNEZ DE LA ROSA, en pie.*)

MARTÍNEZ. ¡Pido a nuestros aliados de la Cuádruple Alianza treinta mil hombres que nos ayuden a extirpar la cizaña del carlismo en armas!

CARNERERO. (*Con un manotazo al periódico.*) ¿A qué lo dirá, si ya se los han negado?

MARTÍNEZ. Señores de la Cámara alta, en sus señorías confío. Lejos de mí el funesto sueño del sufragio universal y de la anarquía. Mi Gobierno se apoyará en las instituciones más firmes: la corona y vuestro Estamento.

LARRA. Convénzase, Espronceda: nos traiciona.

ESPRONCEDA. ¡Tendrá que justificarse en su logia!

LARRA. Espronceda, niño grande, lo probable es que la logia apruebe esas palabras.

MARTÍNEZ. ¡El Estatuto Real es la triaca que curará todo desmán de los exaltados irresponsables!

LARRA. «Los oradores ministeriales se empeñan (...) en sostener (...) que en el Estatuto está todo. Sin duda (...) lo leen en italiano (*statutto*).» (*El Parnasillo ríe. VEGA señala a su folleto.*)

VEGA. ¡Este Fígaro!...

MARTÍNEZ. «El Nacional». «El Eco de la Opinión», «El Tiempo» y «El Universal» atentan contra los sagrados principios monárquicos que el Estatuto defiende y serán suspendidos por decreto. ¡Viva la libertad!

LARRA. ...de imprenta.

CARNERERO (*Nodding assent.*): People are dying in every part of he city.

GALLEGO: It would be dangerous to give way to panic. They say it's nly an outbreak of influenza.

BRETÓN: Exactly. Influenza, also know as Asian cholera.

DÍAZ (*To BRETÓN.*): Then the government is lying to us?

LARRA: Far from it! It says that "it is not a question of cholera, but predominant and suspicious sickness; so much so that those damned uspicions have taken many to their grave, no doubt for being ypercritical". (*VEGA produces a pamphlet which he begins to read.*)

GRIMALDI: And our poor friend Mesonero has fallen ill... he too nay die.

CARNERERO: And the authorities, meanwhile, do nothing. (*He roduces a newspaper and absorbs himself in his reading. Light falls uddenly on the right-hand rostrum, where MARTÍNEZ DE LA ROSA is tanding.*)

MARTÍNEZ: I have requested our allies of the Four-way Alliance to end thirty thousand men to assist us in stamping out the plague of armed Carlism!

CARNERERO (*Slapping the newspaper.*): What's the point when hey've already refused?

MARTÍNEZ: My Lords, I place my trust in this House. I have no ympathy whatsoever with the creeping dream of universal suffrage and narchy. My government rests upon the firmest of all institutions: the rown and this noble Assembly.

LARRA: Face facts, Espronceda: he's betraying us.

ESPRONCEDA: It's because he has to justify himself to his own upporters!

LARRA: Espronceda, you overgrown child, his supporters are bound o applaud his every word.

MARTÍNEZ: The Royal Statute is the potion which will quell the xcesses of irresponsible extremists!

LARRA: "Every minister who speaks is resolute (...) in maintaining ...) that the Statute is all. Doubtless (...) they are reading it in Italian statutto)." (*Laughter in the café. VEGA points at his pamphlet.*)

VEGA: Figaro, as acute as ever!

MARTÍNEZ: "The National", "The Echo of Opinion", "The Times" nd "The Universal" are a calculated insult to the sacred principles of nonarchy as enshrined in the Statute, and it is hereby decreed that they vill cease publication. Long live liberty!

LARRA: ...of the press.

ARRIAZA. (*Entusiasmado.*) ¡Sí, señores! ¡Viva la libertad dentro del orden!

MARTÍNEZ. Señorías... Viva la reina. (*Se sienta, solemne.*)

LARRA. Clarísimo. «Desde que tenemos una racional libertad de imprenta, apenas hay cosa racional que podamos racionalmente escribir.» (*El bloque derecho se oscurece.*)

VEGA. (*Vuelve a señalar a su folleto.*) ¡Este Fígaro!...

BRETÓN. (*Pendiente de la calle.*) ¡Este ruido! ¿No lo nota? (*Está creciendo efectivamente un confuso griterío que atrae la atención de todos.*)

VEGA. ¿Qué pasa?

CARNERERO. Nada bueno. (*GRIMALDI va hasta la puerta para atisbar. Disparos aislados entre la algarabía.*)

GALLEGO. ¡Dios mío! (*Casi todos se levantan. Los gritos se acercan.*)

VOCES. ¡Muerte a los frailes!... ¡Han envenenado las aguas!... ¡Son los culpables de la peste!... ¡Carlistas asesinos!... ¡Nuestros hijos mueren por culpa de esos criminales!... ¡Abajo los conventos!... ¡Muerte, muerte!... (*LARRA y ESPRONCEDA se incorporan y atienden. Todo el gabinete se inunda de contrastadas y frías luces. Las campanas tocan a rebato. Por los huecos del fondo asoman un MERCEDARIO, un DOMINICO y un JESUITA, con caretas completamente blancas de ojos pasmados. Tremendos golpes en puertas invisibles.*)

MERCEDARIO. ¡Piedad!

DOMINICO. ¡En nombre de Nuestro Señor Jesucristo!

JESUITA. ¡Somos inocentes! (*Los ruidos arrecian. Escándalo de puertas destrozadas. Los religiosos se arrodillan. Asoman al tiempo por los laterales del primer término cuatro hombres de la plebe armados de palos, escopetas, algún pistolón. En sus caras, horrendas máscaras bermejas. La luz del café ha decrecido y todos sus clientes miran despavoridos al grupo. LARRA se estremece: armado de un garrote, ha visto entrar por el primer término a su criado PEDRO, sin máscara, como un quinto asaltante.*)

LARRA. ¡Pedro!

ASALTANTES. ¡Muerte a los envenenadores! ¡Acabad con los culpables de la peste! ¡A ellos! (*Irrumpen gritando en el gabinete. Los frailes suplican, pero son pronto acallados. Dos disparos ultiman a DOMINICO y al MERCEDARIO; el propio PEDRO derriba de un garrotazo al JESUITA. Otro rufián le arrebata la estaca y 'remata al caído. Entre el fragor de campanas y gritos, los asaltantes arrastran los cuerpos y se los llevan por los huecos del fondo. PEDRO permanece en*

ARRIAZA (*Zealously.*): Yes, gentlemen! Long live freedom within order!

MARTÍNEZ: My Lords... Long live the Queen. (*He sits down solemnly.*)

LARRA: Crystal clear. "Ever since the inception of our freedom of the press, within reason, there is hardly a reasonable thing which we can reasonably write". (*The right-hand rostrum grows dark.*)

VEGA (*Pointing to his pamphlet again.*): How very true!

BRETÓN (*His attention drawn by events in the street.*): That noise! Don't you hear it? (*A growing clamour is heard, attracting their undivided attention.*)

VEGA: What's happening?

CARNERERO: Nothing good. (*GRIMALDI goes to the door to look out. Occasional shots ring out amidst the hubbub of voices.*)

GALLEGO: Good God! (*They stand up almost to a man. The shouts draw nearer.*)

VOICES: Kill the priests!... They put poison in the water!... It was them who brought the plague on us!... Murderers! Carlists!... Our children are dying because of them!... Criminals!... Burn their convents!... Kill them, kill them!... (*LARRA and ESPRONCEDA stand up to watch. The study is washed with cold, contrasting lights. An urgent pealing of bells. Through the gaps at the back appear a DOMINICAN, a JESUIT and a PRIEST OF THE ORDER OF MERCY, all wearing chalk-white masks with terrified eyes. The sound of doors being battered.*)

PRIEST: Mercy!

DOMINICAN: For the sake of Our Lord Jesus Christ!

JESUIT: We have done nothing! (*The clamour intensifies. The sound of splintering doors. The priests kneel down. At the same time, four men, clearly proletarian, armed with sticks, muskets, perhaps a pistol, appear downstage from the sides. They wear glaring masks of scarlet. The light in the café has dimmed, and all its customers watch them fearfully. LARRA shivers; he has seen a fifth assailant enter downstage. It is PEDRO, unmasked, and armed with a heavy club.*)

LARRA: Pedro!

ASSAILANTS: Poisoners! Kill them, they brought the plague on us! Take them! (*They burst into the study, filling it with their shouts. The priests beg for mercy, but are quickly silenced. Two shots bring down the DOMINICAN and the PRIEST OF THE ORDER OF MERCY; PEDRO himself fells the JESUIT with his club. Another of the rioters snatches the cudgel to finish him off. Amidst the clamour of bells and cries, the assailants drag the bodies through the gaps at the back. PEDRO remains*

escena. Las campanas enmudecen un momento y doblan a muerto. Todos los del Parnasillo se van sentando, sombríos. El PADRE GALLEGO se arrodilló y rezó en silencio durante el asalto. GRIMALDI le ayuda ahora a levantarse. GALLEGO se santigua y se sienta. PEDRO se vuelve hacia su señor.)

LARRA. ¿Qué has hecho?

PEDRO. Tú lo sospechaste.

LARRA. ¡Del anterior criado, no de ti!

PEDRO. *(Se encoge de hombros.)* Quién sabe. *(LARRA apoya su frente en las manos y el gabinete se oscurece un tanto. Dos focos vuelven a iluminar a LARRA y a ESPRONCEDA, meditando en las escaleras, Crece al mismo tiempo la luz en el Parnasillo. Achacoso y apoyándose en su bastón, MESONERO entra por la puerta del café vestido de negro.)*

MESONERO. ¡Qué espanto, señores!

CARNERERO. Todo son calamidades, Mesonero. Pero nos alegra verle. Temíamos...

MESONERO. Y yo. Aún no sé cómo he sanado del cólera. ¡Bendito sea Dios!

GALLEGO. ¡Sea por siempre bendito y alabado!

LARRA. *(Descubre su cara, atiende.)* ¡Todos celebramos su restablecimiento!

MESONERO. Todos..., menos yo. Mi santa madre ha muerto. Le contagié el mal.

GALLEGO. ¡Que el Señor la tenga en su seno!

MESONERO. Muchas gracias. *(Estrechando manos y musitando gratitudes llega a su sitio habitual. Antes de sentarse, interpela a LARRA.)* Ahora no podrá negarlo, Fígaro: la canalla es temible y odiosa. Han asesinado a más de cien religiosos. *(Se sienta. Estrecha otras manos. Callan las campanas.)*

LARRA. No.

MESONERO. ¿Cómo?

LARRA. Esos crímenes son repugnantes. Pero son fruto de la ignorancia. «Toda la dificultad de llevar adelante la regeneración del país consiste en interesar en ella a las masas populares.» «Cuando yo veo a los (...) pueblos de una nación (...) atropellar el orden y propasarse a excesos lamentables (...) difícilmente me atrevo a juzgarlos con ligereza; mientras mayores son los excesos (...) más me empeño en buscarles una causa.» *(ESPRONCEDA levanta su cabeza y le escucha.)*

BRETÓN. ¿Defiende usted esos crímenes?

LARRA. ¡Ni esos ni ninguno! Pero, «¿En dónde ve el pueblo español su principal peligro, el más inminente? (...) En la importancia

nstage. The bells fall silent for a second, then toll mournfully. The men n the café return sombrely to their seats. During the whole duration of he assault FATHER GALLEGO has knelt to pray. Now GRIMALDI elps him to his feet. GALLEGO blesses himself and sits down. PEDRO urns towards his master.)

LARRA: What have you done?

PEDRO: You always suspected.

LARRA: My first servant yes, but not you!

PEDRO (*Shrugging his shoulders.*): Who can ever tell? (*LARRA rests is forehead in his hands and the light in the study dims slightly. Two potlights once again pick out LARRA and ESPRONCEDA, lost in hought on the stairs. At the same time, light grows on Little Parnassus. MESONERO comes in, walking with the aid of a stick. He has a sickly ir, and is dressed in black.*)

MESONERO: The horror of it, gentlemen!

CARNERERO: We are surrounded by horror, Mesonero. But we are glad to see you. We feared...

MESONERO: And I. I still don't know how I recovered from the cholera. Thanks be to God!

GALLEGO: Praise be, indeed!

LARRA: (*Removing his hands from his face, he fixes his attention on the café*): We're all delighted to have you back among us!

MESONERO: I'm afraid I can't share your pleasure. My dear mother passed away. She caught it from me.

GALLEGO: May her soul rest in peace!

MESONERO: Thank you. (*Amidst handshakes and expressions of gratitude he makes his way to his usual seat. Before sitting down, he addresses LARRA.*) There's no denying it now, Figaro: the rabble is appalling and despicable. They've murdered more than a hundred priests. *He sits down, still shaking hands. The bells fall silent.*)

LARRA: No.

MESONERO: What do you mean?

LARRA: Their crimes are repugnant. But they are also the fruit of ignorance. "The real stumbling block in regenerating this country of ours is achieving the involvement in that task of the ordinary people". "Whenever I see (...) the common people of any nation (...) crush public order underfoot with unrestrained acts of unfortunate violence (...) I find it hard to judge them lightly; the greater the violence, the more I insist in looking for its cause". (*ESPRONCEDA raises his head to listen to him.*)

BRETÓN: Are you defending their crimes?

LARRA: I defend no crime! But I ask you, "Where does the Spanish

132]

que de resultas de la indulgencia y de un desprecio inoportuno ha tomado la guerra civil. ¿No veía en los conventos otros tantos focos de esa guerra, en cada fraile un enemigo, en cada carlista un reo de Estado tolerado? ¿No procedía del poder de esos mismos enemigos, dominantes siglos enteros en España, la larga acumulación de un antiguo rencor jamás desahogado?» «Quien pudo dar salida conveniente a ese río no lo supo hacer, y cuando llega la avenida se queja del río.»

GALLEGO. Larra, esos pobres frailes...

LARRA. Toda nuestra compasión para ellos. (*Eleva la voz.*) Como para Torrijos, Iglesias y tantos otros a quienes no fue el pueblo quien mató.

MESONERO. Pero, Larra...

LARRA. «El mayor crimen de los tiranos es el de obligar (...) a los pueblos a recurrir a la violencia contra ellos, y en tales casos sólo sobre su cabeza recae la sangre derramada.» «Asesinatos por asesinatos, ya que los ha de haber, estoy por los del pueblo.»

BRETON. ¡Digo! Mientras la sangre no sea de usted...

DIAZ. (*Desdeñoso.*) Sólo es una frase.

CARNERERO. ¡Si escribe eso alguna vez, Fígaro, no cuente más con mi revista!

LARRA. Como guste. Ustedes no son ignorantes como esas turbas, pero no son menos torpes.

ARRIAZA. ¡Nos llama asesinos!

MESONERO. ¡Delira! ¿No le parece, Espronceda?

ESPRONCEDA. Delira. Pero tiene razón. (*Los del Parnasillo se miran entre sí, estupefactos. La luz les abandona.*)

LARRA. Gracias por su defensa. (*ESPRONCEDA ha vuelto a ensimismarse.*) ¿Le sucede algo, Espronceda? (*Habla su voz en el aire.*)

LARRA. (*Su voz.*) «¿Y quién duda que tenemos libertad de imprenta? Que quieres imprimir una esquela de convite; más una esquela de muerte; más todavía, una tarjeta con todo tu nombre y tu apellido (..) Nadie te lo estorba.» (*ESPRONCEDA lo mira y se levanta lleno de furia.*)

LARRA. (*Habla con su boca.*) No me diga nada: malas noticias.

ESPRONCEDA. (*Desciende al suelo del gabinete.*) ¡Me han prohibido entero el número 14 de «El Siglo»! (*LARRA se incorpora y se acerca.*) ¡Pero no voy a usar por ello de medias palabras! (*Avanza hacia el primer término.*)

LARRA. (*Le sigue.*) También las tachan a menudo. «Nunca escribo

eople feel that its principal, its most immediate, threat lies? (...) In a
ivil war that indulgence and an inordinate degree of contempt have
aused to flare out of all proportions. Did it not see each and every
monastery as a focus of that war, in every monk an adversary, in every
'arlist a tolerated enemy of state? And did the power wielded by those
ame enemies over centuries in Spain not produce a deep groundswell of
esentment which had no possible outlet?" "Those who could have safely
hannelled the river chose not to, and when the river bursts they see fit
nly to blame the river".

GALLEGO: Larra, those poor priests...

LARRA: And all of us feel more than sorry for them. (*Raising his
oice.*) As we do for Torrijos, Iglesias and so many others who were also
illed... but not by the people. [41]

MESONERO: But, Larra...

LARRA: "The greatest crime of tyrants is that they force (...) the
eople to take up arms against them, and when they do, the bloodshed is
n their heads, and theirs alone". "Murder for murder, since murder there
ust be, I choose those of the people".

BRETÓN: Of course! As long as it's not your blood which is spilt...

DÍAZ (*Scornfully.*): Mere words.

CARNERERO: If you ever write that, Figaro, you may no longer
ount on the patronage of my journal!

LARRA: Just as you wish. There are none of you ignorant in the
ame way as the common people are, but you are all no less to blame.

ARRIAZA: He's calling us murderers!

MESONERO: He's mad! Don't you think so, Espronceda?

ESPRONCEDA: He is mad. But he's right. (*The men in the café look
t each other in silent amazement, as the light over them fades.*)

LARRA: Thank you for your support. (*ESPRONCEDA has lapsed
ack into thought.*) Espronceda, is anything wrong? (*His voice is heard in
he air.*)

LARRA (*Voice off.*): "And who can doubt that we have freedom of
he press? You want to print an invitation; then, a death notice; then, a
ard with your entire name and surname (...) And nobody will stand in
our way". (*ESPRONCEDA looks at him and stands up, full of anger.*)

LARRA (*Speaking normally.*): Don't tell me: bad news.

ESPRONCEDA (*Coming down to the floor of the study.*): They've
anned the entire issue of number 14 of "The Century"! (*LARRA stands
p and moves towards him.*) But that doesn't mean to say I'm going to use
alf-words. (*He walks forward.*)

LARRA (*Following him.*): They're censored just as frequently. "I

yo más artículos que cuando ellos (*Señala al Parnasillo.*) no ven ninguno, de suerte que en vez de decir: Fígaro no ha escrito este mes, fuera más arrimado a la verdad decir (...) ¡Cuánto habrá escrito Fígaro este mes!» (*El café se ilumina despacio.*)

ESPRONCEDA. No estoy para bromas.

LARRA. Perdone. Soy un imbécil.

ESPRONCEDA. ¡Publicaré «El Siglo» con todas sus páginas en blanco y los títulos de los artículos solamente!

VEGA. ¡Una idea magnífica!

GRIMALDI. ¡Este mozo es tremendo!

LARRA. Ello demostraría que también usted cree en la fuerza de las medias palabras. Pero en este momento sería una provocación. No lo haga.

ESPRONCEDA. ¿Por qué no? Acabo de abofetear a un censor...

CARNERERO. ¡Inaudito!

ESPRONCEDA. Y esta otra bofetada será más eficaz que todos los artículos prohibidos.

DÍAZ. ¡Esa es la verdadera rebeldía! No los equilibrios en la cuerda floja... de otros.

LARRA. (*Después de un rápido vistazo a DÍAZ.*) Podrían desterrarle...

ESPRONCEDA. Me inmolaré en una acción definitiva si es menester. (*Ríe.*) Pero no osarán hacerme nada.

LARRA. ¡No suicide su propia voz!

ESPRONCEDA. ¡No sea tan miedoso, Fígaro! Publicaré «El Siglo» en blanco.

LARRA. Será un desafío y nos costará caro a todos.

ESPRONCEDA. ¡Sea más valiente!

LARRA. ¡Yo no soy cobarde! Yo sólo pienso. (*Se encamina a la izquierda para sentarse.*)

VEGA. ¡Fígaro, él tiene razón! ¡La campanada será enorme! (*ESPRONCEDA va a sentarse también con ellos.*)

LARRA. Y estéril.

VEGA. (*A ESPRONCEDA.*) ¡Hágalo! Yo lo apruebo. ¡Quizá logremos resultados inesperados!

LARRA. Eso temo. (*PEDRO entró por un hueco del fondo para ir a sentarse en la escalera izquierda.*)

PEDRO. (*Murmura.*) Y a los pocos días se vio lo que se podía esperar. (*La luz invade el café hasta hacerse más viva que nunca. El bloque derecho se ilumina al tiempo. MARTÍNEZ DE LA ROSA aparece en pie y muy irritado. DÍAZ, VEGA, MESONERO, CARNERERO*

never write as many articles as when they (*Indicating Little Parnassus.*) don't see a single one, so that instead of saying 'Figaro hasn't written anything this month', it would be closer to the truth to say 'How much Figaro must have written this month!'" (*Light slowly grows on the cafe.*)

ESPRONCEDA: I'm in no mood for jokes.

LARRA: Forgive me. I wasn't thinking.

ESPRONCEDA: I will publish "The Century", but with all its pages blank and with only the titles of the articles!

VEGA: Magnificent!

GRIMALDI: This young man is phenomenal!

LARRA: That would show that you believe in the power of half words as well. But at a time like this it would be an open provocation. Don't do it.

ESPRONCEDA: Why not? I have just physically struck a censor...

CARNERERO: Incredible!

ESPRONCEDA: And this new blow would have more effect that all the banned articles put together.

DÍAZ: That's real defiance! And not mere balancing on a slack rope, like others contrive to do.

LARRA (*Glancing swiftly at DÍAZ.*): They could send you into exile...

ESPRONCEDA: I am prepared to offer myself up for a decisive blow. (*Laughing.*) But they wouldn't dare touch me.

LARRA: You're commiting suicide as a writer!

ESPRONCEDA: Don't be so faint-hearted, Figaro. I'll publish "The Century" in blank.

LARRA: It would be a provocation that will cost us all dear.

ESPRONCEDA: Have courage!

LARRA: I'm no coward! But I do stop to think. (*He walks towards the left and sits down.*)

VEGA: Figaro, he's right. A resounding blow! (*ESPRONCEDA also walks over to sit with them.*)

LARRA: A fruitless one.

VEGA (*To ESPRONCEDA.*) Go ahead! You have my approval. Perhaps we'll achieve more than we bargain for!

LARRA: That's what I'm afraid of. (*PEDRO enters through a gap at the back and goes to sit on the left-hand stairway.*)

PEDRO (*In a low voice.*): And a few days later they got exactly what they'd bargained for. (*The light grows in the cafe until it is brighter than ever. The right-hand rostrum is illuminated at the same time. MARTINEZ DE LA ROSA is standing there, clearly angry. DÍAZ, VEGA,*

GRIMALDI exhiben «El Siglo» en blanco, repasan sus paginas y ríen.)
VEGA. Todo Madrid se ríe del Gobierno.
DÍAZ. ¡Y de la censura! *(ESPRONCEDA se pavonea y sonríe.)*
LARRA. Y ahora, a esperar.
DÍAZ. A esperar la crisis.
BRETÓN. ¿Qué crisis?
DÍAZ. La del Gobierno. La reina tendrá que relevarlo.
BRETÓN. *(Se acaricia la barbilla.)* No diga sandeces.
MARTÍNEZ. ¿Esos exaltados van a darme lecciones a mí, que he padecido cárceles y destierro? ¡No derruirán mi obra! ¡El orden, ante todo! ¡Suspéndase para siempre la publicación de ese libelo! *(Se sienta y desaparece en la oscuridad. En el Parnasillo siguen mirando «El Siglo», pero se muestran inquietos.)*
GALLEGO. *(A ESPRONCEDA.)* Lamento advertirle de que van a tomar represalias... Ante Dios Nuestro Señor le digo que intenté salvar «El Siglo», pero eligió un mal momento para retar al Gobierno. El cólera no acaba de remitir y en la guerra de Navarra Zumalacárregui obtiene victoria tras victoria. El trono de nuestra amada soberana empieza a peligrar. Y Cabrera... ¿Sabe cómo le llaman?
ESPRONCEDA. El tigre del Maestrazgo.
GALLEGO. Porque ha llegado a la mayor crueldad. Fusila a los prisioneros... y les corta las orejas a los niños, ¡a los niños!, cuando les sorprende llevando partes del ejército... *(LARRA mira con aprensión a su gabinete.)*
ESPRONCEDA. ¿Qué se puede esperar de un faccioso?
GALLEGO. *(Apesadumbrado.)* También los nuestros fusilan sin dar cuartel. Todos somos caínes. *(Silencio. Se abre la puerta del café y entran dos soldados de la MILICIA URBANA. Todos disimulan sus periódicos.)*
MILICIANO 1.° ¿Don José de Espronceda?
ESPRONCEDA. *(Se levanta.)* Yo soy.
MILICIANO 1.° *(Saluda, se acerca y le tiende un pliego lacrado, que el poeta se apresura a abrir.)* Tenemos orden de acompañarle para que recoja lo más necesario.
VEGA. *(Se levanta.)* ¡Esto es un atropello! ¿Qué pretenden?
ESPRONCEDA. Me destierran a Badajoz.
DÍAZ. ¡Qué infamia!

*MESONERO, CARNERERO and GRIMALDI hold blank copies of "The
Century", flicking through its pages and laughing.)*

VEGA: The government is a laughing stock all over Madrid.

DÍAZ: So are the censors. *(ESPRONCEDA preens himself
smilingly.)*

LARRA: And now, we wait.

DÍAZ: We wait for the crisis.

BRETÓN: What crisis?

DÍAZ: In the government. The Queen will have to dissolve it.

BRETÓN *(Stroking his chin.):* Nonsense!

MARTINEZ: Those hotheads think they can teach me a lesson, I who
have suffered exile and imprisonment? They won't stop my work! Order
above all else! Their lampooning little journal is banned once and for all!
*(He sits down and is lost in darkness. In Little Parnassus they continue
reading "The Century", but there is a new air of anxiety.)*

GALLEGO *(To ESPRONCEDA.):* I'm afraid that there are will be
reprisals... I swear by God's name that I tried to save "The Century", but
you chose the wrong moment to defy the government. The outbreak of
cholera continues unabated, and in the war in Navarra Zumalacárregui is
winning victory after victory. The throne of our beloved sovreign is under
increasing threat. And Cabrera... Have you heard what they're calling him?

ESPRONCEDA: The tiger of Maestrazgo.[42]

GALLEGO: Because of his appalling cruelty. He has all his prisoners
shot... and slices the ears off children, children, mind you!, when he
catches them running dispatches... *(LARRA looks apprehensively towards
his study.)*

ESPRONCEDA: What else can you expect from a rebel?

GALLEGO *(Sorrowfully.):* Our own army is no less pitiless when it
comes to executions. All of us carry the mark of Cain.[43] *(Silence. The door
of the café opens and two soldiers from the URBAN MILITIA enter.
They all conceal their newspapers.)*

MILITIAMAN #1: Don José de Espronceda?

ESPRONCEDA *(Rising.):* I'm Espronceda.

MILITIAMAN #1 *(He salutes, and steps forward to hand him a
sealed document, which the poet hurriedly opens.):* We have orders to
accompany you so that you may collect whatever belongings are most
necessary.

VEGA *(Standing up.):* This is outrageous! What do you think you're
doing?

ESPRONCEDA: They're sending me to Badajoz.

DÍAZ: It's a disgrace!

MILICIANO 1.º Caballeros, nosotros tenemos que cumplir la orden. (*LARRA se levanta y le pone una mano en el hombro a ESPRONCEDA.*) LARRA. ¿Lo ve? ESPRONCEDA. (*A todos.*) ¡No podrán conmigo! Vamos. (*El MILICIANO 2.º abre la puerta, sale y la sujeta. ESPRONCEDA sale y, tras él, el MILICIANO 1.º La puerta se cierra y el café se oscurece un tanto.*) LARRA. Le previne. PEDRO. Y le ayudaste. Todos leyeron tu artículo: «El Siglo en blanco.» (*El criado se incorpora y sale por un hueco del fondo mientras se expande la fantasmal voz de LARRA.*) LARRA. (*Su voz.*) «A catorce *Siglos* nos ha dejado este periódico; es decir, en la Edad Media; (...) quedémonos en blanco enhorabuena. Muchos son efectivamente los puntos que ha dejado en blanco nuestro buen *Siglo* (...) *amnistía* (...) *política interior* (...) *Cortes* (...) pero más creemos que hubieran sido aún los puntos en blanco, si conforme era el 14 siglo, hubiera sido el 19. Y por último, deducimos (...) de la muerte que alcanza a nuestro buen *Siglo*, (...) que el siglo es chico como son los hombres, y que en tiempos como estos los hombres prudentes no deben *hablar*, ni mucho menos *callar*.» (*Un foco ha crecido sobre la figura de LARRA. En la semioscuridad del Parnasillo, todos están inmóviles como estatuas. El escritor se muestra deprimido, defraudado. Cargada de desánimo, se oye levemente su voz en lo alto.*) LARRA. (*Su voz.*) Más de sesenta niños desorejados... (*En la puerta del gabinete renace el lento resplandor.*) ADELITA. (*Su voz.*) Papaíto, déjame entrar... (*El fulgor se extingue. LARRA se levanta, angustiado. Va a las mesas, toca a MESONERO...*) LARRA. Despertad... (*Zarandea a BRETÓN, cruza, toca a CARNERERO, a GRIMALDI, a GALLEGO...*) ¡Despertad!... ¡Despertad!... (*Retrocede unos pasos, mira al conjunto del café.*) ¡Despertad! (*Silencio. Sus manos se unen y se oprimen, convulsas. Su voz denuncia la amargura de su decisión.*) ¡Me voy! (*Pasa al gabinete. Junto al velador, toca la pistola. PEDRO aparece al punto por un hueco del fondo llevando una gran maleta que deja en el suelo.*) PEDRO. (*Sonriente.*) La maleta está dispuesta. (*LARRA se estremece.*) ¿La bajo al portal? (*LARRA da unos pasos, turbado.*) LARRA. (*Con dificultad.*) Debo ir a Lisboa, a Londres y a París.. He de cobrar unos dineros de mi padre... PEDRO. No te vas por eso. ¿Piensas volver?

MILITIAMAN #1: Gentlemen, we are simply carrying out orders. (*LARRA stands up and puts his hand on ESPRONCEDA's shoulder.*)

LARRA: You see?

ESPRONCEDA (*To them all.*): They'll never get the best of me! Let's go. (*MILITIAMAN #2 goes out, and holds open the door for ESPRONCEDA, who is followed by the other MILITIAMAN. The door closes and the light dims slightly in the café.*)

LARRA: I warned him.

PEDRO: And you helped him. Everyone read your article "The Century left blank". (*The servant stands up and exits through one of the gaps at the back as the ghostly voice of LARRA fills the air.*)

LARRA (*Voice off.*): "This journal has left us in the fourteenth Century; that is, back in the Middle Ages; (...) and now we've all been left blank. Indeed, many are the areas that our good *Century* has left blank (...) *amnesty* (...) *internal policy* (...) *Parliament* (...) but many more are the areas, we believe, that would have been blank if, instead of the fourteenth, it had been the nineteenth century. And, lastly, we deduce from the oblivion that has befallen our good *Century* (...) that the century is no bigger than individual men, and that in times like these men of wisdom must not *speak*, nor much less *fall silent*". (*A single light has grown on the figure of LARRA. In the semi-darkness of the café, the others sit motionless, like statues. The writer is clearly depressed, disappointed. His voice, laden with despondency, sounds faintly in the air.*)

LARRA (*Voice off.*): More than sixty children mutilated... (*The study door begins to glow once again.*)

ADELITA (*Voice off.*): Papa, let me in... (*The glow subsides. LARRA, deeply distressed, stands up. He goes to the tables and touches MESONERO...*)

LARRA: Wake up... (*He shakes BRETÓN, crosses over and touches CARNERERO, GRIMALDI, GALLEGO...*) Wake up! Wake up! (*He takes several steps backwards and looks at the entire café.*) Wake up! (*Silence. He joins his hands and wrings them in agitation. His voice reveals the bitterness of his resolve.*) I'm leaving. (*He enters the study. He fingers the pistol on the small table. As he does so, PEDRO appears through a gap at the back, carrying a large suitcase which he deposits on the floor.*)

PEDRO (*Smiling.*): Your case is ready. (*LARRA trembles.*) Shall I take it down? (*Disturbed, LARRA takes a few steps.*)

LARRA (*With difficulty.*): I have to go to Lisbon, London and Paris... to collect some debts for my father...

PEDRO: That's not why you're going. Will you come back?

LARRA. No lo sé.

PEDRO. Martínez de la Rosa va a caer. No ha podido terminar la guerra, no ha dado libertades, la economía está hundida... Se habla ya de un sustituto.

LARRA. El conde de Toreno. Otro ilustre liberal perseguido. Será lo mismo: censura, corrupción...

PEDRO. Se van a formar Juntas políticas en las regiones. ¿No deberías quedarte?

LARRA. ¡No puedo! (*PEDRO recoge la capa y se la pone en los hombros. Le ofrece el sombrero y el escritor se lo pone. El criado señala hacia el frente.*)

PEDRO. Algo ocurre. (*Se retira por el hueco derecho del fondo. LARRA avanza hacia el frente. Se está oyendo el confuso fragor de una multitud. Luz en todo el escenario. Los escritores del café se levantan de golpe, alarmados. DON HOMOBONO deja su pluma y escucha. MARTÍNEZ DE LA ROSA se levanta, intranquilo.*)

CARNERERO. Era de esperar.

GRIMALDI. Los carlistas han batido a nuestros generales y todo el país se ha levantado.

GALLEGO. No tanto...

DÍAZ. Padre Gallego, el Regimiento de Aragón ha tomado la Casa de Correos y exige la Constitución del 12.

MARTÍNEZ. (*Le tiembla la voz.*) ¡No nos obligarán a ir más de prisa! ¡El capitán general de Madrid arenga en estos momentos a los amotinados para que se rindan! (*Disparos aislados, gritos. De pronto, una descarga cerrada. Silencio. La puerta del café se abre y entra el camarero PIPÍ.*)

ARRIAZA. ¿Qué ha pasado, Pipí?

PIPÍ. Han disparado contra el general Canterac y lo han matado.

GALLEGO. ¡No es posible!

PIPÍ. Las tropas del Gobierno han huido. ¡Me lo ha dicho un miliciano que venía de Sol!

MARTÍNEZ. (*Cierra los ojos, entristecido.*) Páctese con los sublevados. (*Comienzan a redoblar tambores lejanos que se acercan. MARTÍNEZ DE LA ROSA se va por la escalera oculta. DON HOMOBONO se eclipsa, medroso.*)

PIPÍ. (*Escucha desde la puerta entreabierta.*) Ya salen. Y a tambor batiente. (*Aclamaciones. Se eleva un coro de voces. La luz se va yendo del bloque derecho. Sobre el son de las cajas y con la melodía del Himno de Riego, canta el coro la siguiente letra.*)

VOCES. «Serenos, alegres, valientes, osados,

LARRA: I don't know.

PEDRO: Martínez de la Rosa is about to fall. He hasn't managed to stop the war, he hasn't given us any new freedoms, the economy is stagnant... They're talking about a replacement already.

LARRA: The Count of Toreno. Another illustrious persecuted liberal. It'll be just the same: censorship, corruption...

PEDRO: They're about to form political assemblies in the provinces. Shouldn't you stay?

LARRA: I can't! (*PEDRO collects LARRA's cloak and places it over his shoulders. He offers him his hat, which the writer takes and puts on. The servant points frontwards.*)

PEDRO: Something's happening. (*He exits through the right-hand gap at the back. LARRA walks forward. The sound of the confused clamour of a crowd. The whole stage is lit. The writers in the café jump to their feet in alarm. DON HOMOBONO lays down his pen to listen. MARTÍNEZ DE LA ROSA stands up anxiously.*)

CARNERERO: It was only to be expected.

GRIMALDI: The Carlists have defeated our generals and the whole country has risen.

GALLEGO: You're exaggerating...

DÍAZ: Father Gallego, the Aragón Regiment has taken the Post Office and is demanding the restoration of the Constitution of 1812.[44]

MARTÍNEZ (His voice is shaking.): They will not force us to move more quickly. The Field Marshal of Madrid is at this moment exhorting the mutineers to surrender! (*Isolated shots, cries. A sudden volley. Silence. The door of the café opens and the waiter, PIPÍ, comes in.*)

ARRIAZA: What's happened, Pipí?

PIPÍ: They shot at General Canterac and killed him.

GALLEGO: That's impossible!

PIPÍ: The government troops have fled. I heard it from a soldier coming from the centre of town!

MARTÍNEZ (*Closing his eyes, saddened.*): Make peace with the rebels. (*Distant drums are heard approaching. MARTÍNEZ DE LA ROSA descends the hidden staircase. DON HOMOBONO scuttles fearfully away.*)

PIPÍ (*Listening from the half-open door.*): They're coming out. To the sound of drums. (*A chorus of voices is raised in acclamation. The light leaves the right-hand rostrum. Above the sound of the drums the voices sing the following words to the tune of the Anthem of Riego.*)

VOICES: "Serene, happy, valiant, brave,
            soldiers, let us sing of victory in the fight".

cantemos, soldados, el triunfo en la lid.»
VEGA. ¡Viva la Constitución del 12!
VOCES. «Soldados, la patria nos llama a la lid,
juremos por ella vencer o morir.»
(*ARRIAZA se desploma en su asiento. CARNERERO y GRIMALDI se
sientan, cavilosos. GALLEGO se santigua en silencio. Los tambores se
alejan. Se van sentando los demás. En los bloques y en el gabinete va
menguando la luz. PIPÍ se recuesta en la puerta y oye la conversación.*)
MESONERO. Bueno... Ya pasó el turbión. (*Los tambores apenas
se oyen.*)
GRIMALDI. (*Sonriente.*) Pongan buena cara, *mes amis*. A malos
tiempos, buenas diversiones.
DÍAZ. Tiene razón. ¡Y no nos faltarán! Un pajarito me ha dicho
que la nueva comedia de don Manuel Bretón causará justísimo regocijo...
GRIMALDI. (*Trivial.*) ¿Cuándo me la dará para mi teatro, Bretón?
BRETÓN. (*Con aviesa sonrisa.*) Pronto. ¿Saben ustedes que Fígaro
nos abandona? (*DÍAZ ahoga la risa.*)
VEGA. ¿Se va?
BRETÓN. Al extranjero, naturalmente.
DÍAZ. Ése no vuelve.
MESONERO. También yo me fui y he vuelto, Díaz.
DÍAZ. Porque usted es un buen español.
VEGA. Por favor, Díaz. Hable de ese modo cuando Larra esté
presente.
DÍAZ. Si se ha ido, ¿cómo va a estar presente?
VEGA. Entonces no le nombre.
BRETÓN. ¿Por qué no? Son chanzas sin malicia por la huida de
Fígaro.
MESONERO. ¿Huida?
BRETÓN. Perdón. Partida.
DÍAZ. Huida o partida, ¡al fin España se libra de Fígaro!
MESONERO. ¡Por favor!
BRETÓN. Por cierto, ¡qué casualidad! ¿Saben el título de mi nueva
comedia?
GRIMALDI. ¿Cuál es?
BRETÓN. «Me voy de Madrid».
GALLEGO. No lo hallo de muy buen gusto.
BRETÓN. ¡Si no aludo a nadie! El protagonista se llama don
Joaquín, lo cual deshace cualquier equívoco. Oigan lo que dice cuando se
va:
«Bien, quiero obrar como cuerdo;

VEGA: Long live the Constitution!
VOICES: Soldiers, our country calls us to the fight,
let us swear that there we do or die".
*ARRIAZA falls back into his seat. CARNERERO and GRIMALDI sit
down thoughtfully. GALLEGO blesses himself in silence. The drums grow
distant. The rest gradually return to their places. The light slowly fades
over the study and the rostra. PIPÍ leans against the door and listens to
the conversation.)*
MESONERO: Well... The storm has passed. (*The drums are barely
audible.*)
GRIMALDI (*Smiling.*): Cheer up, *mes amis*. Bad times, good
entertainment.
DÍAZ: Quite right. And no shortage of it. A little bird tells me that
Bretón's new play will cause much well-deserved mirth...
GRIMALDI (*Nonchalantly.*): When will you give it to me for my
theatre, Bretón?
BRETÓN (*With a malicious smile.*): Soon. Did you know, gentlemen,
that Figaro is leaving us? (*DÍAZ stifles a laugh.*)
VEGA: He's going away?
BRETÓN: Abroad, naturally.
DÍAZ: He won't come back... not him.
MESONERO: I went too, Díaz, and I came back.
DÍAZ: Because you're a good Spaniard.
VEGA: Please, Díaz. Speak that way when Larra is present.
DÍAZ: If he's gone, how can he be present?
VEGA: Then don't talk about him at all.
BRETÓN: Why ever not? Harmless fun because Larra has flown.
MESONERO: Flown?
BRETÓN: Sorry. Gone.
DÍAZ: Flown or gone, at last Spain has got rid of Figaro!
MESONERO: Please!
BRETÓN: By the by, as chance would have it... Do you know the
title of my new play?
GRIMALDI: What is it?
BRETÓN: "I'm leaving Madrid".
GALLEGO: I don't find that in good taste.
BRETÓN: But I have nobody in particular in mind. The protagonist is
called don Joaquín, so that there's no possible misunderstanding. Listen to
what he says as he goes:[45]

"Well I would live among the best and the wise;

mas me voy a fastidiar,
porque debo confesar
que no vivo... ¡si no muerdo!»

(*Todos los de la derecha, menos GALLEGO, ríen. En la izquierda, sólo DÍAZ.*)
DÍAZ. ¡Eso es madrugar! (*BRETÓN ríe entre dientes. MESONERO se levanta, molesto.*)
MESONERO. Se me hace tarde. Con Dios, señores.
VEGA. (*Se levanta.*) Le acompaño. (*Ambos se calan sus sombreros y cruzan.*)
BRETÓN. ¡Escuchen todavía lo que dice don Hipólito! (*De mala gana, VEGA y MESONERO se detienen cerca de la puerta. BRETÓN se levanta y señala a los dos que se van, así como a DÍAZ.*)

«Hoy os convido, venid;
y brindad los tres conmigo
por que el común enemigo
no vuelva más a Madrid.»

(*La algazara es general y hasta GALLEGO sonríe, si bien denegando con la cabeza.*)
DÍAZ. ¡Que no vuelva! (*MESONERO y VEGA salen por la puerta que PIPÍ les abre muy servicial.*)
ARRIAZA. ¡Qué picajosos! Un rato de sana risa no debe ofender a nadie.
(*La luz se va del café. LARRA ha permanecido inmóvil en el borde del gabinete, absorto en sus ingratas imaginaciones. Una leve claridad de sueño baña el bloque izquierdo. Sentada al piano, DOLORES empieza a tocar la cavatina de Rossini con sordas, bajas y espaciadas notas. LARRA contempla la aparición con melancolía. La luz mengua en el bloque. Bajo el delirio, el escritor se yergue y va a tomar su valija. Como un autómata de lentos pasos, avanza con ella hacia el frente. Una rojiza claridad se enciende y aumenta en el hueco derecho. Desde el borde del gabinete, LARRA se vuelve y la mira. Con las manos sobre el teclado, el fantasma de DOLORES eleva su cabeza de estatua en la sombra. PEDRO reaparece por el hueco y avanza hacia el frente. Trae en los brazos a un adolescente de catorce años, muerto al parecer. Es un muchacho flaco, sin máscara y sin otra ropa que un mugriento y andrajoso calzón. En su espalda y pecho, una honda herida sanguinolenta. LARRA mira al extraño grupo con ojos desorbitados.*)

so it pains me all the more
to simply have to recognise
that unless I can bite... life's just a bore!"

All those on the right, except GALLEGO, laugh. On the left, only
DÍAZ.)
    DÍAZ: Clever stuff! (*BRETÓN laughs between clenched teeth.*
MESONERO stands up, rather put out.)
    MESONERO: It's getting late. Goodbye, gentlemen.
    VEGA (*Rising.*): I'll go with you. (*Both don their hats and cross the*
café.)
    BRETÓN: Listen again, this time to don Hipólito. (*Reluctantly,*
VEGA and MESONERO stop near the door. BRETÓN stands up and
points to the two about to leave, as well as to DÍAZ.)

"My three friends, today, in happy mood
drink a toast with me;
our common foe is gone for good,
our city Madrid is free".

General hilarity. E   GALLEGO smiles, although shaking his head as he
does so.)
    DÍAZ: Let it be for good! (*MESONERO and VEGA go through the*
door which the ever-obliging PIPÍ holds open for them.)
    ARRIAZA: Kill-joys, the pair of them! Healthy laughter shouldn't
offend anyone.
The light leaves the café. LARRA has remained motionless at the edge of
he study, absorbed in his unpleasant imaginings. A faint, dreamlike light
grows on the left-hand rostrum. Seated at the piano, DOLORES begins to
play the Rossini cavatina with slow, dull, low notes. LARRA gazes at this
apparition with melancholy. The light dims over the rostrum. Lost in his
fantasy, the writer straightens up and goes to lift his case. Mechanically,
slowly, he walks with it towards the front. A reddish light begins to glow
and increase in strength in the right-hand gap. From the edge of the
study LARRA turns round to watch it. With her hands on the keyboard,
he imagined figure of DOLORES raises her motionless head in the
shadow. PEDRO reappears through the gap and walks forward. He is
carrying a young boy of about fourteen, apparently dead. He is thin,
without a mask and wearing nothing other than a grimy, shabby
undergarment. There is a deep, bloody wound in his chest and back.
LARRA looks at them with horrified eyes.)

LARRA. ¡Déjame partir!

PEDRO. ¿A la eternidad?

LARRA. ¡Bórrate! (*Con su mano izquierda, el escritor se tapa los ojos.*)

PEDRO. Te hará volver tu pasión. Tu pasión; no Dolores. (*La imagen de DOLORES gira despacio su cabeza hacia LARRA. El viajero baja el escalón. Da unos pasos hacia la derecha. Se detiene. Sin que se altere la lasitud del cuerpecillo que sostiene el criado, la yerta boca juvenil emite una palabra.*)

JUANÍN. Pa... pá... (*Fuertemente iluminado, PEDRO permanece inmóvil, mirando al vacío con su carga en los brazos. La luz abandona a LARRA y se debilita en la escena entera hasta apagarse. Brillan las estrellas.*)

TELÓN

LARRA: Let me leave!

PEDRO: For eternity?

LARRA: Why don't you just disappear! (*With his left hand the writer covers his eyes.*)

PEDRO: It'll give you your passion back. Your passion; not Dolores. (*The image that is DOLORES slowly turns to face LARRA. He goes down the step and walks towards the right. He stops. Although the boy continues to hang limply in PEDRO's arms, a single word comes from his stiff lips.*)

JUANÍN: Pa...pa... (*Brightly lit, PEDRO stands motionless, staring into space, the boy lying across his arms. The light on LARRA fades, and dims over the rest of the stage until it is left in darkness. The stars shine.*)

CURTAIN

Rehearsal scenes from the first production in 1977 with Juan Diego as Larra. In the right–hand scene Larra points his gun at Cabrera's mother. Note the masks worn by the actors. (Photos by Gyenes, courtesy of Antonio Buero Vallejo)

PARTE SEGUNDA

(*Lenta subida de la luz. LARRA está de pie e inmóvil, con su maleta en el suelo, en el mismo lugar del primer término. El criado PEDRO se halla en el centro del gabinete. El aposento, a media luz. Se ilumina el bloque derecho. Un altivo personaje, de levita y condecorado, se divisa arriba, de pie. Bajo su melena gris, la media máscara muestra rasgos incisivos, nariz aguileña y espesas cejas sobre los ojos hundidos y penetrantes. Es don Juan Alvarez MENDIZÁBAL. Con voz metálica y autoritaria empieza a hablar. La cabeza de LARRA, humillada, se va elevando y una ilusionada sonrisa se dibuja en su boca. DON HOMOBONO aguarda, atento y humildísimo. LARRA saca un periódico de su bolsillo, se sienta en su maleta y lee en él, risueño, las palabras del prohombre.*)

MENDIZÁBAL.   Prometo solemnemente a España y a su majestad la reina Regente la terminación de la guerra en un plazo de medio año. Queda convocada a tal efecto una leva de cien mil hombres. (*El café se iluminó despacio. En el lugar habitual de CARNERERO se sienta ahora otro hombre de mediana edad, de vestido muy diferente aunque también elegante y de bonachona careta. Es el conocido periodista don Andrés BORREGO. Agrupados a ambos lados del Parnasillo, leen todos las Gacetas donde figuran las palabras del político gaditano. A la izquierda y de pie, ESPRONCEDA declama.*)

ESPRONCEDA.   «El pueblo ved que la orgullosa frente
                levanta ya del polvo en que yacía:
                arrogante en valor, omnipotente,
                terror de la insolente tiranía...»

BORREGO. (*Aplaude.*) ¡Sublime!

MENDIZÁBAL.   Se someterá a las Cortes un proyecto de ley electoral que permita la presencia en ellas de la verdadera opinión de nuestros pueblos... (*El Parnasillo aprueba. Enardecidos, unos; algo remisos, otros.*)

ESPRONCEDA.   ¡Viva Mendizábal! (*Excepto ARRIAZA y*

[149

PART TWO

(The light comes up slowly. LARRA is standing motionless in the same spot, downstage, his suitcase on the ground. PEDRO is in the middle of the study, which is bathed in a half light. As light grows on the right-hand rostrum an arrogant figure, dressed in a frock coat adorned with many medals and decorations, appears standing there. Under his grey mane of hair, he wears a half mask of incisive features, an aquiline nose and bushy eyebrows over sunken, penetrating eyes. This is don Juan Álvarez MENDIZÁBAL.⁴⁶ He begins to speak in clipped, authoritarian tones. LARRA's bowed head slowly begins to lift, and he begins to smile expectantly. DON HOMOBONO humbly and attentively awaits instructions. LARRA takes a newspaper from his pocket, sits down on his suitcase and cheerfully begins to read the words uttered by the great man.)

MENDIZÁBAL: I make a solemn pledge to Spain and to Her Majesty the Queen Regent that the war will be concluded within six months. To that end one hundred thousand men have been called to arms. *(The café lights up slowly. A different man now sits in the space usually occupied by CARNERERO, middle-aged and dressed in a very different style, although no less elegant. His mask, like that of CARNERERO, exudes goodwill. This is the well-known journalist don Andrés BORREGO. Sitting round both sides of Little Parnassus, the habitual figures read the journals in which MENDIZABAL's words appear. Standing on the left, ESPRONCEDA.)*
ESPRONCEDA:

"To the People I proclaim, see that noble brow
rise from the dust wherein it lay:
of bold endeavour and undisputed sway,
insolent tyranny in its gaze trembles now".

BORREGO *(Applauding.):* Sublime!
MENDIZÁBAL: An electoral bill will be presented before Parliament which will give due weight to the opinions of all the people of this land... *(General approval in Little Parnassus, some fervently, others with somewhat more restraint.)*
ESPRONCEDA: Long live Mendizábal! *(With the exceptions of*

150]

GALLEGO todos le responden con entusiasmo.)
MENDIZÁBAL. ¡La economía será definitivamente saneada! Os lo afirma un hombre que sabe algo de números.
BORREGO. ¡Y que lo diga! En su dorado exilio inglés amasó un fortunón.
MENDIZÁBAL. Honraré el voto de confianza que se me otorga sin recurrir a empréstitos ni a elevar los impuestos.
ARRIAZA. ¡Habrá que rendirse ante este hombre!
DÍAZ. ¡Ese hombre es España!
MENDIZÁBAL. No se precisa para ello derogar el Estatuto Real.
ARRIAZA. ¡Vaya! Menos mal.
MENDIZÁBAL. Él nos basta para lo más urgente: el decreto, que me honro en presentar, de desamortización de bienes eclesiásticos. (*El PADRE GALLEGO baja la cabeza.*)
ESPRONCEDA. ¡Al fin, la justicia social!
MENDIZÁBAL. Mi ilustre antecesor, el señor conde de Toreno, inició ya la saludable reforma. Bien impuesto del peso terrible de manos muertas y campos baldíos, de bienes que un mal entendido concepto de sus prerrogativas permitió acumular a la Iglesia durante siglos, no vaciló en disolver la Compañia de Jesús ni en suprimir todos los conventos con menos de doce profesos, devolviendo al Estado propiedades tan torpemente improductivas. Pero, sin negar los aciertos de este hombre sabio y probo, que me honró con la cartera de Hacienda, debo decir que nunca tomé posesión; pues parecióme que aquellas disposiciones pecaban de improvisadas. ¡Y no me equivoqué! El conde, persona de estudios y de pluma, no acertó a dar cauce a la exaltación cuyo despertar fomentó. Padecimos nuevos incendios de conventos, ultrajes a sus desdichados moradores convertidos en mendigos, Juntas de rebeldes en las regiones, asesinatos al grito santo de «Constitución» y hasta –penoso es decirlo– insurrecciones de las fuerzas militares encargadas de poner fin a tantos desastres. Incluso los proletarios incendiaron en Barcelona la fábrica de hilados Bonaplata por ver en las nuevas máquinas la amenaza de su miseria futura y sin comprender que sus desventuras procedían de la desorganizada economía de la nación... Yo lamento con todo mi corazón la dura respuesta que sufrieron. Los trabajadores Pardiñas (*Descarga de fusilería.*), Bell (*Otra descarga.*), Prats (*Otra descarga.*), y Joldi (*Otra*

ARRIAZA and GALLEGO, they all echo this enthusiastically.)

MENDIZÁBAL: The economy will be restored to health once and for all. As a man with no little knowledge of mathematics, I can assure you of that.

BORREGO: He may well say that! In his halcyon exile in England he made himself a fortune.

MENDIZÁBAL: I shall honour the trust of this House without resorting to debt or to higher taxation.

ARRIAZA: There'll be no stopping this man!

DÍAZ: This is the man Spain has been waiting for!

MENDIZÁBAL: All of this can be accomplished without repealing the Royal Statute.

ARRIAZA: So! Just as well!

MENDIZÁBAL: It will suffice for our most urgent measures: it is with pride that I present a bill to enforce confiscation of the assets of the Church. *(FATHER GALLEGO lowers his head.)*

ESPRONCEDA: At last, social justice!

MENDIZÁBAL: It was my worthy predecessor, His Excellency the Count of Toreno, who began this wholesome reform. Fully aware of the terrible burden of idle hands and fields left fallow, of a wealth of property that an exaggerated sense of prerrogative had permitted the Church to accumulate over centuries, he did not hesitate to disband the Company of Jesus nor to suppress those monasteries whose community numbered less than twelve, thereby reclaiming for the State properties previously left sadly unproductive. However, whilst I have no wish to deny the accomplishments of this wise and upright man -who, indeed, honoured me with the portfolio of the Exchequer, which I must confess I did not accept- it did seem to me that those measures were not thought through with sufficient rigour. And I was to be proved correct! The Count, a man of letters and of the pen, was not able to channel the strength of feeling which he had stirred. Once again, the country had to suffer the burning of monasteries, with new outrages perpetrated upon their former inhabitants, now reduced to begging, the setting up of Assemblies of rebels in the provinces, murders committed in the hallowed name of the Constitution, and even -painful though it is to say it- mutiny in the very forces charged with putting an end to such a disastrous chain of events. Furthermore, the workers of Barcelona burnt down the Bonaplata Mills, believing their future to be threatened by the instalation of new machinery, blind to the fact that their misery springs from the chaotic economy of the nation... I express my heartfelt regret at the severity of the response they met. The workers Pardiñas *(Burst of gunfire.)*, Bell *(Another volley.)*, Prats

descarga.), fueron fusilados. (*Breve pausa.*) ¡Y esto no se repetirá!
(*Estentóreos aplausos y vivas en el Parnasillo.*)
ESPRONCEDA. (*Recita.*)

«¡El necio audaz, de corazón de cieno,
a quien llaman el conde de Toreno!»

(*VEGA, BRETÓN, DÍAZ y BORREGO lo aclaman.*)
LOS ESCRITORES. ¡Bravo, bravo! ¡Admirable Espronceda!
MENDIZÁBAL. Otros decretos más sensatos nos traerán la salvación
nacional. ¡Y el de la desamortización será el primero! (*Nuevas
ovaciones.*)
BORREGO. ¡Es un gobernante!
MENDIZÁBAL. Sin dejar en el desamparo a esos pobres religiosos,
a quienes se dará un subsidio honroso, serán puestas en venta todas las
propiedades eclesiásticas que tan nulo rendimiento daban al país, y con ese
enorme capital levantaremos a España, pagaremos sus atrasos a nuestros
gloriosos mílites y daremos la batida final al carlismo. (*Ovaciones.*) Y a
vosotras, Juntas que os constituisteis por toda la península para salvar la
libertad que el poder ponía en peligro, os digo: tened confianza. El más
hábil cabecilla faccioso, Zumalacárregui, ha muerto bajo nuestro fuego, y
las fuerzas carlistas ya no son más que hordas indisciplinadas. ¡Yo os pido
un plazo de seis meses! Desde hoy mismo, nuestra heroica Milicia Urbana
recupera su antigua condición de Milicia Nacional. (*Ovaciones delirantes.*)
Desde hoy, vuestras legítimas ansias de ciudadanía darán su mejor fruto en
las Diputaciones Provinciales que se crean al efecto, ¡y vosotras, Juntas,
seréis esas Diputaciones! (*Ovaciones.*) La funesta Intendencia Superior de
Policía creada por el difunto rey queda disuelta, y sus individuos, a las
órdenes del Ministerior de la Gobernación. (*Enorme ovación.*) ¡Los cien
mil españoles que pedimos al país serán reclutados entre todos los
declarados útiles, desde los 18 a los 40 años! ¡Y desde hoy, al fin, será
decretada la libertad de prensa! (*Ovación indescriptible. DON
HOMOBONO se alarma un tanto.*)
ESPRONCEDA. (*Recita.*)

«A par en nuestros brazos
ufanos la ensalcemos

Another volley.), and Joldi (Another volley), were shot. (Short pause.) This will not happen again! *(Furious applause and hurrahs in Little Parnassus.)*
ESPRONCEDA *(Reciting.):*

"A brazen fool, with heart so low,
This is the man known as the Count of Toreno!"

Acclaim from VEGA, BRETON, DÍAZ and BORREGO.)
THE WRITERS: Bravo! Bravo! Well done, Espronceda!
MENDIZÁBAL: Other more circumspect measures will bring about he salvation of our nation. And the Act of Confiscation will be the first of hese! *(Renewed applause.)*
BORREGO: A leader among leaders!
MENDIZÁBAL: Without leaving the men of the Church totally destitute - indeed, we shall provide them with a significant endowment- we intend to put up for sale all those ecclesiastical properties which have given such little return to the country, and with the enormous capital accrued thereby we shall once again make Spain great. We shall pay the monies outstanding to our glorious army and crush the Carlists. *(Applause.)* And to those Assemblies which were formed throughout the country to defend the freedoms which those in power seemed set to usurp, say this: trust me. The most able of the rebel leaders, Zumalacárregui, has fallen in combat and the Carlist troops have been reduced to a rabble. ask you for six months grace! As from this very day, our heroic Urban Militia will be reinstituted as a National Militia. *(Delighted applause.)* And equally from today, the disquiet, which you as citizens of this land have had good reason to feel, will be allayed by the specific creation of Regional Councils, Councils which will be drawn wholly from the former Assemblies! *(Applause.)* The notorious Superior Inspectorate of Police, created by our former King, is hereby disbanded, and its members placed under the authority of the Ministry of the Interior. *(Enormous applause.)* The hundred thousand Spaniards called to their country's service will be recruited from those registred as able-bodied and whose ages range between 18 and 40. And also from today, freedom of the press will at last be guaranteed under law! *(Monumental applause. DON HOMBONO reacts with some alarm.)*
ESPRONCEDA *(Reciting.):*

"Together with open arms
let us proudly raise her high

y al mundo proclamemos:
España es libre ya.»

(*Se acerca a su mesa, toma una copa y bebe.*)
DÍAZ Y VEGA. ¡España es libre ya! (*Beben.*)
MENDIZÁBAL. No quiere el Gobierno detener la revolución, como ha insinuado mi predecesor. ¡Todo lo contrario! ¡Ni está dispuesto a llamar sediciosos a quienes piden la Constitución del 12, porque nosotros contribuimos a forjarla! (*Aplausos, vivas.*)
VEGA. ¡Muy bien!
BORREGO, MESONERO Y GRIMALDI. ¡Muy bien!
ARRIAZA. Mucho carga la mano contra Toreno. Fueron amigos y los dos son masones.
DÍAZ. ¡Ésa es su grandeza! ¡Nada por encima del bien de la patria!
ARRIAZA. (*Menea la cabeza, receloso.*) ¡Hum!
MENDIZÁBAL. Y ahora, todos a trabajar y a salvar a la nación. He dicho. (*Se sienta.*)
DÍAZ. ¿Qué dirá de todo esto Larra? Dicen que ha regresado.
BRETÓN. (*Da un respingo.*) ¿Ha vuelto? (*LARRA se levanta y guarda su periódico. Sonríe, toma la valija y se acerca al gabinete.*)
ESPRONCEDA. Ha vuelto. Queden con Dios. (*Se cubre y sale por la puerta de cristales. La luz huye del Parnasillo. LARRA sube el escalón y deja la maleta en el suelo, atento a lo que sigue oyendo.*)
MENDIZÁBAL. (*Considera fríamente al funcionario.*) ¿Fue Calomarde quien le nombró?
D. HOMOBONO. (*Muerto de miedo.*) Sí, excelencia. Y no puede imaginar mi decepción ante sus severas órdenes de tachar y tachar... Yo procuraba suavizar, pero...
MENDIZÁBAL. Pero tachó usted fielmente. (*LARRA deja capa y sombrero en una silla.*)
D. HOMOBONO. (*Baja la cabeza.*) Tenía que obedecer rigurosamente, excelencia.
MENDIZÁBAL. Estudiaremos qué se hace con su puesto. Siéntese.
D. HOMOBONO. Sí, excelencia. (*Se sienta. Se levanta.*) ¿Continúo mi trabajo?
MENDIZÁBAL. Mientras se resuelve lo que proceda, extreme la prudencia.

as to the waiting world we cry:
Spain is free at last".

(He goes over to his table, lifts a glass and drinks.)
DÍAZ and VEGA: Spain is free at last! *(They drink.)*
MENDIZÁBAL: The Government has no wish to impede the revolution, as my predecessor has implied. Indeed, the reverse is true! Nor is it prepared to condemn those who demand the restoration of the 1812 Constitution, because we are the very people who helped to forge that Constitution. *(Applause and cheers.)*
VEGA: Excellent!
BORREGO, MESONERO and GRIMALDI: Excellent!
ARRIAZA: He's playing a heavy hand with Toreno. They used to be friends and they're both masons.
DÍAZ: That's the measure of his greatness! The good of the country above all else!
ARRIAZA *(Shaking his head, suspiciously.)*: Hmm!
MENDIZÁBAL: Now, all hands to the wheel and let us save this nation of ours. I have nothing more to say. *(He sits down.)*
DÍAZ: What will Larra have to say about all this? I hear he's back.
BRETÓN *(With a start.)*: Back? *(LARRA stands up and folds away his newspaper. He smiles, picks up his case and moves towards his study.)*
ESPRONCEDA: He's back. Goodbye, gentlemen. *(He puts on his hat and goes out through the glass door. The light over the café fades. LARRA steps up into his study and puts his case down, absorbed in the conversation that he hears.)*
MENDIZÁBAL *(Contemplating the clerk coldly.)*: You were appointed by Calomarde?
D. HOMOBONO *(Paralysed with fear.)*: Yes, Excellency. You cannot imagine my disappointment at the severity of his instructions to cut hither and thither... I endeavoured to be circumspect, but...
MENDIZÁBAL: You cut away faithfully. *(LARRA puts his hat and cloak on a chair.)*
D. HOMOBONO *(Looking down.)*: I had no choice but to follow my orders to the letter, Excellency.
MENDIZÁBAL: We will have to consider what to do with your position. Sit down.
D. HOMOBONO: Yes, Excellency. *(He sits down and immediatel stands up again.)* Shall I continue with my work?
MENDIZÁBAL: Whilst we decide upon an appropriate course oı action, proceed with exceeding caution.

D. HOMOBONO. Como vuestra excelencia disponga. (*Se sienta y lee sin atreverse a tachar. LARRA sonríe y mira a todos lados.*)

LARRA. Mi difunta y mis hijos, atendidos. Veinte mil reales al año me va a dar Borrego por mi colaboración en «El Español». Nadie cobró nunca tanto: seré aún más envidiado... Baldomerita quizá no sea hija mía. ¿Quién puede saber si su mujer le ha sido fiel cuando no se entiende con ella? Pero también será atendida. ¡Vida nueva!... Mendizábal es nuestra esperanza. «Las Juntas sometidas, el crédito levantado, la facción abatida, la quinta verificada (...) son cosas que hacen bastantemente su elogio. Así que todos hemos abandonado la oposición» (*Entretanto, PEDRO se pone una máscara de zafio y ladino aldeano cuarentón. LARRA termina de hablar y repara en el criado. PEDRO se inclina.* ¿Te ha dicho María cuál será tu salario?

PEDRO. Sí, señor. Es un buen salario, señor.

LARRA. (*Mientras va a la chimenea.*) ¿Sabes leer?

PEDRO. Lo corriente.

LARRA. (*Ríe.*) ¿Sabrás leer por lo menos las señas de los recados y de las cartas?

PEDRO. Sí, señor. (*En la chimenea, LARRA destapa un frasquito de esencia y se perfuma levemente orejas y barba.*)

LARRA. ¿Tu nombre?

PEDRO. Pedro, señor, para servirle.

LARRA. ¿Tu tierra?

PEDRO. Asturias.

LARRA. Asturiano o de la Montaña. Tu antecesor era montañés. Todos venís de allá... ¿Tienes familia?

PEDRO. No, señor.

LARRA. Al montañés tuve que despedirle. Era un borrachín y me robaba.

PEDRO. (*Se yergue.*) Yo no robo, señor.

LARRA. (*Se acerca a él.*) Y beber, ¿bebes?

PEDRO. (*Titubea.*) Todo hombre bebe algo, señor. Un vasito nunca viene mal.

LARRA. (*Ríe.*) Sobre todo, si es de las botellas del amo.

PEDRO. (*Ríe.*) Sólo cuando el amo lo permita, señor.

LARRA. (*Risueño.*) Labia no te falta. Me alegro. No quiero tontos a mi lado. ¿Qué edad tienes?

PEDRO. Para agosto cumpliré los 40, señor.

LARRA. Pareces más viejo.

D. HOMOBONO: As Your Excellency wishes. *(He sits down and reads without daring to cross anything out. LARRA smiles and looks all around.)*

LARRA: My dead wife and children, well provided for. Borrego is going to give me twenty thousand reales a year for working on "The Spaniard". An unheard of amount: they'll be more envious than ever... Baldomerita mightn't be my daughter. How can you tell if your wife has been faithful to you or not when there's nothing left between you? But she'll be well provided for nonetheless. A new life!... Mendizábal has given us hope. "The suppression of the Assemblies, the end of the national debt, the crushing of the rebels, the raising of an army (...) are all things which do him great credit. And so we have all come out of opposition". *(PEDRO, meanwhile, has put on the mask of a rough, cunning peasant of about forty years of age. LARRA finishes speaking and notices him. PEDRO bows.)* Did María tell you what the wages are?

PEDRO: Yes, sir. It's a good wage, sir.

LARRA *(As he walks over to the chimney.)*: Can you read?

PEDRO: Enough to get by.

LARRA *(Laughing.)*: At least, you can descipher the addresses on messages and letters?

PEDRO: Yes, sir. *(Beside the chimney, LARRA uncorks a small bottle of scent and lightly perfumes his beard and ears.)*

LARRA: Your name?

PEDRO: Pedro, sir, at your service.

LARRA: Where are you from?

PEDRO: Asturias.

LARRA: Asturias... Cantabria. Your predecessor was from Cantabria. You all come from up there... Do you have any family?

PEDRO: No, sir.

LARRA: I had to sack him. He was a petty drunkard, and he stole from me.

PEDRO *(Stiffening.)*: I don't steal, sir.

LARRA *(Drawing closer to him.)*: And drinking... do you drink?

PEDRO *(Hesitating.)*: Everyone takes a drink sometime, sir. A small glass never does any harm.

LARRA *(Laughing.)*: Especially if it comes from the master's cellar.

PEDRO *(Laughing.)*: Only with the master's permission, sir.

LARRA *(Cheerfully.)*: You have a quick tongue. I'm glad. I have no wish to be surrounded by fools. How old are you?

PEDRO: I'll be forty in August, sir.

LARRA: You look older.

PEDRO. Sí, señor. Ya lo sé.

LARRA. Quedas admitido. (*Lo despide con un ademán y le da la espalda.*)

PEDRO. Gracias, señor. Con su licencia. (*Va a la maleta y la levanta. LARRA se vuelve y le observa. El criado recoge capa y sombrero, y sale con todo por el hueco izquierdo del fondo. LARRA medita.*)

LARRA. Fue así. ¿Y qué?

PEDRO. (*Su voz, en el aire.*) Nada. No te quedan ni dos minutos.

LARRA. ¿No te dejas ver?

PEDRO. (*Su voz.*) Eres el público de tu propio teatro y te resistes a imaginarme... hasta la plática que tuvimos.

LARRA. ¡Acabemos! (*Da unos pasos hacia el velador.*)

PEDRO. (*Su voz.*) Cuando quieras. (*LARRA se detiene. Luz sobre MENDIZÁBAL.*)

MENDIZÁBAL. (*Sentado.*) El convenio que Martínez de la Rosa concertó con la facción para que se respetasen las vidas de los prisioneros volverá a entrar en vigor. ¡Y lo respetaremos, aun cuando el enemigo siga sin cumplirlo! (*Entretanto, la luz fue sacando a ARRIAZA de la sombra del café. Está leyendo un periódico. LARRA se sienta en una silla junto al velador y atiende, iluminado por un foco.*)

ARRIAZA. Se le olvidan los cien carlistas presos en la Ciudadela de Barcelona y asesinados por las turbas. (*Luz sobre BORREGO, que también lee.*)

BORREGO. Usted lo ha dicho. Las turbas, no el ejército. (*Se ilumina el resto del café.*)

VEGA. ¡Y fue una represalia! Deplorable, pero comprensible.

ARRIAZA. ¿Represalia?

VEGA. ¡Por los prisioneros que los carlistas arrojaron a un abismo el mes anterior! ¡Y eso sí lo hicieron hombres de uniforme!

ARRIAZA. A saber si en la matanza de Barcelona no intervino la Milicia Nacional.

VEGA. (*Se levanta.*) ¡No le consiento infundios!

ARRIAZA. ¿Infundio? Será porque el Gabinete de Prensa no ha permitido publicarlo.

GALLEGO. ¡Ciertas noticias serían peligrosas en estos momentos!

ARRIAZA. ¡Lo sé! Sólo se permiten las que don Andrés Borrego da

PEDRO: Yes, sir. I know.

LARRA: All right, the position is yours. *(He dismisses him with a gesture and turns his back on him.)*

PEDRO: Thank you, sir. With your permission. *(He goes to lift the suitcase. LARRA turns round and watches him. The servant picks up his master's cloak and hat, and carries them through the left-hand gap at the rear. LARRA is deep in thought.)*

LARRA: That's the way it happened. So what?

PEDRO *(His voice sounds in the air.):* Nothing. You have barely two minutes left.

LARRA: Will you not show yourself?

PEDRO *(Voice off.):* You're the audience of your own theatre and you refuse to imagine me... or even the conversation we had.

LARRA: Let's finish it once and for all! *(He takes a few steps towards the occasional table.)*

PEDRO *(Voice off.):* Whenever you want. *(LARRA stops. Light falls on MENDIZÁBAL.)*

MENDIZÁBAL *(Sitting down.):* The agreement signed by Martínez de la Rosa with the rebels to safeguard the lives of prisoners will once again come into effect. And we shall respect it, even though the enemy may constantly choose to flout it! *(Meanwhile, a single spotlight has picked out ARRIAZA in the shadow of the café. He is reading a newspaper. LARRA, similarly lit, sits down to watch on a chair near the occasional table.)*

ARRIAZA: He's forgetting about the hundred Carlists held in Barcelona, and murdered to a man by the rabble. *(A light picks out BORREGO, also reading.)*

BORREGO: That's precisely it. The rabble, not the army. *(The rest of the café is lit up.)*

VEGA: And it was an act of reprisal! Appalling, but understandable.

ARRIAZA: Reprisal?

VEGA: For the prisoners the Carlists threw down a ravine the month before! And they were in uniform!

ARRIAZA: It's still to be proved that the National Militia weren't involved in the massacre in Barcelona.

VEGA *(Rising.):* I won't tolerate slurs of that nature!

ARRIAZA: A slur? Only because the Press Bureau has forbidden its publication.

GALLEGO: There are certain items of news which would not be expedient at this time.

ARRIAZA: I'm fully aware of that! The only news which sees the

a la prensa. (*VEGA se vuelve a sentar de mala gana.*)

MESONERO. (*De buen humor.*) Ayer era Carnerero; hoy, Borrego. Hasta en los apellidos se parecen. (*BRETÓN y DÍAZ ríen.*)

BORREGO. (*A ARRIAZA.*) Usted olvida que Mendizábal ordenó una investigación y no se hallaron culpables.

ARRIAZA. Nunca se hallan si no le conviene al Gobierno. Y con las noticias sucede lo mismo. Se publica, eso sí, que Cabrera ha fusilado a treinta prisioneros de la Columna de Valdés.

BORREGO. ¿Desea usted el triunfo de don Carlos, señor de Arriaza? Sabíamos que era usted absolutista, pero no carlista.

ARRIAZA. (*Se levanta descompuesto.*) ¡Caballero!

GALLEGO. ¡Señores, por favor! ¡No rompan la paz de nuestro amistoso cenáculo! (*ARRIAZA se sienta de mala gana. BORREGO murmura algo ihinteligible y se sienta a su vez. Huye la luz del Parnasillo y en el primer término se cruzan misteriosas claridades.*)

UNA VOZ. ¡Formen el pelotón! ¡Paso a su excelencia el general Cabrera! (*Un sordo redoblar de tambores inquieta a LARRA, que se levanta. Por la izquierda del primer término aparece una extraña figura militar fuertemente iluminada. Es el general Ramón CABRERA: máscara felina, boina blanca, gran tabardo sobre su uniforme. LARRA siente el batir de los tambores como una implacable llamada y comienza, a su pesar, a marcar levemente el paso.*)

CABRERA. (*Ríe.*) ¿Quieres formar en el pelotón? (*LARRA deniega, estremecido, pero sigue marcando el paso con creciente intensidad.*) ¡Corre a buscar tu fusil! (*LARRA deniega otra vez, sobrecogido. Y otra vez resistiéndose, marcha hacia el fondo al son de las cajas. El brazo del criado asomó por el hueco de la derecha sosteniendo un fusil, que el escritor coge. Desaparece el brazo. LARRA pone el arma sobre su hombro en un vago remedo de los movimientos de ordenanza y vuelve al primer término marcando el paso. Baja del gabinete, da media vuelta y queda en posición de firmes. Todo él tiembla.*) ¡Descansen, armas! (*LARRA baja el fusil al suelo. Los tambores enmudecen y dan en seguida un prolongado redoble de atención.*) ¡Soldados! Tenéis enfrente a dos bribones de la ralea cristina. Son los alcaldes de Torrecilla y Valdeagorta. Ya han visto apalear hasta la muerte a otro peor aún que ellos: al alcalde que se atrevió a oponerse por las armas a quienes iban a rescatar su pueblo para nuestra sagrada causa. A estos dos traidores, que delinquieron al no pasarse a nuestras filas, se les fusilará solamente. Nuestro capellán les ha dado ya los auxilios espirituales. ¡En el nombre de Nuestro Señor Jesucristo y de su majestad el

light of day comes from the pen of don Andrés de Borrego. *(VEGA turns round and sits down with a bad grace.)*

MESONERO *(Cheerily.):* Carnerero yesterday, Borrego today. Two very influential peas in a pod.*⁴⁷ (BRETÓN and DÍAZ laugh.)*

BORREGO *(To ARRIAZA.):* You seem to forget that Mendizábal ordered an inquiry which found that nobody was to blame.

ARRIAZA: Nobody ever is, if that's what suits the government. The same thing happens with the news. Oh yes, they were quick enough to publish that Cabrera shot thirty prisoners from Valdés's column.

BORREGO: Señor de Arriaza, am I to conclude that you support don Carlos? We have always taken you for an absolutist, but not a Carlist.

ARRIAZA *(Standing up furiously.):* Sir!

GALLEGO: Gentlemen, please! Let's not shatter the harmony of our little gathering! *(ARRIAZA reluctantly sits down. BORREGO mutters something unintelligible and sits down in turn. The café falls into darkness as strange gleaming pools of light begin to play in the foreground.)*

VOICE: Firing squad... fall in for His Excellency General Cabrera! *(A dull drum roll startles LARRA, who stands up. From the left foreground appears a bizarre military figure, brightly lit. It is General Ramón CABRERA: a feline mask, the white beret of the Carlists, a large tabard over his uniform. LARRA feels the rhythm of the drums drawing him inexorably and. against his own will, he begins, almost unobtrusively, to mark time.)*

CABRERA *(Laughing.):* You want to join the firing squad? *(LARRA shakes his head fearfully, but continues marking time with growing intensity.)* Get your rifle, at the double! *(LARRA, terrified, refuses once again. Still resisting, he marches upstage to the beat of the drums. His servant's arm appears through the right-hand gap, holding a rifle, which LARRA takes. The arm disappears. LARRA hoists the weapon over his shoulder in a fashion broadly reminiscent of arms drill, turns towards the front and continues marking time. He comes down from the study, performs a half turn and stands to attention. His whole body is shaking.)* Stand easy! *(LARRA lowers his gun. Silence, punctuated immediately by a new and prolonged drum roll.)* Men! You see in front of you two of the Queen's scum -the mayors of Torrecilla and Valdeagorta. Another of their sort, but even more depraved than them, has already been beaten to death in front of their very eyes: the mayor who dared to take arms against those who offered the liberation of his village for our sacred cause. These two traitors, whose offence was to refuse to join our ranks, will simply be shot. The Chaplain has already administered the last rites. In the name of Our

rey don Carlos, apunten! (*Luchando contra sí mismo, LARRA se coloca en posición de apuntar.*) ¡Fuego! (*Dispara el escritor y se oye al tiempo una descarga de fusilería.*) ¡Descansen, armas! (*Desmadejado, resollante, LARRA baja el fusil. CABRERA se retira por la izquierda. En uniforme cristino, con media máscara que recuerda a un dogo, el BRIGADIER NOGUERAS aparece por la derecha y adopta una postura semejante a la que tomó su adversario.*)

NOGUERAS. (*Hacia la derecha.*) Escriba, capitán. Del brigadier Nogueras, comandante de Teruel, al excelentísimo señor capitán general. Mi general: A los crímenes que los facciosos vienen cometiendo se han sumado recientemente el apaleamiento hasta la muerte de un alcalde leal a nuestra causa y el fusilamiento de otros dos bajo el pretexto de que, pudiendo hacerlo, no se pasaron al bando carlista. Para reforzar la moral de nuestra tropa y desalentar al enemigo, encarezco a vuecencia la necesidad de dar al criminal cabecilla Cabrera un escarmiento ejemplar. Por ello suplico a vuecencia me autorice a pasar por las armas a doña María Griñó, prisionera desde 1834 y madre del cabecilla. Aunque dicha señora no se ha significado en la política, es indudable su adhesión a la causa de su monstruoso hijo. Su fusilamiento no será sino la eliminación de otro enemigo. Lo que me honro en pedir a vuecencia, etcétera, etcétera. (*LARRA lo mira con horror. Sordo redoble de tambores.*)

LARRA. ¡No!... (*Aparece un capitán ayudante por la derecha, saluda y tiende a NOGUERAS un pliego abierto. Su media máscara es cadavérica. EL BRIGADIER lee el pliego. Leve cambio de luz.*)

NOGUERAS. El general Mina autoriza el fusilamiento. (*LARRA arroja el fusil al suelo.*) ¿Qué haces, bisoño? ¡Recoge tu arma! (*LARRA vacila.*) ¡Obedece! (*LARRA recoge el fusil.*) ¡Fir...mes! (*El escritor obedece.*) Suspendan... ¡armas! (*LARRA suspende su fusil.*) ¡De...recha! (*Gira LARRA y se enfrenta con el lateral izquierdo.*) Descansen... ¡armas! (*El fusil de LARRA golpea el suelo. Redoblan los tambores. Una anciana sin máscara y pobremente vestida, de dulce expresión y mortecina mirada, entra por la izquierda conducida por los dos MILICIANOS Nacionales, quienes la sitúan de perfil y se retiran por donde entraron. Callan los parches.*) Señora: ¿desea formular ante el mando alguna petición?

MARÍA GRIÑÓ. (*Después de un momento.*) Sólo quiero decir... que os perdono a todos... y os ruego que perdonéis a mi hijo. (*EL BRIGADIER y el CAPITÁN se miran.*)

NOGUERAS. ¡Apunten! (*LARRA apunta a la madre de CABRERA.*)

LARRA. ¡Es un crimen repugnante!

..ord Jesus Christ and of His Majesty King Carlos, take aim! *(Fighting against himself, LARRA takes up position.)* Fire! *(The writer fires and a volley of shots is heard at the same time.)* Stand easy! *(Faint and gasping for breath, LARRA lowers his rifle. CABRERA exits from the left. In the uniform of the loyalist army, and wearing a half mask whose features are reminiscent of those of a huge dog, Brigadier NOGUERAS appears from he right and adopts a stance similar to that of his enemy.)*

NOGUERAS *(Speaking towards the right.):* Captain, write this down. From Brigadier Nogueras, Commander of Teruel, to His Excellency, the Field Marshal. Sir: To the long list of crimes committed by the rebel forces we must append the recent beating to death of a mayor loyal to our cause and the shooting of two others, under the pretext of their wilfully refusing to join the Carlist ranks. In order both to strengthen the morale of our own troops and to weaken that of the enemy, I impress upon Your Excellency the urgency of teaching their criminal leader, Cabrera, a salutary lesson. I therefore request Your Excellency to authorize me to courtmartial doña María Griñó, the mother of the enemy leader, held in custody since 1834. Although she has played no active role in political affairs, her adherence to the cause of her monstruous son is beyond question. Her execution would simply be the elimination of one more of the enemy, and I earnestly entreat Your Excellency to consider this request favourably, etcetera, etcetera. *(LARRA looks at him in horror. A muted drum roll.)*

LARRA: No! *(An ADJUTANT appears from the right, salutes and hands NOGUERAS an unsealed message. His half mask is corpse-like. NOGUERAS reads the message. Slight change of lighting.)*

NOGUERAS: General Mina has authorized the execution. *(LARRA throws his rifle to the floor.)* What are you doing, soldier? Pick up your gun! *(LARRA hesitates.)* Do it! *(LARRA picks up the rifle.)* Atten...tion! *(The writer obeys.)* Rest... arms! *(LARRA rests his rifle.)* Right... turn! *(LARRA turns to face left.)* Stand... easy! *(LARRA lets his rifle bang against the floor. The drums sound again. An old woman is led in from the left by two National MILITIAMEN who place her facing right before leaving by the same entrance. She is poorly dressed and her unmasked face reveals fading eyesight and a gentle expression. The drums fall silent.)* Madam: do you have any last request to make?

MARÍA GRIÑÓ *(After a moment.):* Just that... I forgive you all... and I beg you to forgive my son. *(NOGUERAS and his ADJUTANT look at each other.)*

NOGUERAS: Take aim! *(LARRA aims at CABRERA's mother.)*

LARRA: This is an unspeakable crime!

164]

NOGUERAS. ¿Ha hablado alguien?... ¿No?... Ayudante, tome nota de la ejecución que se verifica hoy, 16 de febrero de 1836, en Tortosa, y oficie dando cuenta de su cumplimiento. (*EL CAPITÁN saluda y sale.*)

MARÍA GRIÑÓ. Soy inocente.

NOGUERAS. ¡Fuego! (*LARRA dispara y vuelve a oírse la descarga del pelotón. MARÍA GRIÑÓ se dobla y cae.*) Esa fiera no olvidará que aún tenemos como rehenes a sus dos hermanas. (*Se retira por la derecha. LARRA suelta el fusil, se acerca al cadáver y lo zarandea suavemente un par de veces como si quisiese despertarlo. Reaparecen los dos MILICIANOS Nacionales.*)

MILICIANO 1.º ¿Qué haces? No lleva nada encima.

LARRA. Yo nunca... he fusilado.

MILICIANO 2.º Ya te acostumbrarás. ¡Aparta! (*El escritor se incorpora. Ellos recogen el cuerpo y se lo llevan por la izquierda. LARRA retrocede.*)

LARRA. No... No... (*Reaparece iracundo CABRERA, ahora por la derecha. Asustado, el escritor se vuelve al oírle.*)

CABRERA. ¡Oficiales! ¡Soldados! El castigo por el vil asesinato de mi infeliz madre, a vosotros lo encomiendo. ¡La sangre cristina tiene que subir hasta las cumbres del Maestrazgo! Vuestro general lo manda y lo jura. (*Va a irse.*)

LARRA. ¡No!

CABRERA. (*Lo mira.*) ¿Qué dices?

LARRA. ¡Sus dos hermanas están presas! Las fusilarán si usted toma venganza!

CABRERA. (*Sonríe con malicia.*) Ya hemos logrado hacerlas escapar. (*Hacia la derecha.*) ¡Ayudante, redacte una orden! Se fusilará inmediatamente a la señora del coronel Fontiveros, a Cinta Foz, a Mariana Guardia y a Francisca Urquizo, con otros prisioneros del campo cristino hasta el número de treinta, que expiarán con su muerte el infame castigo que ha sufrido la mejor de las mujeres. ¡Pelotón, firmes! ¡Apunten!... (*LARRA se tapa la cara con las manos.*) ¡Fuego! (*Truenan los fusiles. Ayes. Tiros de gracia. CABRERA sale por la derecha. Cede la luz irreal y el café se ilumina.*)

BRETÓN. ¡Espantoso!

VEGA. ¡Horrendo!

ARRIAZA. Pero... el fusilamiento de una madre...

GALLEGO. Dios nos asista.

VEGA. ¡Así titula su artículo Fígaro! Oigan lo que escribe: «...Otra pequeña arbitrariedad ejecutada oficialmente en una vieja, en

NOGUERAS: Did someone say something?... No?... Adjutant, take
note of the execution which is being carried out today, 16th February
836, in Tortosa, and communicate that it has been duly accomplished.
The ADJUTANT salutes and leaves.)
MARÍA GRIÑÓ: I have done nothing.
NOGUERAS: Fire! *(LARRA fires and another volley of shots is
heard. MARIA GRIÑÓ doubles over and falls.)* That savage won't forget
that we still hold his two sisters hostage. *(He exits from the right. LARRA
drops his gun, goes over to the dead body and gently shakes it once or
twice as though trying to wake it. The two National MILITIAMEN
reappear.)*
MILITIAMAN #1: What are you up to? She hadn't a thing.
LARRA: It's the first time... I've ever shot anyone.
MILITIAMAN #2: You'll soon get used to it. Move! *(The writer
stands up. They lift the body and leave from the left. LARRA draws
back.)*
LARRA: No... No... *(CABRERA reappears furiously, this time from
the right. The writer spins round in fear upon hearing him.)*
CABRERA: Officers! Men! I entrust to you the retribution for the
vile murder of my poor mother. Enemy blood must flow until the very
peaks of these mountains are awash with it. Your General both orders this
and swears it. *(He makes to leave.)*
LARRA: No!
CABRERA *(Looking at him.):* What do you mean?
LARRA: They're holding your two sisters! They'll shoot them if you
take revenge!
CABRERA *(Smiling maliciously.):* We've got them out. *(Speaking to
the right.)* Adjutant, take note of an order. The following are to be shot
forthwith: the wife of Coronel Fontiveros, Cinta Foz, Mariana Guardia,
Francisca Urquizo and other enemy prisoners up to a total of thirty, who
will atone with their death for the crime perpetrated upon the most noble
and best of women. Firing squad, attention! Take aim!... *(LARRA covers
his face with his hands.)* Fire! *(The guns thunder out. Cries of pain and
fear silenced by single shots. CABRERA leaves from the right. The cafè
lights up as the unreal lighting fades.)*
BRETÓN: Hideous!
VEGA: Horrible!
ARRIAZA: To shoot... a mother...
GALLEGO: God preserve us.
VEGA: That's the title Figaro gives his article! Listen to what he
says: "...Another small act of despotism officially executed on the person

virtud de un *cúmplase* de un héroe.» (...) «Dios me libre de caer en manos de héroes!... Es así que la primera causa de que existan facciosos fueron las madres que los parieron; ergo quitando de en medio a las madres, lo que queda. (...) De resultas el otro no ha fusilado más que a treinta. (...) ¡Bienaventurados en tiempos de héroes los incluseros, porque ellos no tienen padre ni madre que les fusilen!» (*El BRIGADIER NOGUERAS reaparece, ahora por la izquierda, LARRA no se ha movido.*)

GALLEGO. (*Caviloso.*) Tal vez ese artículo sea la causa...

GRIMALDI. ¿De qué?

GALLEGO. El general Mina ha sido destituido.

BORREGO. Entonces no todo está perdido. Aún somos hombres frente a bestias.

VEGA. ¡Y escritores capaces de hacerse oír! (*Se oscurece el café. NOGUERAS interpela al escritor.*)

NOGUERAS. (*Indica el arma en el suelo.*) ¿Es tuyo ese fusil?

LARRA. (*Descubre su rostro y lo mira.*) Yo soy Larra.

NOGUERAS. Sé quién es Larra: un reptil que se ha atrevido a picar a nuestro heroico general Mina. (*Se abalanza, recoge el arma y encañona al escritor.*) ¡Traidor!

LARRA. ¡No! (*Retrocede. EL BRIGADIER se echa el fusil a la cara. LARRA retrocede aprisa hacia el gabinete.*) ¡No! (*Se aplasta contra la escalera izquierda. NOGUERAS dispara. LARRA gime y se deja caer en los peldaños. EL BRIGADIER se va por la izquierda con el fusil, al tiempo que ESPRONCEDA entra por la puerta del fondo. El aposento se ilumina. Al ver al poeta, LARRA se esfuerza en incorporarse.*)

ESPRONCEDA. ¿Qué le sucede? (*LARRA logra ponerse en pie.*) ¿Soñaba?

LARRA. (*Se aparta unos pasos hacia el frente.*) Muero.

ESPRONCEDA. (*Impasible, mirando al vacío.*) Tal vez. (*LARRA se vuelve bruscamente y lo mira.*)

LARRA. (*Se pasa la mano por la frente y habla pensando en otra cosa.*) ¿Le han... readmitido... en la Guardia de Corps?

ESPRONCEDA. Desde hace unos días.

LARRA. Usted venía a hablarme de Teresa y de Dolores... Y ya no importan ni Teresa ni Dolores.

ESPRONCEDA. ¿Está seguro? (*Corta pausa.*)

LARRA. Tome asiento.

of an old woman, at the behest of a hero". (...) "God preserve me from falling into the hands of heroes!... It is a fact that the prime cause of the existence of rebels were the mothers who bore them: therefore, the removal of the mothers removes the cause. (...) As a result, the other hero ordered a mere thirty to be executed. (...) Blessed are waifs and strays in times of heroes, because they have no mother or father to be shot!" *(Brigadier NOGUERAS reappears, this time from the left. LARRA has not moved.)*

GALLEGO *(Thoughtfully.)*: Perhaps that article was the reason...

GRIMALDI: For what?

GALLEGO: General Mina has been cashiered.

BORREGO: Then all is not lost. There are still men among us to face up to the savages.

VEGA: And writers who can make themselves heard! *(The café falls dark. NOGUERAS addresses LARRA.)*

NOGUERAS *(Pointing to the weapon on the floor.)*: Is that your rifle?

LARRA *(Taking his hands away from his face to look at him.)*: I am Larra.

NOGUERAS: I know exactly who Larra is: a snake who dared to bite our heroic General Mina. *(He rushes forward, snatches the gun and points it at the writer.)* Traitor!

LARRA: No! *(He steps backwards. NOGUERAS pushes the gun right into his face. LARRA retreats quickly towards the study.)* No! *(He is pressed against the left-hand staircase. NOGUERAS fires. LARRA groans and falls onto the steps. The Brigadier exits with the gun from the left just as ESPRONCEDA enters through the door at the back. The room is lit up. When he sees the poet, LARRA makes an effort to get up.)*

ESPRONCEDA: What's wrong? *(LARRA struggles to his feet.)* A dream?

LARRA *(Moving a few steps towards the front.)*: I'm dying.

ESPRONCEDA *(Impassively looking into space.)*: Perhaps. *(LARRA spins round to look at him.)*

LARRA *(He passes his hand to his forehead and speaks as though his mind were elsewhere.)*: Have they accepted you back into the Military Guard.

ESPRONCEDA: Some days ago?

LARRA: You came here to talk about Teresa and Dolores... but neither of them matters any more.

ESPRONCEDA: Are you quite sure? *(Brief silence.)*

LARRA: Sit down.

ESPRONCEDA. Estoy mejor de pie... Me arde la sangre.

LARRA. (*Mientras se encamina a una silla y se sienta, desfallecido.*) Y a mí. Pero debemos serenarnos. Que el diablo se lleve a las mujeres. Y hasta a los horrores de la guerra. Nosotros debemos pensar. (*Ruido lejano de fusilería.*)

ESPRONCEDA. No lo dice muy convencido...

LARRA. No. (*Suspira.*) Porque «lo malo es lo cierto. Sólo los bienes son ilusión».

ESPRONCEDA. ¿Quiere decir que el mal somos nosotros?

LARRA. Todos nosotros.

ESPRONCEDA. (*Se acerca y le pone una mano en el hombro.*) Si lo comprendemos, aún podemos vencerlo.

LARRA. ¿Cómo? El artículo de Flórez Estrada debería haber tumbado al Ministerio y apenas se ha comentado.

ESPRONCEDA. Muy cierto. La desamortización parece algo y es una burbuja.

LARRA. Peor aún. Una farsa indignante.

ESPRONCEDA. (*Pasea.*) Seremos polichinelas de esa farsa si no protestamos.

LARRA. Tres españoles cuerdos contra millones de idiotas. Tres despiertos contra un país dormido. ¿Se puede ganar esa partida?

ESPRONCEDA. Si le visitamos, tal vez.

LARRA. ¡Es un decreto! ¡No lo derogará!

ESPRONCEDA. Mendizábal es masón. Tendrá que oírnos. (*Pasea.*)

LARRA. Le veo tan ingenuo como cuando se empeñó en sacar en blanco «El Siglo». ¿Quiere ganarse otro destierro?

ESPRONCEDA. ¡Tiene que oírnos!

LARRA. Tiene que leernos.

ESPRONCEDA. También así podría deportarnos.

LARRA. Sin duda.

ESPRONCEDA. ¡Entonces, intentémoslo! ¡Hablemos con él! (*Larga pausa.*)

LARRA. (*Se levanta.*) ¡Está bien! Lo haremos. (*Cambia la luz. Crece arriba sobre MENDIZÁBAL. LARRA y ESPRONCEDA se encaminan hacia la escalera derecha y aguardan. DON HOMOBONO mira al presidente y se escandaliza en silencio cuando lo ve actuar; el prohombre se levanta con su mejor sonrisa.*)

MENDIZÁBAL. ¿Espronceda y Larra? ¡Qué honor para mí! (*Baja al otro nivel. Ellos van a subir.*) ¡No se molesten en subir! Estaremos

ESPRONCEDA: I prefer to stand... My blood's boiling.

LARRA *(As he walks towards a chair, where he flops down weakly.)*: And mine. But we must stay calm. To the devil with women. And even with war and its horrors. You and I must think. *(A distant burst of gunfire.)*

ESPRONCEDA: You don't sound very convinced...

LARRA: I'm not. *(He sighs.)* Because "evil is our sole reality. What's right is mere delusion".

ESPRONCEDA: You mean that we're part of the evil?

LARRA: All of us.

ESPRONCEDA *(He goes over and puts his hand on LARRA's shoulder.)*: If we understand it, we can still overcome it.

LARRA: How? Flórez Estrada's article should have toppled the whole ministry, and it went virtually unnoticed.

ESPRONCEDA: Indeed. The Act of Confiscation seems solid enough, and yet it's turned out to be a mere bagatelle.

LARRA: Worse than that. It's an outrageous farce.

ESPRONCEDA *(He begins to pace to and fro.)*: And you and I will become buffoons in the farce unless we protest.

LARRA: Three sane Spaniards against millions of fools. Three men awake while the whole country sleeps. What chance is there?

ESPRONCEDA: If we were to visit him, perhaps.

LARRA: It's been decreed by law! He's not going to repeal it!

ESPRONCEDA: Mendizábal is a mason. He has no choice but to listen to what we have to say. *(Pacing to and fro.)*

LARRA: I think you're being as naive now as when you insisted on bringing out the blank edition of "The Century". Do you want to risk being exiled again?

ESPRONCEDA: He has to hear us!

LARRA: He has to read us.

ESPRONCEDA: Even then he could exile us.

LARRA: Of course.

ESPRONCEDA: Then, let's try at least! Let's speak to him! *(Long silence.)*

LARRA *(Standing up.)*: All right! We will. *(Change in lighting. MENDIZÁBAL is illuminated. LARRA and ESPRONCEDA walk towards the right-hand staircase and wait. DON HOMOBONO watches his superior and is silently outraged when he sees what he does; the great man puts on his best smile and rises.)*

MENDIZÁBAL: Espronceda and Larra? An honour, indeed. *(He descends to the level below. They are about to come up.)* Please, don't

más cómodos en la salita. (*Baja con los brazos abiertos.*) ¡Cuánto me complace su visita! (*Abajo ya, abraza a LARRA.*) ¡Nuestro admirable satírico! (*Abraza a ESPRONCEDA.*) ¡Y nuestro más excelso vate! (*Les indica las sillas. Ellos se sientan. Él vuelve el sillón y se acomoda junto al bufete.*) ¿Puedo ordenar que les sirvan algo?

LARRA. No, muchas gracias.

ESPRONCEDA. Nosotros, excelencia...

MENDIZÁBAL. ¡Por favor, apeen el tratamiento! ¿No somos amigos?

ESPRONCEDA. Usted sabe que sí.

MENDIZÁBAL. Díganme en qué puedo servirles. (*ESPRONCEDA va a hablar.*) Pero, antes, una palabrita. He pensado hartas veces que ustedes hacen mucha falta en la arena política. ¿Qué les parecería ganar sus actas de diputados en las primeras elecciones?

ESPRONCEDA. (*Cambia una mirada con su amigo.*) Lo pensaremos. Hoy veníamos a hablarle de nuestros temores ante asuntos muy graves.

MENDIZÁBAL. ¿Temores?

LARRA. Terribles certezas. (*El Ministro los mira fijamente.*)

MENDIZÁBAL. ¡Ah, ya comprendo! La libertad de imprenta. Tienen razón al quejarse. (*Ríe.*) ¡Y también mucha chispa! (*A LARRA.*) ¿Comó era aquello de usted...? Algo así: «¿Ha leído vuesa merced *El Pobrecito Hablador*? Yo le publicaba en tiempos de Calomarde y de Cea; ahora, como ya tenemos libertad racional, probablemente no se podría publicar.» (*Ríe más fuerte.*) ¡Es divertidísimo!

LARRA. Su memoria me honra.

MENDIZÁBAL. Muy justa queja, amigo Fígaro. Pero, ¿qué quiere? Estamos en guerra y no puedo suprimir la censura. Convengan, sin embargo, en que se ha dulcificado todo lo posible. Pese a todo, Larra, ya no estamos en los tiempos de Calomarde. Madrid tiene ahora unos cincuenta periódicos y revistas. Y ustedes escriben a menudo contra mis disposiciones...

LARRA. Señor don Juan...

MENDIZÁBAL. ¡Lo recuerdo para que vean que somos tolerantes! Usted, por ejemplo, ha escrito: «Habla la reina y se hace lenguas de la libertad de imprenta; hablan los ministros y para ellos no hay altar donde ponerla (...) y hablo yo y digo como don Basilio en la ópera de mi tocayo ¿A quién engañamos, pues, aquí?»

LARRA. Me asombra usted.

MENDIZÁBAL. (*Sonriente.*) ¿Se lo habría dejado publica

trouble yourselves. We'll be much more comfortable in the reception room. *(He descends with arms open.)* I find your visit particularly gratifying. *(Upon reaching the bottom level, he embraces LARRA.)* Our admirable satirist! *(Embracing ESPRONCEDA.)* And our finest bard! *(He points to the chairs, and they sit down. He turns the armchair round and settles himself next to the bureau.)* Can I order anything for you?

LARRA: No, thank you.

ESPRONCEDA: Your Excellency, we...

MENDIZÁBAL: Please, let's not be so formal. We are all friends, are we not?

ESPRONCEDA: You know we are.

MENDIZÁBAL: Tell me what I can do for you. *(ESPRONCEDA is about to speak.)* But permit me first to say that I have long thought that the world of politics has much need of men like you. What would you say to a safe seat at the next elections?

ESPRONCEDA *(Exchanging a look with his friend.):* We must think it over. We've come here today to express our fears over certain very serious matters.

MENDIZÁBAL: Fears?

LARRA: Terrible certainties. *(The minister stares at them.)*

MENDIZÁBAL: I think I understand. The freedom of the press. You have every right to complain. *(He laughs.)* And you do it with such spirit! *(To LARRA.)* What was it you said...? Something along these lines: "Sir, have you read The Poor Little Babbler. I used to publish it in the days of Calomarde and Cea; now that we enjoy rational liberty, it would probably be banned". *(He laughs even louder.)* Very witty!

LARRA: I'm flattered that you should remember it.

MENDIZÁBAL: A just grievance, my dear Figaro. But, what can I do? We are at war and I cannot lift censorship. But you will agree, nonetheless, that it has been greatly tempered. In spite of everything, Larra, we are no longer in the times of Calomarde. There are now over fifty journals and newspapers in Madrid. And both of you frequently attack my decrees in print...

LARRA: Sir...

MENDIZÁBAL: I mention it so that you are aware of just how tolerant we are. You, for example, wrote this: "The Queen speaks, and freedom of the press is on everyone's lips; the ministers speak, and it is sacrosanct (...) and I speak and I ask like don Basilio in the opera of that other Figaro: who's fooling who here?".

LARRA: You surprise me.

MENDIZÁBAL *(Smiling.):* Would Calomarde have permitted that?

Calomarde? No. Ni otras muchas cosas que recuerdo. Usted ha dicho de mí que prometo, o sea que no cumplo; usted se ha burlado de mi ley electoral y de la disolución de las Cortes que hube de ordenar... Se le ha dejado que lo diga y, que yo sepa, todavía no le han multado.

ESPRONCEDA. Señor presidente, no hemos venido a quejarnos de su paternal libertad de imprenta, sino de cuestiones más graves.

MENDIZÁBAL. (*Frío.*) ¿Por ejemplo?

LARRA. Quisiéramos hablarle... de la desamortización.

MENDIZÁBAL. (*Se envara.*) ¡No pretenderán criticarla!

ESPRONCEDA. Al hecho en sí, no.

MENDIZÁBAL. (*Se levanta, excitado.*) ¡Entonces...! (*Ellos van a levantarse.*) Sigan sentados, se lo ruego. Y escúchenme. (*Pasea.*) Desde las Cortes de Cádiz se viene estudiando ese problema. Y ya se efectuaron desamortizaciones parciales... (*Se vuelve y los mira.*) Mi decreto de desamortización definitiva de los bienes del clero y la reducción implacable de sus comunidades culmina esa obra. ¡Las tierras, al pueblo! (*Se acerca.*) Para recobrar títulos de la deuda interior, sí; para atender a los gastos de guerra... Pero también para que nuestra revolución se lleve a cabo.

LARRA. ¿Qué revolución?

MENDIZÁBAL. ¡La suya y la mía! Luchamos por una revolución que haga de España una nación civilizada, moderna y rica. ¿O no?

LARRA. Naturalmente.

MENDIZÁBAL. Entonces no la estorben.

LARRA. Si quisiera escucharnos con calma...

MENDIZÁBAL. ¡No se quejará de mi calma! (*Se vuelve a sentar.*) ¡Hable!

LARRA. Señor presidente, usted ha sacado a pública subasta toda la inmensidad de tierras baldías y mal trabajadas...

MENDIZÁBAL. Divididas en pequeñas parcelas adecuadas a las familias campesinas.

LARRA. ¿Y cree que van a parar a esas familias?

MENDIZÁBAL. Nadie les impide adquirirlas.

LARRA. Todo les impide adquirirlas. Ni tienen dinero, ni los títulos depreciados de la deuda con los que también se pueden comprar.

MENDIZÁBAL. No lo crea. Los títulos están muy repartidos.

No. Nor many other things I could mention. You have said that I promise much, meaning that I accomplish little; you sneered at my electoral law and at the dissolution of parliament that was forced upon me... You enjoy total licence to say these things and, as far I am aware, you have not been penalised in any way.

ESPRONCEDA: Sir, we have not come here to take issue with your benevolent restoration of freedom of the press, but rather about matters of greater import.

MENDIZÁBAL *(Coldly.):* Such as?

LARRA: We would like to speak to you about... the Act of Confiscation.

MENDIZÁBAL *(Stiffening.):* Surely you can't mean to criticize that?

ESPRONCEDA: Not in itself, no.

MENDIZÁBAL *(Rising in agitation.):* Well then...? *(They make to stand up.)* No, please remain seated. Listen to what I have to say. This problem has been under scrutiny ever since the Parliament of Cadiz.⁴⁵ At that time certain partial confiscations were carried out. *(He turns round to face them.)* My law authorising the complete confiscation of the properties of the Church and the inexorable diminution of their communities is the culmination of that work. The land will be returned to the people! *(He draws closer to them.)* To recover the deeds to the internal debt as well, of course; to meet the cost of the war... But also so that our revolution may be completed.

LARRA: What revolution?

MENDIZÁBAL: Yours and mine! We are fighting for a revolution which will transform Spain into a modern, civilized, wealthy nation. Or am I mistaken?

LARRA: Of course not.

MENDIZÁBAL: Then don't stand in its way.

LARRA: If you would only listen calmly to what we have to say...

MENDIZÁBAL: You shall have no complaints about my calm! (He sits down again.) I am listening.

LARRA: Sir, you have put up for public auction all those vast tracts of land left to lie waste or which were insufficiently worked...

MENDIZÁBAL: Broken into small lots as befits the means of peasant families.

LARRA: And do you think they can be acquired by those families?

MENDIZÁBAL: Nobody's preventing it.

LARRA: Everything is preventing it. They have neither money nor the depreciated deeds of the debt, which can also be used for the purchase.

MENDIZÁBAL: You are quite mistaken. The deeds are widely

¡Están ustedes hablando con un economista!

ESPRONCEDA. Yo he asistido a una de esas subastas. Larra y yo pensamos que usted desconoce lo que en ellas sucede.

MENDIZÁBAL. ¿Qué sucede?

ESPRONCEDA. Los augurios de don Álvaro Flórez Estrada se están confirmando.

MENDIZÁBAL. ¡Bah! Ese teorizante...

LARRA. Otro economista, don Juan.

ESPRONCEDA. En las subastas está pasando lo que él previó. Los más adinerados, o sus hombres de paja, adquieren parcela tras parcela y forman así grandes propiedades. Los pobres ni siquiera asisten, y si algún campesino modesto se obstina en pujar, hay partidas de la porra que lo maltratan y lo echan.

LARRA. Ya ve en lo que está parando su reforma agraria.

ESPRONCEDA. ¿No sería mejor el procedimiento de enfiteusis propuesto por Flórez Estrada? El Estado distribuiría todas esas tierras entre los campesinos pobres y se las arrendaría mediante pagos a plazos bien calculados.

LARRA. «La guerra misma de Navarra es (...) un efecto de lo poco o nada que se ha tratado de interesar al pueblo en la causa de la libertad. ¿Cómo se le quiere interesar trasladando los bienes nacionales (...) de las manos muertas (...) a manos de unos cuantos comerciantes, resultado inevitable de la manera de venderlos adoptada?»

MENDIZÁBAL. (Sombrío.) Ustedes piden la anarquía. De pronto, los pobres, propietarios, y los verdaderos hombres de empresa, anulados. Sería utópico... y fatal. ¡Nuestra revolución se apoya en la libertad de acumular bienes! Sólo así obtendremos un poder central fuerte que acabe con tanto privilegio, tanto fuero, tanta aduana interior, tanto retraso. Eso es lo que defienden los facciosos.

LARRA. ¿Y no ha pensado usted que los fueros de ciertas regiones son antiguos derechos populares que no hay que destruir, sino perfeccionar?

MENDIZÁBAL. ¡No puedo creer a mis oídos! ¡Ustedes... hablan como carlistas!

ESPRONCEDA. Nadie ha escrito con mayor sarcasmo que Larra acerca de la facción. Con su corte de frailes, don Carlos sólo lucha por sentarse en el trono de su hermano, como un ídolo impasible ante el que se prosterne un país mantenido en lo que él llama la bendita ignorancia. Pero si los pueblos del norte le apoyan es porque él, para embaucarlos, les reconoce fueros y costumbres... ¿No deberíamos quitarle esa bandera?

dispersed. Remember you are speaking to an economist.

ESPRONCEDA: I have attended one of those auctions. Larra and I are of the opinion that you're not really aware of what goes on there.

MENDIZÁBAL: What does go on there?

ESPRONCEDA: The prophecies of FlSrez Estrada are proving well founded.

MENDIZÁBAL: Bah! A mere theoretician...

LARRA: Another economist, don Juan.

ESPRONCEDA: What's taking place in the auctions is exactly what he predicted. Those with money, or their straw men, acquire lot after lot, so that they amass huge properties.⁴⁹ The poor don't even bother to attend, and if some peasant of modest means stands firm in his bid, then there are ruffians at hand to assault him and throw him out.

LARRA: So you see what's become of your agrarian reform.

ESPRONCEDA: Wouldn't the leasing system that Flórez Estrada suggested not be better? The State would distribute all the land among the peasants and rent it to them for carefully calculated payments.

LARRA: "The war in Navarra is (...) in itself a result of the little or nothing which has been done to involve the people in the cause of freedom. And how can we involve the people when the property of the nation (...) is transferred from the hands of the idle (...) to those of a few merchants, the inevitable result of the chosen manner by which it is sold?"

MENDIZÁBAL (Sombrely.): You're asking for anarchy. At a stroke, the poor become proprietors, and the real men of business are wiped out. It would be a utopia... and a disastrous one. Our revolution is based upon liberty of acquisition! It's the only way by which we can create a strong centralist power to eradicate so much privilege, so many unfair charters, so many internal tariffs, so much backwardness. Those are the very things the rebels seek to defend.

LARRA: Have you never thought that the charters of some of the provinces are ancient popular rights which should be perfected, not destroyed.

MENDIZÁBAL: I can't believe what I'm hearing! You're both speaking... like Carlists!

ESPRONCEDA: Nobody has been more caustic than Larra in his treatment of the rebels. With his entourage of priests, don Carlos's only reason for fighting is to be able to sit on his brother's throne like an inscrutable demigod with the country kept in what he calls blessed ignorance lying prostrate at his feet. But if the people in the north support his cause it's because he wins them over by recognising their charters and customs... Shouldn't we stop him from brandishing that particular banner?

MENDIZÁBAL. Imposible. Perjudicaríamos el desarrollo de la nación.

LARRA. ¿Quiere decir el desarrollo de los potentados?

MENDIZÁBAL. Deje esas bromas para sus artículos, Larra.

LARRA. El único y tremendo bromazo es el de una guerra supuestamente motivada por un problema de sucesión. Pero, en confianza, señor de Mendizábal: ¿qué nos importa a nosotros la persona que vaya a reinar? Cuando una reina se acuesta con un palafrenero, el heredero del trono puede ser hijo del palafrenero.

MENDIZÁBAL. ¡Cuide sus palabras! Yo soy un leal súbdito de su majestad la reina.

LARRA. Pues yo soy un leal servidor del pueblo.

MENDIZÁBAL. ¡No más que yo! La soberanía reside en el pueblo. Pero la reina y su Gobierno son sus mandatarios.

LARRA. Ya veremos qué dice de eso mañana la soberanía nacional..., si es que puede manifestarse en los comicios.

MENDIZÁBAL. (Irónico.) ¿Insiste en criticar mi ley electoral?

LARRA. La ley y su aplicación. Usted sólo concede el voto a los que pasen de los doce mil reales de renta anual, y prohíbe votar a los menores de treinta años, que son, sin embargo, capaces de escribir, de hablar con usted ahora y hasta de ser diputados.

MENDIZÁBAL. Ustedes sí, pero la plebe... Seamos sensatos, Larra. La plebe es ignorante. Darle hoy el voto sería el caos. Y todos hemos visto lo que sucede entonces. Asesinatos, motines...

LARRA. El poder también asesina.

MENDIZÁBAL. ¿Qué dice?

LARRA. No olvide a María Griñó, ni a los prisioneros de Barcelona.

MENDIZÁBAL. ¡Es inaudito! ¿Ignora usted que el general Mina ha sido destituido?

ESPRONCEDA. El Gobierno ha cerrado los ojos ante los desmanes de otros que no han sido destituidos.

MENDIZÁBAL. ¡No podemos quedarnos sin jefes!

LARRA. Si quiere ganar la guerra, interese al pueblo en nuestra causa, no a los jefes. Modifique las disposiciones de desamortización y amplíe la ley electoral.

MENDIZÁBAL. Sería el desastre, y el carlismo triunfaría. Y. pueden seguir soñando cuanto quieran. Yo debo estar muy alerta. (Se levanta. LARRA y ESPRONCEDA se ponen de pie.)

LARRA. ¿Así, pues, no?

MENDIZÁBAL: Impossible. We would be jeopardising the entire future of the country.

LARRA: Don't you mean the future of the wealthy?

MENDIZÁBAL: Keep that sort of jest for your articles, Larra.

LARRA: The only jest, and a prodigious one it is, is that of a war supposedly caused by a problem of succession. But, between ourselves, Señor de Mendizábal, what can the person who is going to reign possibly matter to us? A queen goes to bed with a groomsman, and the heir to the throne may well be a groomsman's son.

MENDIZÁBAL: Weigh your words! I am a loyal subject of Her Majesty the Queen.

LARRA: In that case, I am a loyal servant of the people.

MENDIZÁBAL: No more than I! Sovreignty resides in the people. But the Queen and her government are its instruments.

LARRA: We'll soon see what national sovreignty has to say about that..., that is if it can manage to make its presence felt in the elections.

MENDIZÁBAL: Do you still insist on attacking my electoral reforms?

LARRA: In theory and in practice. You only give the vote to those whose annual income exceeds twelve thousand reales, whilst those under thirty years of age remain without a vote, yet among them are people capable of writing, of talking with you, as we are doing now, even of sitting in parliament.

MENDIZÁBAL: You two gentlemen, yes, but the common people... Let's be sensible, Larra. The commonalty is ignorant. To give it the vote would be to invite chaos. And we have all of us witnessed what happens then. Murders, riots...

LARRA: Power also murders.

MENDIZÁBAL: What do you mean?

LARRA: Let's not forget María Griñó or the prisoners in Barcelona.

MENDIZÁBAL: This is monstrous! You know full well that General Mina has been cashiered.

ESPRONCEDA: The government has turned a blind eye to the outrages of others who have not been.

MENDIZÁBAL: We can't leave ourselves without leaders!

LARRA: If you want to win the war, involve the people in our cause, not the leaders. Change the operation of the Act of Confiscation and widen the electoral reform.

MENDIZÁBAL: It would lead to disaster... and to a Carlist victory. You can both continue dreaming as much as you wish. But I have to be very alert. (*He stands up, followed by LARRA and ESPRONCEDA.*)

LARRA: So your answer is no.

MENDIZÁBAL. Categóricamente, no.

LARRA. Entonces, señor de Mendizábal, oiga mis últimas palabras. (*Se acerca y, mientras le habla, le desprende muy suavemente la careta y se la pone en una mano.*) Usted ha sido un político desterrado por servir a la libertad, pero no nos ha dado libertad. Usted ha defendido la causa popular en sus discursos, pero es usted un millonario opulento, y su desamortización es otra hábil jugada de bolsa a favor de los ricos, no de los braceros. En resumen: usted inaugura otra sustanciosa etapa de privilegios. Y nosotros, aunque nos multe o nos encarcele, lo diremos.

ESPRONCEDA. Hago mías las palabras de Larra. Y agrego que acaso nadie haya querido ayudarle mejor que nosotros.

MENDIZÁBAL. (*Seco.*) Gracias, caballeros. (*LARRA y ESPRONCEDA se inclinan. MENDIZÁBAL sube la escalera. DON HOMOBONO se levanta. Sobre su verdadero semblante una faz de párpados muy fruncidos sobre los ojos huidizos y suspicaces, de mejillas cuajadas de plaquetas, de nariz olfateadora y ávida el ministro se apresura a ajustar rápidamente su máscara.*)

D. HOMOBONO. Excelencia... (*MENDIZÁBAL se detiene.*) El señor de Larra trajo hace cuatro días un artículo asaz irrespetuoso...

MENDIZÁBAL. ¡Prohíbalo!

D. HOMOBONO. (*En sus glorias.*) ¡Sí, excelencia! (*Se inclina y corre a su mesa.*)

MENDIZÁBAL. Espere. (*DON HOMOBONO se detiene.*) No lo prohíba entero. Pero tache sin temor.

D. HOMOBONO. (*Triste.*) Como vuestra excelencia mande. (*Se sienta y empieza a tachar. El ministro sube hasta su sillón y se sienta, desazonado. La luz se va yendo del bloque y crece en el Parnasillo. Apiñados en dos o tres grupos, leen todos ejemplares de un folleto. LARRA y ESPRONCEDA se han sentado, desalentados, en el gabinete.*)

LARRA. ¿Qué se puede hacer?

ESPRONCEDA. ¡Escribir!

LARRA. ¿Nos dejarán?

ESPRONCEDA. Recordaré palabras suyas: «El escritor (...) debe (...) remitir a la censura tres artículos nuevos por cada uno que le prohíban.» (*Leve cambio de luz. LARRA se levanta y pasea con las manos en la espalda.*)

LARRA. Tan desanimado como yo. (*El poeta baja la cabeza. LARRA se vuelve hacia el frente y mira al vacío.*) Y no obstante, logró publicar «El Ministerio Mendizábal». Y yo defendí ese folleto en un artículo. (*Se vuelve hacia su amigo.*) Así vamos cerrándonos el camino.

MENDIZÁBAL: Most definitely, no.

LARRA: In that case, Señor de Mendizábal, hear my final words. *(He goes over to him and, while he is speaking, gently removes his mask and places it in his hand.)* You were a politician who suffered exile in the service of liberty, but you have not brought liberty to us. You have defended the cause of the people in your speeches, but you are a man of power and wealth, and your Act of Confiscation is merely another market ploy to benefit the rich, and not those who work the land. In short, you're opening the door to a new, substantial era of privilege.[50] And even though you penalise us or imprison us, that's what we shall say.

ESPRONCEDA: Larra speaks for me on this as well. And I would add that nobody has sought to help you more than us.

MENDIZÁBAL *(Drily.)*: Thank you, gentlemen. *(LARRA and ESPRONCEDA bow. MENDIZÁBAL climbs the staircase. DON HOMOBONO stands up. The minister hurriedly replaces his mask over a face which reveals frowning eyebrows above shifty, suspicious eyes, pockmarked cheeks, an alert snout-like nose.)*

D. HOMOBONO: Excellency... *(MENDIZÁBAL stops.)* Several days ago Señor de Larra brought in an article which was veritably insolent...

MENDIZÁBAL: Ban it!

D. HOMOBONO *(In his element.)*: Yes, Excellency! *(He bows and hurries to his desk.)*

MENDIZÁBAL: Wait. *(DON HOMOBONO stops in his tracks.)* Don't ban it in its entirety. But cut whatever you see fit.

D. HOMOBONO *(Sadly.)*: As Your Excellency pleases. *(He sits down and begins to erase. The minister proceeds to his armchair and sits down, clearly displeased. The light on the rostrum fades and grows over Little Parnassus. Huddled together into two or three groups, the regulars are all reading copies of a pamphlet. LARRA and ESPRONCEDA, discouraged, have sat down in the study.)*

LARRA: What can we do?

ESPRONCEDA: Write!

LARRA: Will they let us?

ESPRONCEDA: Let me recall something you once wrote: "The writer (...) must (...) submit another three articles to the censor for every one he has banned". *(Slight change in the lighting. LARRA rises and paces up and down, his hands behind his back.)*

LARRA: He's lost heart every bit as much as I have. *(The poet lowers his gaze. LARRA turns towards the front and stares into space.)* Even so, he still managed to publish "The Ministry of Mendizábal". And I supported his pamphlet in an article of mine.[51] *(He turns towards his

(*Sigue paseando. La luz vuelve al bloque derecho. LARRA mira a MENDIZÁBAL y, a poco, torna a sentarse en su silla.*)

MENDIZÁBAL. ¿Cómo se ha podido autorizar ese inmundo folleto de Espronceda?

D. HOMOBONO. (*Se levanta, asustadísimo.*) Vuestra excelencia recomendó amplios criterios para sus escritos...

MENDIZÁBAL. ¡Antes de que me visitase!

D. HOMOBONO. Después, vuestra excelencia no me dijo nada.

MENDIZÁBAL. Y de Larra, ¿no le dije algo?

D. HOMOBONO. Sí, excelencia.

MENDIZÁBAL. ¡Pero ustedes le autorizan también el artículo de apoyo a ese folleto!

D. HOMOBONO. Como vuestra excelencia dijo que no se le prohibiesen cosas y que solamente se le tachase..., se tachó bastante.

MENDIZÁBAL. (*Le considera.*) ¿Quiere que le diga una cosa, don Homobono? Es usted un imbécil.

D. HOMOBONO. Excelencia, yo le suplico...

MENDIZÁBAL. ¡Debí sustituirle! Ya lo hará mi sucesor.

D. HOMOBONO. ¿Su sucesor?

MENDIZÁBAL. (*Se levanta y pasea.*) Esos escritos son como navajazos. Milagro será que no me rocen.

D. HOMOBONO. (*Casi al borde de las lágrimas.*) ¡La culpa es de don Juan Nicasio Gallego! Siempre me recomienda indulgencia con Larra.

MENDIZÁBAL. (*Se detuvo.*) Cualquiera sabe a lo que juega ese galápago. ¿O será tan necio como usted? Es igual. Usted lamentará su imprudencia. (*Baja por las gradas ocultas.*)

D. HOMOBONO. (*Se sienta, abrumado.*) ¡Santísima Virgen de los Desamparados, ayúdame! (*Apoya los codos en la mesa y esconde su rostro entre las manos. Oscuridad en el bloque. Aumenta la luz en el gabinete.*)

ESPRONCEDA. Sólo una verdad entre tanta mentira: debemos presentarnos a las elecciones.

LARRA. ¡Nosotros somos escritores!

ESPRONCEDA. Mientras nos dejen. En las Cortes seremos invulnerables, y la censura no podrá silenciar nuestra palabra.

LARRA. Si hay que convertirse en procurador, lo haré. Pero, ¿con quién deberíamos presentarnos?

friend.) And so we close down our horizons. *(He continues to pace. The light returns to the right-hand rostrum. LARRA looks at MENDIZÁBAL, before returning to his seat.)*

MENDIZÁBAL: How did Espronceda manage to get permission to publish that unspeakable pamphlet of his?

D. HOMOBONO *(Rising, terrified.):* Your Excellency recommended a certain indulgence with his writings...

MENDIZÁBAL: That was before he came to see me!

D. HOMOBONO: Your Excellency said nothing afterwards.

MENDIZÁBAL: And did I say anything about Larra to you?

D. HOMOBONO: Yes, Excellency.

MENDIZÁBAL: Then why did you authorise his article supporting the pamphlet?

D. HOMOBONO: Your Excellency had said not to prohibit anything in its entirety, only to excise... and we excised a great deal.

MENDIZÁBAL *(Contemplating him.):* Shall I tell you something, don Homobono? You are a fool.

D. HOMOBONO: Excellency, I beg you...

MENDIZÁBAL: I should have got rid of you. My successor will.

D. HOMOBONO: Successor?

MENDIZÁBAL *(He stands up and begins pacing to and fro.):* Those two pieces are full of barbs, razor-sharp. It'll be a miracle if I come out of this unscathed.

D. HOMOBONO *(Almost on the verge of tears.):* It's don Juan Nicasio Gallego... he's to blame! He's always urging me to be lenient with Larra.

MENDIZÁBAL *(Standing still.):* Who knows what that lumbering windbag is up to... Perhaps he's as much a fool as you are. You will live to regret your indiscretion. *(He goes down the hidden stairway.)*

D. HOMOBONO *(He sits down, overcome.):* Oh, Holy Mother of the Defenceless, help me now! *(He rests his elbows on the table and hides his face between his hands. Darkness falls over the rostrum. Light in the study.)*

ESPRONCEDA: Just one clear truth in the midst of so many lies: we must stand for parliament.

LARRA: But we're writers!

ESPRONCEDA: Only for as long as they let us be. Nobody will be able to touch us in parliament, and the censors won't be able to silence our words.

LARRA: If I have to become a member of parliament, then I will. Who can we stand with?

ESPRONCEDA. ¿No le han hablado Istúriz y el duque de Rivas?

LARRA. Vagamente.

ESPRONCEDA. Cuentan con nosotros.

LARRA. «Istúriz es un verdadero radical...»

ESPRONCEDA. ¡Y adversario de Mendizábal! No pasa día en el Estamento sin que le zarandee con sus ataques. (*LARRA se levanta, pasea.*)

MESONERO. ¿Un desafío público en las Cortes entre el presidente del Gobierno y el jefe de la oposición? (*LARRA se adelanta y escucha.*)

DÍAZ. Y en el campo del honor. Mendizábal no ha podido tolerar tamañas insidias.

VEGA. Diga mejor que Istúriz no ha podido sufrir tanta soberbia.

DÍAZ. ¡Si el retado ha sido él! (*LARRA va a su escritorio y recoge unos papeles.*)

VEGA. ¡Ha sido Mendizábal! (*Se levanta y se encara con DÍAZ.*)

BRETÓN. Señores... Da lo mismo. (*VEGA se sienta de mala gana.*)

GRIMALDI. ¡Pipí! ¡Sirve a todos! ¡Yo convido!... Lo malo es que el duelo se verifica hoy.

GALLEGO. Para mayor risa en el extranjero. No tenemos hombres de Estado.

BORREGO. (*A GALLEGO.*) ¿Deberemos comentar el lance en los periódicos?

DÍAZ. Si el presidente despacha a Istúriz, tendrá que hacerlo.

BRETÓN. ¡Mocito fantasioso! Ya verá como el duelo es sólo a primera sangre. (*LARRA ha vuelto al primer término y, sin bajar el escalón, ofrece sus papeles a BORREGO. El periodista se levanta sorprendido, los toma y lee un poco.*)

BORREGO. ¿Dos barateros que se desafían en la cárcel?

LARRA. (*Ríe.*) Una fabulita inocente. Uno de ellos mata al otro y, para reconvenirlo, le dan garrote. Entonces habla la sociedad. (*BORREGO lee. La voz de LARRA, en el ambiente.*)

LARRA. (*Su voz.*) «Algún día, baratero, tendrás razón; pero por el pronto te ahorcaré...»

LARRA. (*Habla con su boca.*) «... Y el baratero murió... Y la sociedad siguió, y siguieron con ella los duelos, y siguió vigente la iey, y barateros la burlarán, porque no serán barateros de la cárcel, ni barateros

ESPRONCEDA: Have Istúriz and the Duke of Rivas not spoken to you?[52]

LARRA: Vaguely.

ESPRONCEDA: They're counting on us.

LARRA: "Istúriz is a genuine radical...".

ESPRONCEDA: And Mendizábal's sworn opponent! There's not a day passes in the house that he doesn't rattle him with his attacks. *(LARRA stands up and begins to pace to and fro.)*

MESONERO: The Prime Minister and the leader of the opposition have challenged each other publicly, in parliament? *(LARRA steps forward to listen.)*

DÍAZ: A question of honour. Mendizábal couldn't put up with such insidious lies any longer.

VEGA: It would be more accurate to say that Istúriz couldn't tolerate such brazen arrogance.

DÍAZ: But he was the one who was challenged! *(LARRA goes to his writing desk to collect some papers.)*

VEGA: It was Mendizábal! *(He stands up to face DÍAZ.)*

BRETÓN: Gentlemen... What difference does it make? *(VEGA sits down reluctantly.)*

GRIMALDI: Pipí! A drink for everyone! On me!... The trouble is that the duel is to take place today.

GALLEGO: To turn us into laughing-stocks abroad. There's not a single statesman in the whole country.

BORREGO *(To GALLEGO.):* Should we make any public comment on the quarrel?

DÍAZ: If the Prime Minister dispatches Istúriz, you'll have no choice.

BRETÓN: The delusions of youth! You'll see... the duel will be to the first blood, and nothing more. *(LARRA has walked forwards and, without stepping down from the study, hands his papers to BORREGO. The journalist stands up in surprise, takes them and reads them briefly.)*

BORREGO: Two rag and bone men challenge each other in prison?[53]

LARRA *(Laughing.):* An innocent little fable. One kills the other and then, for his own good, he's executed. Then we hear the voice of society. *(BORREGO reads. LARRA's voice sounds in the air.)*

LARRA *(His voice.):* "Some day, rag and bone man, you will be in the right; but, for the time being, I'll hang you..."

LARRA *(Speaking normally.):* "...And the rag and bone man died... And society carried on, and duelling with it, and the law was still enforced. And the rag and bone men will continue to ignore it, because they have no fear of prison and no regard for the people, although they

del pueblo, aunque cobren el barato del pueblo.»

BORREGO. Larra, no olvide que mi revista es ministerial.

LARRA. ¿Y si vence Istúriz?

BORREGO. ¡Con Mendizábal o con Istúriz, ministerial!

LARRA. «Bastante censura nos ponen los gobiernos (...) sin que se nos añada otra doméstica en nuestro mismo periódico (...) En el Ministerio Mendizábal he criticado cuanto me ha parecido criticable.» Y lo mismo estoy haciendo ya con Istúriz. Todo lo cual, señor Borrego, se lo pienso repetir en otro artículo. Conque muévase y procure que aprueben los dos si quiere recibir más. (*BORREGO se guarda a disgusto los papeles y LARRA se vuelve hacia ESPRONCEDA. Leve cambio de luz.*) Lo publiqué en abril.

ESPRONCEDA. (*Asiente.*) Y en días muy tensos.

BORREGO. Fígaro no se quejará de mí. Le he publicado «Los barateros». Pero ya publiqué yo días antes que ese duelo era «la más justa y honorífica explicación que dos hombres podían y debían darse.»

BRETÓN. Claro. Por si acaso.

BORREGO. ¿Qué ha dicho?

ARRIAZA. No haga caso, es un guasón. Usted procedió perfectamente.

GALLEGO. Sin embargo, la ley prohíbe el duelo. Y la religión lo condena.

DÍAZ. Será ahora. (*GALLEGO no se digna contestar. Leve cambio de luz. Entra el PADRE FROILÁN muy contento.*)

P. FROILÁN. ¡Ya cayó el anticristo! Pipí, lo mío. (*Se sienta en su sitio acostumbrado.*)

DÍAZ. ¿A quién se refiere?

BORREGO. (*Preocupado.*) A Mendizábal. Istúriz le ha pedido cuentas del voto de confianza otorgado por la Cámara y no ha acertado a justificar los descalabros de la campaña del norte. (*DÍAZ se levanta, trémulo.*)

GALLEGO. Perdone. El motivo ha sido que quiso inculpar de esos reveses a nuestros mejores generales y propuso a la reina nuevos mandos. Ella se ha negado y él ha tenido que dimitir.

MESONERO. ¡Qué tragedia!

BRETÓN. ¡Qué comedia!

P. FROILÁN. (*Farfulla.*) ...todos del mandil... ¡Al fuego con todos! (*DÍAZ se ha acercado.*)

live off the people's .ags and bones".

BORREGO: Larra, you must not forget that my journal is loyal to the government*

LARRA. And if Istúriz wins?

BORREGO: Loyal, whether to Mendizábal or to Istúriz is irrelevant.

LARRA: "There is sufficient censorship directed at us from the government (...) without adding the self-imposed censorship of our own press (...) In Mendizábal's ministry I've attacked everything that I believed demanded to be attacked". I'm doing the same with Istúriz. All of which, Señor Borrego, I intend to restate in another article. So I advise you to get moving and make sure that they are both given authorisation, that is if you want any more pieces from me. *(BORREGO unwillingly puts the papers away. LARRA turns towards ESPRONCEDA. A slight change in lighting.)* It came out in April.

ESPRONCEDA *(Nodding.):* And at a very tense moment.

BORREGO: Figaro need have no quarrel with me. I published his "The rag and bone men". But a few days previously I wrote that the duel was "the most fair and honourable explanation that two men could and should give each other".

BRETÓN: Of course. One can never be sure of these things

BORREGO: What do you mean by that?

ARRIAZA: Pay no heed, his usual heavy-handed sarcasm. You behaved quite correctly.

GALLEGO: Even so, the law prohibits duelling. And religion condemns it.

DÍAZ: That's a recent development, is it? *(GALLEGO does not deign to reply. Slight change in lighting. FATHER FROILAN enters, clearly very happy.)*

F. FROILÁN: The anti-Christ has fallen! Pipí, my usual. *(He sits down in his normal place.)*

DÍAZ: Who are you talking about?

BORREGO *(Worried.):* Mendizábal. Istúriz demanded a reply to the vote of confidence taken by the house, and he wasn't able to account for the setbacks in the northern campaign. *(DÍAZ stands up nervously.)*

GALLEGO: If you'll forgive me... The reason was that he tried to turn our best generals into scapegoats for the defeats, and he proposed new commanders to the Queen. She refused and he was forced to resign.

MESONERO: What a tragedy!

BRETÓN: What a comedy!

F. FROILÁN *(Muttering.):* ... all round her apron strings... Burn the lot of them! *(DÍAZ has drawn nearer.)*

VEGA. ¿Y quién va a gobernar?

BORREGO. La reina ha llamado a Istúriz.

BRETÓN. Muy natural. A quien más ha podido. (*DÍAZ murmura un sordo saludo y sale del café. Los de la izquierda ríen.*)

ARRIAZA. Vamos de desastre en desastre.

GRIMALDI. Y la comida empieza a escasear...

MESONERO. Y el café de este café ya es achicoria...

BRETÓN. O malta... (*Se va yendo la luz del Parnasillo.*)

LARRA. (*A ESPRONCEDA.*) Accedo a ser procurador.

ESPRONCEDA. (*Se levanta.*) ¡Corro a decírselo a Istúriz!

LARRA. ¡Dígale que no olvide mis artículos! No seré ministerial n con él, y no callaré si hay que criticar su gestión.

ESPRONCEDA. Se avendrá. Nos necesita. (*Sale por uno de lo huecos del fondo. La luz se amortigua en el centro e ilumina el bloqu derecho. Muy nervioso, DON HOMOBONO se levanta y espera humildísimo. Por el hueco derecho del fondo aparece ISTÚRIZ. E mismo vestido civil de MENDIZÁBAL. Es un cincuentón de noble port y cabello todavía oscuro. Su media máscara, muy diferente en cambio d la de su antecesor, parece la de un bilioso sapo. En su camino hacia l escalera se detiene un instante.*)

ISTÚRIZ. Escriba lo que quiera, Larra. Cuento de todos modos co usted. Le presentaremos por Ávila. (*LARRA se inclina levemente ISTÚRIZ sube despacio. En el gabinete, la voz de LARRA.*)

LARRA. (*Su voz.*) ¿Sabrá este viejo zorro que Dolores vive all (*ISTÚRIZ se detiene un segundo y lo mira, risueño.*) ¿Se vuelv proxeneta para ganar mi voluntad? (*El nuevo presidente sigue subiendo. Trabajo le mando. (*ISTÚRIZ llega al descansillo. El censor se inclina El ministro lo mira de arriba abajo. LARRA atiende muy interesado.*)

ISTÚRIZ. Tengo malos informes de su conducta. Mientras s determina qué se hace con usted, procure no disgustarme. (*Va a subir su despacho.*)

D. HOMOBONO. Excelencia... (*Su excelencia se detiene.*) Es qu uno... ya no sabe a qué atenerse... ¿Los escritos del señor de Larra y d señor Espronceda, por ejemplo..., ¿se deben prohibir?

ISTÚRIZ. (*Airado.*) ¡Esos dos señores van a ser diputados! No l olvide.

D. HOMOBONO. (*Hecho un lío.*) No, si yo no olvido nada. (*ISTÚRIZ sube y se sienta. El hombrecillo se sienta a su vez, mu perplejo.*) Ni entiendo ya nada. Que el Señor se apiade de mis cuatro

VEGA: And who will take over the government?

BORREGO: The Queen has summoned Istúriz.

BRETÓN: A matter of course. Who else is there? *(DÍAZ mutters his goodbyes and leaves the café. Those on the left laugh.)*

ARRIAZA: We're stumbling from one disaster to another.

GRIMALDI: Food's starting to become scarce...

MESONERO: The coffee here is pure chicory...

BRETÓN: Or malt... *(The light fades gradually over the café.)*

LARRA *(To ESPRONCEDA.):* I accept. I'll stand.

ESPRONCEDA *(Rising.):* I'll go and tell Istúriz at once.

LARRA: Tell him as well that I just won't forget my articles! I won't be loyal to anyone, not even him, and if his actions justify it, I shan't pull any punches.

ESPRONCEDA: He'll agree to that. He needs us. *(He exits through one of the gaps at the back. The light on the centre softens as the right-hand rostrum is lit. The nervous DON HOMOBONO stands up and humbly waits. Through the right-hand gap at the back appears ISTÚRIZ, wearing the same civilian attire as MENDIZÁBAL. He is a man of about fifty years of age, of noble bearing and hair that is still dark. His half mask, in this case very different from that of his predecessor, suggests a bilious toad. He stops for a moment as he walks towards the stairs.)*

ISTÚRIZ: You may write what you please, Larra. I shall rely upon you in any event. You will stand in Avila. *(LARRA bows slightly. As ISTÚRIZ climbs the stairs, LARRA's voice is heard in the study.)*

LARRA *(Voice off.):* Is it possible the old fox knows that's where Dolores lives? *(ISTÚRIZ stops for a second and looks at him cheerfully.)* Is he turning himself into a go-between to win me over? *(The new Prime Minister continues climbing.)* He'll have his work cut out with me. *(ISTÚRIZ reaches the first level. The censor bows. The Prime Minister looks him up and down. LARRA watches with great interest.)*

ISTÚRIZ: I have received negative reports about you. While your future is being decided, try not to irritate me further. *(He makes to go up to his office.)*

D. HOMOBONO: Excellency... *(His Excellency stops.)* It's just that one... isn't quite sure of how to proceed... The writings of Señor de Larra and Señor Espronceda, for example..., should they be banned?

ISTÚRIZ *(Angrily.):* Those particular gentlemen will soon be members of parliament. Bear that in mind.

D. HOMOBONO *(Lost in confusion.):* I bear everything in mind, I assure you. *(ISTÚRIZ continues to his office, where he sits down. DON HOMOBONO also sits, deeply perplexed.)* I can't make any sense of it.

hijitos. (*Se pone a trabajar mecánicamente.*)

LARRA. ¿Y quién entiende ya nada? (*Se ilumina el Parnasillo.*)

GALLEGO. ¿Y quién entiende ya nada?

BRETÓN. Nadie. Porque nuestro zoilo, no sé si lo saben, quiere ser procurador.

VEGA. También se presenta Espronceda.

BORREGO. ¿Por qué no? ¡Hay que ayudar a Istúriz! (*ARRIAZA rompe a reír.*) Esa risa, ¿va por mí?

ARRIAZA. No, no. Me río... de los peces de colores. (*Sofoca su risa.*)

P. FROILÁN. (*Farfulla.*) ...masones! (*Se levanta.*)

GALLEGO. Caridad, padre Froilán...

P. FROILÁN. (*Con sorpresa de todos se le oye bien.*) ¡Con Fernando VII vivíamos mejor!

GALLEGO. Padre, hubo muchas muertes y destierros. Yo mismo...

P. FROILÁN. ¡Usted también es masón!

GALLEGO. (*Se levanta.*) ¿Está loco?

P. FROILÁN. ¡Y el masón, al paredón!

GALLEGO. (*Indignado.*) ¡No le consiento...!

VEGA. (*Irónico.*) Mansedumbre, padre Gallego...

GALLEGO. (*Se reporta.*) Tiene usted razón. (*Se cala la teja.*) Buenas tardes.

P. FROILÁN. ¡Soy yo quien se va y para no volver! (*Farfulla.* Banda de... sacrílegos... arreglará... don Carlos. (*Se encasqueta su teja y sale del café. GALLEGO se descubre y se sienta, meneando la cabeza con pesar. Se oscurece el Parnasillo, al tiempo que entra ESPRONCEDA muy agitado por la puerta del fondo del gabinete.*)

ESPRONCEDA. ¡Larra, no vayamos a las elecciones!

LARRA. ¿Ahora sale con ésas?

ESPRONCEDA. ¡Istúriz es un vanidoso! ¡Las Cortes le han dado un voto de censura, se ha irritado y las ha disuelto!

LARRA. Otro Mendizábal...

ESPRONCEDA. ¡El poder ensoberbece a todos! ¡Pero si Istúri gallea, se le responderá! (*Señala con un dedo, al tiempo que se expand un ruido de disparos y gritos lejanos.*) ¡Vuelven a formarse Juntas! ¡H sonado la hora de la acción!

May the Good Lord look kindly upon my four little ones. *(He sets to work mechanically.)*

LARRA: Can anyone make any sense of it? *(Light on Little Parnassus.)*

GALLEGO: Can anyone make any sense of it?

BRETÓN: Nobody. In case you didn't know, our young pundit wants to enter parliament.

VEGA: Espronceda is standing with him.

BORREGO: And why not? Istúriz must be supported as well. *(ARRIAZA laughs out loud.)* Is that laughter for my benefit?

ARRIAZA: No, no. I'm just laughing at... nothing in particular. *(He stifles his laughter.)*

F. FROILÁN *(Muttering.):* ...masons! *(He gets up.)*

GALLEGO: Be charitable, Father Froilán...

F.FROILÁN *(To the surprise of all those who hear him with clarity.):* Life was better under Fernando VII!

GALLEGO: Father, many people were killed, sent into exile. I myself...

F.FROILÁN: You're a mason as well!

GALLEGO *(Rising.):* Have you gone mad?

F. FROILÁN: Shoot every last mason!

GALLEGO *(Indignant.):* I will not stand for...!

VEGA *(Ironically.):* Be meek, Father Gallego...

GALLEGO *(Restraining himself.):* Yes, of course. *(He puts on his hat.)* Good day.

F. FROILÁN: Don't leave on my account. I'm going and I won't be back. *(He mutters.)* Bunch of... blasphemers... show them... don Carlos. *(He puts on his hat and leaves the cafe. GALLEGO takes his off and sits down, shaking his head regretfully. Little Parnassus grows dark at the same time as ESPRONCEDA, in a state of considerable agitation, enters through the back door of the study.)*

ESPRONCEDA: Larra, we mustn't stand.

LARRA: You've changed your tune!

ESPRONCEDA: Istúriz is conceited beyond belief. Parliament took a vote of censure against him, he flared up and simply dissolved the house.

LARRA: Another Mendizábal...

ESPRONCEDA: Power turns all their heads! But if Istúriz wants to be cock of the walk, he'll soon have his answer! *(He points with his finger at the same time as the noise of distant shooting and screaming begins to rise.)* They're forming Assemblies again! The time for real action has arrived!

LARRA. ¡¿Qué acción?

ESPRONCEDA. Barricadas en las calles. Como en París.

LARRA. Siéntese.

ESPRONCEDA. No tengo tiempo.

LARRA. ¡Para mí, sí! (*Va a su lado y le fuerza amistosamente a sentarse.*) Las provincias se van a levantar: bueno está. ¿Quiénes mueven la insurrección?

ESPRONCEDA. ¿A quién apunta?

LARRA. A Mendizábal y a sus adictos. Desde que cayó está conspirando contra Istúriz. Prefiero a Istúriz.

ESPRONCEDA. ¿No ha dicho que es otro Mendizábal?

LARRA. ¿Y qué? (*Pasea, pensativo. Los disparos menudean. Radiante, aparece DIAZ en la puerta del café, al tiempo que éste se ilumina. ESPRONCEDA taconea impaciente, en espera de las palabras de su amigo.*)

DIAZ. ¡Comenzó la danza, señores! Han asesinado en Málaga al gobernador y al capitán general.

GRIMALDI. ¿Es cierto, señor Borrego?

BORREGO. Puede serlo. Toda Andalucía se ha levantado.

DIAZ. (*Avanza.*) ¡Y Zaragoza, y Valencia, y Murcia! ¡Y Cataluña!

GALLEGO. ¿Y eso le alegra?

DIAZ. ¡Llorar no lloro! ¡Ustedes sigan bien! (*Y sale del café como un cohete.*)

BRETÓN. (*Por DIAZ.*) Periquito bailón. (*Ríen los de la izquierda.*)

BORREGO. El general don Evaristo San Miguel se va a sublevar también.

VEGA. ¡No!

BORREGO. Mocito, yo suelo estar bien informado.

GALLEGO. En fin: que la guerra se perderá.

MESONERO. El poder siempre es fuerte... (*La luz se va del café poco a poco.*)

LARRA. (*A ESPRONCEDA.*) ¿Disolución de Cortes? Bien. Seremos procuradores en las nuevas.

ESPRONCEDA. ¡Hay que dar una sola bandera a esas insurrecciones! ¡Yo me sublevo con mi regimiento!

LARRA. ¿Y si ganamos mañana la elección?

ESPRONCEDA. Poco importa. (*Va a levantarse.*)

LARRA. ¡Razone! Mendizábal y su camarilla no han vacilado en llevar a soldados y menestrales a la muerte por una oculta cuestión de intereses. Recuerde su famosa ley electoral: elecciones por distritos, o sea,

LARRA: What action?

ESPRONCEDA: Barricades in the streets. Like Paris.

LARRA: Sit down.

ESPRONCEDA: I haven't got time.

LARRA: You have time for me. *(He goes to his side and gently forces him onto a seat.)* The provinces are about to rise: that's clear. Who's behind it?

ESPRONCEDA: Who are you thinking of?

LARRA: Mendizábal and his followers. Ever since he fell he's been plotting against Istúriz. And I prefer Istúriz.

ESPRONCEDA: But you've just said that he's another Mendizábal.

LARRA: What of it? *(He paces to and fro pensively. The shooting grows in intensity. Just as Little Parnassus is lit up, DÍAZ appears in the doorway, positively radiant. ESPRONCEDA taps his feet impatiently as he waits for his friend to speak.)*

DÍAZ: The cat is well and truly among the pigeons, gentlemen! They've assassinated both the Governor and Field Marshal of Malaga.

GRIMALDI: Is that correct, Señor Borrego?

BORREGO: It could well be. The whole of Andalusia has risen.

DÍAZ: So have Zaragoza, Valencia and Murcia! And Catalonia!

GALLEGO: And you're pleased about it?

DÍAZ: I'm not exactly heartbroken. Good day to you, gentlemen. *(He dashes out of the café.)*

BRETÓN *(Referring to DÍAZ):* Off the parrot prances. *(Laughter from those on the left.)*

BORREGO: General don Evaristo San Miguel is about to mutiny as well.

VEGA: I don't believe it!

BORREGO: Young man, I usually know what I'm talking about.

GALLEGO: So... the war is lost.

MESONERO: Power is always resilient... *(The light gradually fades over the café.)*

LARRA *(To ESPRONCEDA.):* Dissolve parliament? All right. We'll sit in the new one.

ESPRONCEDA: We have to unite all the uprisings behind one banner! I'm bringing my regiment out!

LARRA: And if we win these elections, then what?

ESPRONCEDA: It makes no difference. *(He makes to rise.)*

LARRA: Consider for one moment! Mendizábal and his cronies didn't think twice before sending soldiers and workers to their death for an obscure question of self-interest. Remember his famous electoral reform:

poniéndolas en manos de los caciques. El duelo de estos dos barateros va a desangrar a España. ¿Y por qué riñen? Mendizábal favorece a sus amigos ricos de Cádiz defendiendo el libre cambio; Istúriz, a la industria catalana, para cuyos tejidos pide leyes protectoras. Y es de suponer que los dos saquen sabrosas tajadas de sus respectivas políticas... No se deje arrastrar a motines sangrientos por ninguno de ellos.

ESPRONCEDA. (*En pie.*) ¡Yo me sublevo!

LARRA. ¡Como quiera! Pero no retire la candidatura.

ESPRONCEDA. No voy a pensar ahora en tales niñerías.

LARRA. Pensaré yo por los dos. Su elección podría librarle mañana de un tribunal militar.

ESPRONCEDA. Me fugaré si llega el caso. ¿No viene?

LARRA. No.

ESPRONCEDA. Adiós. (*Se va por la puerta del fondo, que deja abierta. Se oye, muy suave y remota, la cavatina de Rossini, ejecutada por una orquesta. LARRA mira hacia la salita del piano, pero allí no hay nadie.*)

LARRA. ¡Dolores, si tú no vienes, yo iré a Ávila! Pero si no me escuchas y he de luchar solo, lucharé. (*Se sume en sus reflexiones. La luz cambia levemente. PEDRO entra por el fondo con una carta en bandeja.*)

PEDRO. Señor... Han traído esta carta.

LARRA. ¡La credencial! (*Abre la carta presuroso y lee.*) ¿Qué día es hoy, Pedro?

PEDRO. 6 de agosto de 1836, señor.

LARRA. Dentro de dieciocho días me sentaré en las Cortes, y España me oirá. Lástima que Espronceda no haya sido elegido... ¡Corazón ardiente y generoso! (*Pausa. Se abstrae y musita, intemporalmente.*) También morirá joven. (*Leve cambio de luz. PEDRO deniega repetidamente, suspira, toma el sombrero del escritor y se lo ofrece, al tiempo que se sienten disparos lejanos. Los dos escuchan: los rumores bélicos aumentan. El bloque derecho se ilumina. ISTÚRIZ y DON HOMOBONO, llenos de zozobra, se levantan y aguzan el oído. LARRA se cala la chistera y se dirige al primer término. Al oír a DÍAZ, se detiene sin bajar el escalón. Luz vivísima en el Parnasillo. El criado se retira por un hueco del fondo. DÍAZ entró por la puerta y va, exultante, de una a otra mesa.*)

district elections, in other words, hand it to the local landowners on a plate. Those two rag and bone men, with their constant duelling, are going to bleed Spain dry. And what are they fighting about? Mendizábal is protecting the interests of his rich friends in Cadiz by fighting for free trade: Istúriz, those of the Catalan cloth manufacturers by demanding tarrifs. And you can be sure that both of them make a pretty penny from their respective policies... Don't allow yourself to be dragged into a bloody battle on their account.

ESPRONCEDA: I'm going to join them!

LARRA: Do what you want! But don't withdraw your candidature.

ESPRONCEDA: I'm not going to even think about such nonsense now!

LARRA: I'll think for both of us. If you're elected it'll save you from a court martial.

ESPRONCEDA: I'll make a run for it if it comes to that. So you won't join me?

LARRA: No.

ESPRONCEDA: Goodbye. (He leaves through the door at the back, leaving it ajar. Rossini's cavatina sounds, distantly, softly, played by an orchestra. LARRA looks over at the room where the piano is, but there is nobody there.)

LARRA: If you won't come here, Dolores, then I'll go to Avila! But if you won't listen to me and I have to fight alone, then fight I will! (He loses himself in thought. There is a slight change in the lighting. PEDRO enters from the rear with a letter on a tray.)

PEDRO: Sir... this letter has just been delivered by hand.

LARRA: My credentials! (He tears the letter open and reads its contents.) What's today's date, Pedro?

PEDRO: 6th of August, 1836, sir.

LARRA: In eighteen days time, I will take my seat in parliament, and all of Spain will hear me. A pity that Espronceda wasn't elected... Such a generous, warm heart! (Pause. He ponders and murmurs, out of chronology.) He'll die young as well. (Slight change in the lighting. PEDRO shakes his head repeatedly, sighs, lifts the writer's hat and holds it out to him, at the same time as distant shots are heard. They both listen: the sounds of war grow nearer. The right–hand rostrum lights up.ISTÚRIZ and DON HOMOBONO stand up in alarm, listening attentively. LARRA puts on his hat and walks forwards. Upon hearing DÍAZ he stops, without stepping down from the study. Very bright light on Little Parnassus. PEDRO exits through a gap at the back. DÍAZ has entered the café and goes exultantly from table to table.)

DÍAZ. ¡Tres sargentos! ¡Tres sargentos! Higinio García...

GRIMALDI. ¡No nos aturda, *mon Dieu*!

DÍAZ. ¡Alejandro Gómez!

ARRIAZA. (*Sombrío.*) Y Juan Lucas, ya lo sabemos.

DÍAZ. ¿No lo comprenden? ¡Al fin, la revolución! Todos los oficiales de La Granja vinieron a Madrid a la ópera...!

BRETÓN. Sospechosa unanimidad.

DÍAZ. Justo. Ellos preferían que lo hicieran los sargentos. O sea, el pueblo.

ARRIAZA. La horda.

DÍAZ. ¡Límpiese la boca antes de insultar al pueblo, señor Arriaza! ¡Los sargentos de La Granja, amenazando a la reina con sus propios soldados! ¡Ahí es nada! Y ella ha tenido que prometer la Constitución del 12. (*LARRA se decide y pasa directamente de su sala al café.*)

LARRA. Buenos días, señores. ¿Hay novedades?

BRETÓN. Según el señor Díaz, nada menos que la revolución.

LARRA. Ya. (*Se sienta a la izquierda y se descubre. DÍAZ lo mira con irónica sonrisa de superioridad.*)

BORREGO. Bien mirado, es un paso.

DÍAZ. ¿No les recuerda nada ese regreso de la reina a Madrid custodiada por los amotinados?

MESONERO. (*Preocupado.*) El regreso de Varennes.

DÍAZ. Usted lo ha dicho. (*Mira a LARRA y grita.*) ¡Abajo Istúriz! ¡Abajo la censura! (*Sobresaltados, ISTÚRIZ y DON HOMOBONO se miran, bajan la cabeza y descienden de sus dos niveles por la parte oculta. El bloque sigue iluminado.*)

BORREGO. Nuestro joven amigo no ignora la historia. Y tampoco hay que echar en saco roto las prendas literarias y morales del señor Díaz. Nuestras revistas van a necesitar sus colaboraciones. ¿Eh, Mesonero? («*El Curioso Parlante» sonríe ambiguamente.*)

DÍAZ. (*Derretido.*) Son ustedes muy amables...

GALLEGO. Yo fui doceañista y no negaré que la nueva vigencia de esa Constitución me es muy grata.

DÍAZ. Pues bien, señores, ¡viva la Constitución y viva el pueblo! (*BORREGO, GRIMALDI, GALLEGO, VEGA, MESONERO, responden con sus ovaciones.*)

BRETÓN. (*Con una ojeada de soslayo a LARRA, que escucha impasible.*) Y también, amigo Díaz, ¡viva el nuevo presidente! Don José María Calatrava. Un patriota. (*CALATRAVA aparece en el nivel*

DÍAZ: Three sergeants! Three sergeants! Higinio García...[54]
GRIMALDI: Mon Dieu, you made us all jump!
DÍAZ: Alejandro Gómez!
ARRIAZA *(Darkly.):* And Juan Lucas, yes, we know.
DÍAZ: Don't you see? Revolution, at last. All of the officers from the palace at La Granja came to Madrid, for the opera...!
BRETÓN: A suspicious consensus of opinion.
DÍAZ: Indeed. They preferred their sergeants to do it. In other words, the people.
ARRIAZA: The rabble.
DÍAZ: Señor Arriaza, think carefully before you insult the people! Three sergeants in La Granja threatening the Queen with her own soldiers! It doesn't happen everyday! She had no choice other than promise to restore the constitution of 1812. *(LARRA makes up his mind and crosses straight from his room to the café.)*
LARRA: Good day, gentlemen. Anything new?
BRETÓN: According to Señor Díaz, nothing less than revolution.
LARRA: Indeed? *(He sits down on the left and removes his hat. DÍAZ watches him with an ironic smile of superiority.)*
BORREGO: All things considered, it's a step in the right direction.
DÍAZ: The Queen being escorted back to Madrid by mutineers... something vaguely familiar about the scene, don't you think?
MESONERO *(Worriedly.):* The return of Varennes.
DÍAZ: Indeed. *(He looks at LARRA and shouts.)* Down with Istúriz! An end to censorship! *(ISTÚRIZ and DON HOMOBONO look at each other, startled. With bowed heads, they descend from both levels by means of the hidden stairs. The rostrum remains illuminated.)*
BORREGO: Our young friend has no mean knowledge of history. Señor Díaz has many literary and moral qualities that we must not allow to go to waste. Our journals are going to have need of a pen like his. Don't you think so, Mesonero? *(MESONERO smiles ambivalently.)*
DÍAZ *(Won over.):* You are too kind, gentlemen.
GALLEGO: I fought for the constitution as well, and I'm delighted to see it come back into effect.
DÍAZ: In that case, gentlemen. Long live the constitution and long live the people! *(BORREGO, GRIMALDI, GALLEGO, VEGA and MESONERO echo his acclamation.)*
BRETÓN *(With a sideways glance at LARRA, who continues listening impassively.):* And let's not forget our new Prime Minister, my dear Díaz! Don José María Calatrava.[55] A true patriot. *(CALATRAVA appears on the upper level of the left-hand rostrum and stands there*

superior del bloque izquierdo y se detiene en actitud solemne. Tiene unos cincuenta y seis años, y los cabellos, plateados y revueltos. Su media máscara congestiva, casi roja, es muy diferente de la de sus predecesores. El traje civil es en cambio idéntico.)

MESONERO. Seis años pasó en el penal de Melilla.

DÍAZ. Y en el destierro ganó su pan trabajando como zapatero. ¡Él, un jurista eminente! *(CALATRAVA levanta su mano: va a hablar. DÍAZ se sienta junto a GALLEGO y todos escuchan.)*

CALATRAVA. Istúriz y yo formamos parte de la Junta de Bayona. Los dos queríamos abatir la tiranía fernandina... Con pesar hube de alejarme de mi predecesor. Su moderantismo nos llevaba a un callejón sin salida. Afortunadamente el pueblo ha hablado y su majestad se ha dignado confiarme el timón en esta nueva singladura... Se decreta un empréstito forzoso de doscientos millones de reales. Todos los bienes muebles e inmuebles del clero ingresarán en el Tesoro. ¡Se efectuará una nueva quinta de cincuenta mil hombres!... Todos los ciudadanos serán calificados como leales o sospechosos, y es justo que los daños y privaciones sufridos por los primeros se remedien a costa de los segundos.

DÍAZ. *(Que ha escuchado todo con gestos y ademanes entusiastas.)* ¡Como en Francia!

CALATRAVA. Se abrirán las Cortes el 24 de octubre, y en ellas la nación refrendará la Constitución del 12 que se le ha otorgado o redactará otra si así lo prefiere.

DÍAZ. ¿Qué más se puede pedir?

BORREGO. Muy bien, muy bien... *(CALATRAVA se sienta. La luz le abandona.)*

GRIMALDI. ¡Pipí, sirve a todos un buen jerez por mi cuenta!

GALLEGO. *(Se levanta.)* Espero que me disculpen... No puedo entretenerme... Tengo que hacer. Buenos días. *(Se cala la teja y sale por la puerta.)*

DÍAZ. *(Ríe.)* Su reacción es la mejor señal.

ARRIAZA. ¿De qué?

DÍAZ. De que hemos entrado en la senda revolucionaria.

ARRIAZA. Sin duda. En la senda de las logias.

DÍAZ. ¿Tiene algo que afear a las logias?

ARRIAZA. ¿Yo? Dios me libre. Pero Istúriz también es masón.

DÍAZ. *(Desdeñoso.)* Hay masones y masones.

VEGA. Larra, usted no ha abierto la boca. ¿Será cierto que estamos

solemnly. A man of about fifty-six years of age, his hair is silvery and disordered. His half mask is congestive, almost red, and very different from that of his predecessors. His clothing, on the other hand, is identical.)

MESONERO: He spent six years in prison in Melilla.

DÍAZ: And during his exile he earned his daily bread as a shoemaker. A lawyer of his stature! *(CALATRAVA lifts his hand: he is about to speak. DÍAZ sits down beside GALLEGO, and they all listen.)*

CALATRAVA: Istúriz and I were both members of the Assembly of Bayona. Both of us sought to oppose the tyranny of Fernando... So it was with considerable regret that I found myself forced to distance myself from my predecessor. His indecisive sense of moderation was leading the country into a blind alley. Happily, the people spoke out and Her Majesty has graciously appointed me to the helm as this new day dawns... Essential state borrowing of the sum of two hundred million reales has been approved. All the assets of the clergy, moveable and non-moveable, are to be impounded by the Treasury. A new army of fifty thousand men will be raised!... All citizens will be officially classified as Patriot or Suspect, and justice demands that the damages and losses incurred by the first group be remedied at the cost of the second.

DÍAZ *(Who has been listening with looks and gestures of enthusiasm.):* Just like in France!

CALATRAVA: Parliament will re-convene on the 24th of October, and then the nation will sanction the constitution of 1812 in the form submitted or write a new one, as it sees fit.

DÍAZ: What more can we ask for?

BORREGO: Excellent, excellent... *(CALATRAVA sits down. The light over him fades.)*

GRIMALDI: Pipí, bring out your finest sherry. A glass all round, on me!

GALLEGO *(Standing up.):* I hope you'll excuse me... I can't stay... Certain matters I must attend to. Good day. *(He puts on his hat and leaves.)*

DÍAZ: A very telling reaction.

ARRIAZA: Of what?

DÍAZ: That we are on the true path of revolution.

ARRIAZA: Without question. On the path of the masonic lodges.

DÍAZ: Have you anything against them?

ARRIAZA: Me? God forbid! But Istúriz is a mason as well.

DÍAZ *(Disdainfully.):* There are masons and masons.

VEGA: You've said nothing, Larra. Are we really on the threshold of

a las puertas de un cambio revolucionario?

DÍAZ. Fígaro no puede opinar. Es un moderado. (*LARRA lo mira fijamente, pero calla. Silencio embarazoso.*)

MESONERO. (*A media voz.*) Larra, acepte mi sentimiento por no haber llegado a sentarse en las Cortes.

LARRA. Al contrario. Déme la enhorabuena.

DÍAZ. (*A media voz.*) Presuntuoso.

VEGA. Le hice una pregunta, Larra.

LARRA. Y le contestaré al estilo del señor Díaz que hay revoluciones... y revoluciones.

DÍAZ. Es tan ingenioso que ni se le entiende. ¿Qué ha querido decir?

LARRA. Que el señor Calatrava *parece* un revolucionario. Y que los *heroicos* sargentos de La Granja también lo parecen. Y que todo el mundo lo parece ya, menos yo. ¿Cómo voy a parecerlo, si obtuve del *moderado* Istúriz el acta que he perdido? Todo es parecer. El señor Díaz *parece* ahora un revolucionario y yo, pobre de mí, un moderado. A pesar de haber escrito que para el 36 se necesita una Constitución más avanzada que la del 12. Lo dije, eso sí, con gran moderación. Sin aspavientos, como los de los sargentos de La Granja al exigir la del 12..., después de haber sido comprado cada uno con dos onzas de oro.

MESONERO. (*Inquieto por su amigo.*) Larra...

DÍAZ. ¿He oído bien?

BRETÓN. (*Retiene un brazo de MESONERO, que va a hablar de nuevo.*) Deje hablar a Fígaro, Mesonero.

LARRA. ¡Lo saben igual que yo! Dieciocho sargentos, a dos onzas por cabeza, treinta y seis onzas. Para tan gran resultado, muy barato. Treinta y seis onzas del bolsillo de Mendizábal. (*Un silencio.*) El cual ha vuelto al poder como ministro de Hacienda. ¡Tanto él como su presidente Calatrava parecen verdaderos revolucionarios, ya lo creo! ¿Quién osaría afirmar que vayan a hacer la revolución de las bolsas repletas y no la del pueblo?

MESONERO. Larra, por favor.

LARRA. ¿No estoy diciendo que quien lo afirme es un orate? Calatrava y Mendizábal son revolucionarios. Certísimo. Y yo, un moderado impenitente. Fígaro. Andrés Niporesas. ¡Y tan ni por ésas!

DÍAZ. (*Se levanta.*) ¡Como que están verdes, Bachiller!

LARRA. Sé como están las uvas, señor Díaz. Podridas.

MESONERO. ¡No se hable más de política! Aquí viene Pipí. (*El camarero aparece por la izquierda con una bandeja llena de copas de jerez.*)

a revolution?

DÍAZ: Figaro has nothing to say. He's a moderate. (*LARRA gazes at him fixedly, but says nothing. An embarrassed silence.*)

MESONERO4 (*Speaking softly*): Larra, I wanted to tell you how sorry I am that you won't be able to take your seat in parliament after all.

LARRA: Not at all. You should congratulate me instead.

DÍAZ (*In a low voice.*): Arrogant fool.

VEGA: I asked you a question, Larra.

LARRA: And I shall answer, like Señor Díaz, that there are revolutions... and revolutions.

DÍAZ: He's so ingenious that none of us can understand him. What is that supposed to mean?

LARRA: That Señor Calatrava appears to be a revolutionary. And that the heroic sergeants of La Granja also appear to be revolutionaries. In fact, everyone does, except me. How can I be, when it was Istúriz, another moderate, who sponsored the seat which I've just lost? Nothing is what it seems. Señor Díaz now seems to be a revolutionary and I, for my sins, a moderate. And that in spite of having written that in '36 we need a constitution that goes far beyond that of 1812. Of course, I said it with a remarkable degree of moderation. Without the song and dance of the sergeants in La Granja -bought to a man with two pieces of gold.

MESONERO (*Worried for his friend.*): Larra...

DÍAZ: I can hardly believe what I'm hearing.

BRETÓN (*Holding MESONERO by the arm just as he prepares to speak again.*): Let Figaro have his say, Mesonero.

LARRA: It's common knowledge. Eighteen sergeants, two pieces a head, thirty-six in all. Cheap enough for such a successful outcome. Thirty-six pieces of gold from Mendizábal's purse. (Silence.) Mendizábal, back in power as Chancellor. Both he and his Prime Minister, Calatrava, seem real revolutionaries indeed! And who would be foolhardy enough to believe that theirs is a revolution for the wealthy, not for the people?

MESONERO: Larra, please.

LARRA: But am I not saying that only a fool would believe that? Calatrava and Mendizábal are revolutionaries. Of course, they are. And I am simply an unrepentant moderate. Figaro. Andrés Notevenso. More than ever, not even so!

DÍAZ (*Rising.*): They're well and truly sour, eh Figaro?

LARRA: I know exactly how the grapes are, Señor Díaz. Rotten.

MESONERO: Let's have no more talk of politics. Here comes Pipí. (*The waiter appears from the left with a tray full of glasses of sherry.*)

DÍAZ. Para un brindis político. ¿Usted no va a brindar?

MESONERO. (*Prudente.*) ¿Por qué no?

DÍAZ. ¡Pues a ello! (*PIPÍ ha ido dando copas a las manos que se le tienden. DÍAZ le ayuda; lleva otras a la derecha y toma la suya. En la bandeja queda una copa. Tímido, PIPÍ se la ofrece a LARRA.*) ¡Pipí! ¿Has traído una copa al señor de Larra?

PIPÍ. Claro, señor Díaz.

DÍAZ. Puedes llevártela. (*PIPÍ mira a LARRA sin saber qué hacer.*)

LARRA. Espera. Yo también brindaré.

DÍAZ. (*Mordaz.*) ¿Será posible?

LARRA. Después de ustedes.

DÍAZ. (*Con desprecio.*) Como quiera. Señores... (*Alza su copa. Todos se levantan.*)

GRIMALDI. *Mais non, mon cher ami!* ¡Soy yo quien invita!

DÍAZ. (*Un tanto corrido.*) Cierto, don Juan. Discúlpeme.

GRIMALDI. (*Alza su copa.*) ¡Por el mayor acierto en la gestión del Ministerio Calatrava!

DÍAZ. ¡Y por la revolución! ¡Y por la supresión de la censura! (*Todos beben, menos LARRA. Se van sentando.*)

LARRA. Éste es mi brindis. ¿Nadie me acompaña? (*VEGA no se atreve a mirarlo. Al fin, él mismo se quita la careta y aparece una fisonomía acobardada, casi llorosa, en lucha consigo misma. LARRA lo advierte y sonríe, amargo.*) «¡Ministerio Calatrava, los escritores que vas a desterrar te saludan!» (*Apura su copa y la deja de golpe sobre una mesa.*)

DÍAZ. ¡Esa insolencia...! (*Se levanta y da un paso hacia el pobrecito hablador. Casi todos se levantan.*)

BORREGO. ¡Díaz, repórtese!

DÍAZ. ¡Deslenguado! (*BORREGO lo sujeta.*)

MESONERO. ¡Calma, señores!

BRETÓN. ¡Si no ha pasado nada!

VEGA. (*Que no se ha levantado y sigue eludiendo la mirada de LARRA.*) Sí ha pasado...

ARRIAZA. Serenidad, por favor...

MESONERO. (*Algo le inquieta.*) ¡Silencio!...

DÍAZ. ¡Víbora!

MESONERO. ¡Callen, les digo! ¿No oyen? (*Señala al exterior, donde se oía un confuso griterío que las voces de dentro tapaban. El ruido crece, entreverado por dos o tres disparos. Todos se levantan.*)

BORREGO. ¿Qué pasa? (*Va hacia la puerta, que se abre de*

DÍAZ: A political toast. Will you join us?
MESONERO *(Cautiously.):* Why not?
DÍAZ: Well, take your glass. *(PIPI has distributed glasses to the*
outstretched hands. DÍAZ helps him, carrying some over to the right
before taking his own. Only one glass is left on the tray. Timidly PIPI
offers it to LARRA.) Pipí! Did you bring a glass for Señor de Larra.
PIPI: Of course, Señor Díaz.
DÍAZ: Well, you can take it away. *(PIPI looks at LARRA in*
confusion.)
LARRA: Wait. I'll drink a toast as well.
DÍAZ *(Bitingly.):* Will you indeed?
LARRA: After you.
DÍAZ *(Scornfully.):* As you wish. Gentlemen... *(He raises his glass,*
as the others stand up.)
GRIMALDI: Mais non, mon cher ami! It is I who have invited you.
DÍAZ *(Somewhat taken aback.):* Of course, don Juan. Forgive me.
GRIMALDI *(Raising his glass.):* To the greater wisdom of Calatrava's
ministry!
DÍAZ: And to revolution! And the end of censorship! *(With the*
exception of LARRA, they all drink and return to their seats.)
LARRA: This is my toast. Will anybody join me? *(VEGA doesn't*
dare look at him. Finally, he removes his mask to reveal the cowardly,
almost tearful face of a man in constant battle with himself. LARRA
notices and smiles bitterly.): "Calatrava, those writers you are about to
exile salute you!" *(He drains his glass and bangs it down on the table.)*
DÍAZ: Of all the effrontery...! *(He rises and steps towards the poor*
little babbler. Almost everyone else gets up.)
BORREGO: Díaz, control yourself!
DÍAZ: Scurrilous liar! *(BORREGO restrains him.)*
MESONERO: Gentlemen, calm down!
BRETÓN: A fuss about nothing... nothing of any importance.
VEGA *(Who has remained seated, still avoiding LARRA's gaze.):* No.
It was important...
ARRIAZA: Please, gentlemen, control yourselves...
MESONERO *(Disturbed by something.):* Silence!
DÍAZ: Muckraker!
MESONERO: Be quiet, I said. Can't you hear anything? *(He points*
outside, where an uproar of shouting voices, previously hidden behind
those raised inside the café, begins to be heard. The noise grows,
interspersed with one or two shots. They all stand up.)
BORREGO: What's going on? *(He goes towards the door, which*

improviso. El PADRE GALLEGO vuelve horrorizado.)

GALLEGO. *(Cierra.)* ¡No se asomen! ¡Son temibles!

ARRIAZA. ¿Quiénes?

GALLEGO. *(Se sienta, tembloroso.)* Vienen arrastrando el cadáver del general Quesada.

BORREGO. ¿El capitán general de Madrid?

GALLEGO. Sacó a las tropas a la calle contra Calatrava.

DÍAZ. Pero él había huido.

GALLEGO. *(Asiente.)* Lo acechaban por el camino y lo han asesinado. *(Todos callan y escuchan. La algarabía decrece.)*

ARRIAZA. Parece que se alejan.

BRETÓN. Sí. *(Se van sentando. Ya apenas llegan ruidos.)*

LARRA. La revolución... de las talegas.

DÍAZ. *(Que ha tomado su sombrero, se vuelve hacia él.)* ¡Moderado!

LARRA. *(Para sí.)* No hay remedio.

DÍAZ. ¡Viva Calatrava! *(Abre la puerta y sale aprisa.)*

GRIMALDI. Señores, creo que debemos abandonar el café y volver a nuestras casas aprisa. La calle está peligrosa. *(Se cubre.)*

ARRIAZA. Es lo más prudente. Vámonos. *(Se levanta. Le imitan todos, menos LARRA, y van saliendo por la puerta. Al pasar junto a LARRA, MESONERO le oprime el hombro con afecto. Ningún otro se ha despedido de él. VEGA es el último. Desenmascarado, se detiene cerca de LARRA y, sin mirarlo, habla.)*

VEGA. Perdóneme.

LARRA. No hay nada que perdonar.

VEGA. Debí brindar con usted y no me atreví. No soy lo que aparento.

LARRA. No se preocupe. Lo raro sería no acobardarse en esta época.

VEGA. Gracias, Larra. Adiós.

LARRA. Adiós. *(Sale VEGA. El café vacío se va oscureciendo. Sobre el escritor, un vivo foco. Una vaga figura, que lleva una vela encendida en una palmatoria, aparece por el hueco izquierdo del fondo en el oscuro gabinete. Es PEDRO, enmascarado pero con el torso desnudo. En espalda y pecho muestra la profunda marca de una herida ya vieja que, de momento, se distingue mal. Viene leyendo un folleto y trae una botella bajo el brazo. Absorto en la lectura, se sienta en una de las sillas contiguas al velador, sobre el que deja la palmatoria. LARRA lo divisa. Sin dejar de leer, PEDRO echa un trago de la botella y la deja en el*

suddenly opens. FATHER GALLEGO returns horrified.)

GALLEGO *(Closing the door.):* Don't go out! They're capable of anything!

ARRIAZA: Who are?

GALLEGO *(He sits down trembling.):* They're dragging the body of General Quesada through the streets.

BORREGO: The military commander of Madrid?

GALLEGO: He and his men took to the street against Calatrava.

DÍAZ: But Quesada had already fled.

GALLEGO *(Nodding.):* They were waiting along the way, and they killed him. *(They all fall silent to listen. The hubbub grows distant.)*

ARRIAZA: It seems to have passed.

BRETÓN: Yes. *(They return to their seats. Hardly a sound now reaches the café.)*

LARRA: Revolution... for the men of substance.

DÍAZ *(He has taken his hat, and now turns to face him.):* Moderate!

LARRA *(To himself.):* There's no hope now.

DÍAZ: Long live Calatrava! *(He opens the door and hurries out.)*

GRIMALDI: Gentlemen, I think we should leave the café and get home as speedily as possible. It is dangerous to be on the streets. *(He puts on his hat.)*

ARRIAZA: That's clearly the wisest thing to do. Shall we go? *(He stands up. As he passes close to LARRA, MESONERO squeezes his shoulder affectionately. The rest ignore him. VEGA is the last to leave. Unmasked, he stops beside LARRA and, without looking at him, addresses him.)*

VEGA: Forgive me.

LARRA: There's nothing to forgive.

VEGA: I should have drunk with you and I didn't dare. I'm not everything I seem.

LARRA: Don't worry. Fear at a time like this is natural enough.

VEGA: Thank you, Larra. Goodbye.

LARRA: Goodbye. *(VEGA leaves. Darkness has slowly returned to the empty café. A bright light illuminates the writer. A shadowy figure, carrying a lit candle in a holder, enters the study from the left-hand gap at the back. It is PEDRO, masked but naked to the waist. His back and chest reveal the deep scar of an old wound which, for the moment, cannot be seen with full clarity. He is reading a pamphlet and he carries a bottle under his arm. Absorbed in his reading, he sits down on one of the chairs beside the occasional table, upon which he sets the candlestick holder. LARRA notices him. Without stopping reading, PEDRO drinks from the*

suelo. LARRA sube el peldaño y va, sigiloso, a encender el quinqué del bufete. Aumenta la luz en la salita. LARRA deja su sombrero sobre el mueble. PEDRO levanta la cabeza. Se miran.)

LARRA. (*Baja la cabeza y cierra los ojos.*) Así te encontré una noche en que todo se había vuelto contra mí. Encendí el quinqué... y te dije... (*Calla. Levanta el rostro.*) ¿Qué haces aquí? (*PEDRO se levanta.*)

PEDRO. (*Tartajoso por el vino.*) Perdone. Como el señor tardaba...

LARRA. La casa es tuya, ¿no?

PEDRO. (*Ríe groseramente.*) ¡Es que estamos en Navidad!

LARRA. ¡Y medio desnudo!

PEDRO. Tengo calor.

LARRA. ¡Está nevando!

PEDRO. Pues yo tengo calor.

LARRA. (*Seco.*) Del vino. Mañana hablaremos. (*PEDRO se inclina y va hacia el fondo.*) Espera. (*PEDRO se detiene. El escritor se acerca y mira la cicatriz.*) ¿Qué es esto?

PEDRO. Una herida antigua.

LARRA. ¡Y en la espalda tienes otra!

PEDRO. Es la misma, señor.

LARRA. (*Atónito.*) ¿Atravesado de parte a parte?

PEDRO. Sí, señor.

LARRA. Y has sobrevivido...

PEDRO. De milagro, sí, señor. Eso dijo el médico.

LARRA. ¿Cómo te hirieron?

PEDRO. En el Maestrazgo.

LARRA. ¿Tú has combatido en el Maestrazgo?

PEDRO. Sí, señor. Poco antes de entrar a su servicio.

LARRA. No me lo dijiste.

PEDRO. No me lo preguntó.

LARRA. (*Por el folleto que ve en la mano de PEDRO.*) ¿Estabas leyendo?

PEDRO. Cuando el señor no está, leo.

LARRA. (*Molesto.*) Ese folleto es una entrega de «El Redactor General».

PEDRO. Lo dejaré en su sitio.

LARRA. Dame. (*Le arrebata el folleto y pasa una página hacia atrás.*) «Yo y mi criado». (*Mira a PEDRO.*) Has visto que hablaba de ti y te ha entrado curiosidad...

*bottle and sets it down on the floor. LARRA steps up into the study and stealthily goes to light the lamp on the bureau. The light in the room grows. LARRA sets down his hat on top of the bureau. PEDRO lifts his head, and their gazes meet.*⁵⁶*)*

LARRA *(Lowering his gaze and closing his eyes.):* That's how I found you that night when everything had gone against me. I lit the lamp... and I said... *(He falls silent and looks up.)* What do you think you're doing here? *(PEDRO gets to his feet.)*

PEDRO *(The wine causes him to slur his words.):* Excuse me. As you were late coming home, sir...

LARRA: The house is yours, eh?

PEDRO *(With a guffaw.):* It's Christmas!

LARRA: You're half naked!

PEDRO: I'm hot

LARRA: It's snowing outside!

PEDRO: Well, I'm hot.

LARRA *(Drily.):* The wine. We'll discuss it in the morning. *(PEDRO bows and walks towards the back of the study.)* Wait. *(PEDRO stops. The writer goes to him and looks at the scar.)* What's this?

PEDRO: An old wound.

LARRA: There's another one on your back.

PEDRO: It's the same one, sir.

LARRA *(Astonished.):* You were run right through?

PEDRO: Yes, sir.

LARRA: And you survived...

PEDRO: A miracle, sir. That's what the doctor said.

LARRA: How did it happen?

PEDRO: In the Maestrazgo.

LARRA: You fought there?

PEDRO: Yes, sir. Not long before coming to work for you.

LARRA: You didn't tell me.

PEDRO: You never asked.

LARRA *(Referring to the pamphlet he sees PEDRO holding.):* You were reading?

PEDRO: I read whenever you're out, sir.

LARRA *(Put out.):* That pamphlet is for an edition of "The Writer General".

PEDRO: I'll put it back.

LARRA: Give it to me. *(He snatches the pamphlet and glances at its first page.)* "My servant and I". *(He looks at PEDRO.)* So your curiosity got the better of you when you noticed you were mentioned in the article?

PEDRO.   También he leído otros artículos.   (*LARRA está muy sorprendido.*)   Los leo casi todos.   (*Mirándolo de tanto en tanto, LARRA va a dejar el folleto sobre el bufete.*)

LARRA.   Este último te habrá dado buenos quebraderos de cabeza... (*Vuelve hacia él.*)   Porque ese diálogo entre tú y yo es inventado.

PEDRO.   Ya me he dado cuenta.

LARRA.   (*Divertido.*)   Me sorprendes...   ¿Lo has entendido?

PEDRO.   Creo... que sí.

LARRA.   ¡Pero tú no me habrías hablado como te he hecho hablar yo!

PEDRO.   Creo... que no.

LARRA.   (*Irónico, superior.*)   Veamos.   ¿Qué me habrías dicho? (*Silencio.*)   ¡Habla!

PEDRO.   Puede... que le dijera: si sus murrias le han dejado sin amigos en Nochebuena, podemos distraernos aquí, con Adelita y cantando asturianadas.   Yo sé hacerlo.

LARRA.   ¿Así me habrías hablado?

PEDRO.   Como el señor está tan solo...   ¡Y por eso no entiende a los demás!

LARRA.   (*Irritado.*)   ¿Quieres decir que no te he entendido a ti?

PEDRO.   (*Por el folleto.*)   Ahí lo dice...   Verá.   (*Corre al escritorio, recupera el cuaderno y pasa páginas.*)   Aquí...   No.   (*Eructa.*)

LARRA.   Vete a tu catre.

PEDRO.   Perdone   Es el vino...   ¡Aquí!   Aquí dice que yo soy un animal que sólo sabe comer y dormir y que, si no soy feliz, tampoco soy desgraciado.   (*Mira a su señor.*)   Como si un criado fuese menos que un perro.   Y como si las penas fueran sólo cosa de gente fina.   (*LARRA se acerca al velador y se sienta, eludiendo la mirada del criado.*)

LARRA.   Sigue.

PEDRO.   (*Ríe, mostrando el folleto.*)   En lo de borracho sí tiene razón...   ¿Me puedo acostar?

LARRA.   No.   Siéntate.   (*Da unos golpes sobre la silla contigua.*)

PEDRO.   (*Estupefacto.*)   ¿Qué me siente?

LARRA.   Por favor.   (*Indica la silla.   Muy sorprendido, PEDRO se sienta.*)   Y háblame...   como si fuera un hijo tuyo.

PEDRO.   (*Bruscamente herido, casi grita.*)   ¿Un hijo?

LARRA.   (*Toma la botella del suelo.*)   Echa un trago.   (*Ante la vacilación del criado.*)   ¡Bebe, hombre!   (*PEDRO se decide, toma la*

PEDRO: It's not the first óne I've read. *(LARRA is very surprised.)* I read nearly all of them. *(LARRA goes to leave the pamphlet down on the bureau, turning to look back at his servant as he does so.)*

LARRA: This last one will have had you puzzled. *(He goes towards him.)* Because that dialogue between you and me is entirely imaginary.

PEDRO: I realized that.

LARRA *(Amused.):* You surprise me... Did you understand it?

PEDRO: I... think so.

LARRA But you would never have spoken to me as I made you speak there!

PEDRO: I don't... think so.

LARRA *(In superior, ironic tones):* Well then. What would you have said? *(Silence.)* Go on!

PEDRO: Perhaps... I might have said that if your usual misersable nature means you haven't got a friend in the world on Christmas Eve, then we could celebrate here, together with Adelita, singing songs. The ones I know from Asturias.

LARRA: Is that what you would have said?

PEDRO: With you being so lonely, sir... That's why you don't understand people!

LARRA *(Irritated.):* Don't you mean why I don't understand you?

PEDRO *(Referring to the pamphlet.):* It says it there... I'll show you. *(He runs to the writing desk, takes the pamphlet and turns its pages.)* Here... No. *(He belches.)*

LARRA: Get off to bed.

PEDRO: Sorry. It's the wine... Here it is! This is where you say that I'm like an animal that's only interested in eating and sleeping, and that if I'm not exactly happy, at least I'm not particularly unhappy either. *(He looks at his master.)* As if a servant was less than a dog. And as if only the gentry feel pain. *(LARRA goes to the occasional table and sits down, avoiding the gaze of his servant.)*

LARRA: Go on.

PEDRO *(He laughs as he holds up the pamphlet.):* At least you were right about the drunk bit... Can I go to bed?

LARRA: No. Sit down. (He pats the chair beside his.)

PEDRO *(In amazement.):* You want me to sit down?

LARRA: Please. *(He indicates the chair. PEDRO sits down, very surprised.)* And talk to me... as if I were your son.

PEDRO *(Suddenly hurt, he almost screams.):* My son?

LARRA *(Lifting the bottle from the floor.):* Take a drink. *(As the servant hesitates.)* Go on, drink. *(PEDRO makes up his mind, takes the*

botella y bebe. LARRA habla lentamente.) Y ahora, piensa que soy un niño ignorante, y que mi padre eres tú. (*Silencio. PEDRO se libera de su careta, que abandona sobre la mesita, y rompe a llorar. Intrigado y conmovido, LARRA no lo pierde de vista. PEDRO se oprime frente y ojos con su ruda mano. Después muestra su rostro humedecido: el de un recio campesino de ingenuas pupilas.*) ¿Por qué lloras?

PEDRO. Perdí un hijo.

LARRA. Sigue.

PEDRO. ¿Qué pueden saber los señorines de ciertas cosas?

LARRA. (*Pone su mano sobre el brazo del criado.*) ¿De qué cosas?

PEDRO. Ustedes no van a la guerra.

LARRA. (*Retira su mano.*) ¿Cómo?

PEDRO. Ninguno del café se bate contra los carlistas.

LARRA. (*Vacila.*) Algunos... sí. Espronceda es oficial.

PEDRO. Para lucir el uniforme por Madrid.

LARRA. ¡O donde le manden! Escosura es alférez de Artillería. Pezuela, oficial de Caballería. Estébanez Calderón sirve en el cuartel general del Ejército del Norte. (*Se emociona.*) Y mi inolvidable amigo el conde de Campo Alange...

PEDRO. He leído lo que ha dicho de su muerte. Ése sí fue un valiente.

LARRA. Más que eso. Un hombre abnegado y bueno. ¡Quizá mi único amigo verdadero!... ¡Y qué poco me he acordado de él!

PEDRO. Pero también peleó por su gusto. Si no quieren, ustedes no tienen que pelear.

LARRA. ¿Nosotros?

PEDRO. Los nobles, los ricos, los abogados, los escritores, los fabricantes... Los propietarios de animales o tierras, tampoco. Las tropas se forman con jornaleros, aprendices y mendigos. ¡A la fuerza y para morir! El refrán lo dice: «Quinto, enganche y escorpión, muerte sin extremaunción»

LARRA. ¡Te confundes! ¡El reclutamiento abarca ya a todos!

PEDRO. Entonces, ¿por qué no está usted en campaña? (*LARRA va a hablar.*) No lo diga. Cualquier triquiñuela de la ley. O están dispensados, o se pueden librar por dinero si los enganchan... Por eso los cien mil hombres de Mendizábal se quedaron en cincuenta mil... Usted no sabe lo que es una leva. Entran en los pueblos y, al que calza alpargatas, se lo llevan. Al que lleva zapatos, no: ése es respetable. Yo me he salvado de la quinta de Calatrava por mi herida... No puedo correr. Pero

bottle and drinks. LARRA speaks slowly.) Now, imagine that I'm just an ignorant child and you're my father. *(Silence. PEDRO takes off his mask, which he leaves on the little table, and begins to weep. LARRA watches him, intrigued and moved. PEDRO presses his rough hand over his brow and eyes. When he takes his hand away, his face is tear-stained, in his eyes the uncomplicated look of a simple, honest peasant.)* Why are you crying?

PEDRO: I lost a son.

LARRA: Tell me.

PEDRO: How could a fine young gentleman like you understand things like that?

LARRA *(Putting his hand on his servant's shoulder.):* Things like what?

PEDRO: Your sort doesn't go to war.

LARRA *(Taking his hand away.):* What?

PEDRO: Nobody in your café has fought against the Carlists,

LARRA *(Hesitating.):* Some... have. Espronceda is an officer.

PEDRO: So that he can strut around Madrid in his uniform.

LARRA: Or wherever they happen to send him. Escosura is a corporal in the artillery. Pezuela, a cavalry officer. Estébanez Calderón serves in the general headquarters of the Northern Division. *(With emotion.)* And my dearest friend, the Count of Campo Alange...

PEDRO: I read what you said about his death. He was a brave man.

LARRA: And much more. A good man, a selfless one... Perhaps my only real friend!... And how rarely I think of him now!

PEDRO: But he fought because he chose to. If you and your friends don't want to, nobody will make you.

LARRA: Me and my friends?

PEDRO: The aristocracy, the rich, the lawyers, the writers, the factory owners... those who have land or animals. Armies are made up of working men, apprentices and beggars. Press-ganged cannon fodder! As the old saying goes: "Soldier boy, take the shilling and then feel war's sting, die without a priest the very next morning".

LARRA: You're wrong! No one is exempt from recruitment!

PEDRO: Then, why aren't you there? *(LARRA is about to speak.)* No, don't say it. Some little loophole in the law... special immunity or, if it comes to it, you buy your way out... Which is why Mendizábal's hundred thousand men were reduced to fifty thousand... You don't know how they go about recruiting. They go into the villages and take anyone wearing rope sandals. Nobody with shoes, they're respectable folk. It was only my wound which saved me from Calatrava's men... I can't get about quickly

los pobres vamos a la guerra. Ustedes, no.

LARRA.   Yo no soy rico, Pedro.

PEDRO.   Mucho más que yo, sí.   Como el señor Mesonero, como e
señor duque de Rivas...

LARRA.   ¿Por qué esos nombres?

PEDRO.   (*Lo mira y rie. Se levanta y pasea torpemente.*)   Sí que
hay que hablarle como a un niño, sí.   ¿Tampoco sabe lo de las quintas y
Barcelona?

LARRA.   ¿De qué hablas?

PEDRO.   Allí siempre madrugan, y ya han formado una sociedad de
seguros contra las quintas. (*Se detiene. LARRA lo mira con asombro.*)
Sí, señor.   Los pobres también pueden librarse de sentar plaza, o pagarse
un sustituto.   Y como no tienen dinero, la sociedad lo presta.   Aunque se
entrampen de por vida, salvan al menos al hijo, al hermano –
.,.   Y el dinero lo ponen quienes lo tienen. (*Breve pausa.*)   Como e
señor duque de Rivas y el señor Mesonero.

LARRA.   ¿Qué?

PEDRO.   (*Se acerca, confidencial.*)   Esos señores van a poner aquí
el negocio.   Y el Gobierno lo permite porque también sacará su buen
pellizco.   Si no lo hicieran los ricachos lo haría él solito...   Así que
nosotros, o muertos, o inútiles, o endeudados hasta reventar.

LARRA.   (*Se levanta.*)   Has nombrado a dos personas honorables.
¿Quién dice que andan en esas granjerías?

PEDRO.   (*Rie.*)   ¡Los criados!   Ellos oyen hablar a sus amos con los
visitantes.

LARRA.   ¿Será posible?

PEDRO.   A usted no le cabe en la cabeza porque no es capaz de esas
cochinadas.

LARRA.   (*Se aparta, amargo.*)   *In vino veritas...*

PEDRO.   Déjese de latinajos.   Si me gusta el vino, mejor.   Sepa que
ese artículo me ha hecho daño.   Yo no soy un animal.

LARRA.   (*Se vuelve y le mira a los ojos.*)   Perdónamelo.

PEDRO.   (*Con simpatía.*)   Yo tampoco quiero hacerle daño.   En ese
artículo no hay más que ideas negras... (*Se acerca y le palmea el hombro
con rudo afecto.*)   ¡A sacudírselas! (*Señala el bufete.*)   Y a no pensar en
esa caja amarilla. (*LARRA se estremece.*)   Y menos, hablar de ella en los

:nough. No, it's the poor who go to war. Not you and yours.

LARRA: I'm not rich, Pedro.

PEDRO: You have a lot more than me. Like Señor Mesonero, like he Duke of Rivas...

LARRA: Why them in particular?

PEDRO *(He looks at him and laughs. He gets up and walks unsteadily.):* You really do have to be spoken to like a child. So you haven't heard about the conscription in Barcelona?

LARRA: I don't know what you're talking about.

PEDRO: Well, the early birds in Barcelona have formed a society which insures people against conscription. *(He stands still. LARRA looks at him in amazement.)* Yes, indeed. So now the poor really can escape it, or pay soemone to go in their place. And as they don't have any money, the society lends it to them. And even though they get into debt for the rest of their days, well at least they've kept their son or their brother out of it... And the money comes from those who've got plenty to spare. *(Brief silence.)* Like the Duke of Rivas or Señor Mesonero...

LARRA: What?

PEDRO *(Drawing closer and speaking in confidential tones.):* The same gentlemen are going to set up business here. With the blessing of the government, because it gets its slice of the cake as well. If those with the cash to spare didn't do it, then the government would take over itself... So there's our choice... dead, maimed, or in debt up to our eyes.

LARRA *(Standing up.):* You've accused two honourable gentlemen. What proof do you have that they're involved in these despicable activities?

PEDRO *(Laughing.):* Their servants! They hear their masters talking to visitors.

LARRA: I don't believe it.

PEDRO: You won't believe it because you wouldn't be capable of that sort of dirty business.

LARRA *(Turning aside, bitterly.):* In vino veritas...

PEDRO: Away with your Latin gibberish! So I like wine? All the better! But I want you to know that that article hurt me. I'm not an animal.

LARRA *(Turning round and looking him straight in the eye.):* I'm sorry.

PEDRO *(Sympathetically.):* I don't want to hurt you either. But that article is full of black thoughts... *(He comes over and pats LARRA's shoulder with rough affection.)* You've got to shake them off! *(He points towards the bureau.)* And stop brooding about that yellow box. *(LARRA shivers.)* And whatever you do, stop writing about it. And what do you

papeles. ¿Y qué es eso de que Madrid es un cementerio, y de que media España murió de la otra media?

LARRA. ¿Tampoco hay que escribir esas cosas?

PEDRO. ¡Sí, pero sin desanimarse!

LARRA. Tú no puedes comprender. mis sufrimientos.

PEDRO. ¿Otra vez con ésas? Me va a hacer reír.

LARRA. Tienes razón. Me has dicho que perdiste un hijo...

PEDRO. ¡Para qué hablar de eso!

LARRA. Te lo ruego.

PEDRO. (*Cierra los ojos. Al cabo de unos segundos empieza a hablar con dificultad.*) Yo vine de mi tierra hace muchos años. A trabajar en lo que saliera. El campo es duro y todos queríamos escapar de las levas... Pero aquí también enganchaban. Y me agarraron para luchar contra los carlistas... Antes se me había muerto mi Paquita... (*Calla, sombrío.*) Se reía de mí, me llamaba zafio... Por eso me empeñé en aprender las letras. Pero nos queríamos bien. Ya lo creo. (*Se sienta junto al velador.*)

LARRA. (*Suave.*) ¿De qué murió?

PEDRO. De un mal que la tomó entera. Calenturas, toses... Moza y bonita que era, se me fue. (*Calla un momento.*) Habíamos tenido un nenín hermoso. Juan le pusimos. Un año tenía cuando se quedó sin madre. (*Bebe un trago.*) Lo crié como pude. Muy despierto que era el rapaz, y tan alegre... Le enseñé yo a leer; quería meterle de aprendiz en una imprenta. Y a los trece añitos ya me traía un salario... Vino la guerra. Decían que los casados mayores de veinticinco años estaban libres, pero yo era viudo y, por lo visto, no contaba tener un hijo tan tierno. Metiéronme en la Infantería... Y, con permiso de mi capitán, me llevé al muchacho.

LARRA. ¿Cómo?

PEDRO. De corneta.

LARRA. ¡Era un niño!

PEDRO. ¿Iba a dejarle solo? Yo no tenía parientes. Y en la tropa había otros como él, incluso hijos de oficiales... (*Absorto en su recuerdo.*) Me lo mató el tigre.

LARRA. ¿Cabrera?

PEDRO. (*Asiente.*) Nos sitió en Nogueruelas y tuvimos que rendirnos. Había dicho que respetaría las vidas. Y no bien salimos con bandera blanca se puso a fusilar. Como nosotros también lo hacíamos...

LARRA. ¿Has formado tú en algún pelotón de fusilamiento?

PEDRO. ¡A ver! Nos obligaban. (*LARRA se sienta junto al*

mean by saying that Madrid is a cemetery, and that one half of Spain died at the hands of the other half?

LARRA: I shouldn't write about such things either?

PEDRO: Yes, but without losing heart!

LARRA: How can you understand my suffering?

PEDRO: Not again! You'll have me laughing next.

LARRA: You're right. You said that you'd lost your son...

PEDRO: What's the point in talking about it?

LARRA: Please, do...

PEDRO *(Closing his eyes. After a few seconds he begins to speak with difficulty.)*: I left home many years ago. To work at whatever happened to turn up. Life in the country can be hard, and none of us wanted to be conscripted... But they were conscripting here as well. And they took me to fight against the Carlists... Paquita, that's my wife, had just died... *(Sombre, he falls silent.)* She used to laught at me, call me a yokel... That's why I made myself learn to read. But we were... very fond of each other. We were. *(He sits down beside the occasional table.)*

LARRA *(Softly.)*: What did she die of?

PEDRO: Some illness that took her whole body. Fevers, coughing... Young and pretty as she was, I lost her. *(He falls silent for a moment.) We'd had a youngster, beautiful he was. We called him Juan. Just a year old when he lost his mother. (He takes a drink from the bottle.)* I brought him up as best I could. A clever little lad, full of life... I taught him how to read; I thought I might get him an apprenticeship in a printing press. He was only thirteen and he was already bringing money in... And then the war came. They said that married men over twenty-five were exempt, but I had no wife and it seemed that having such a young son didn't make any difference. So they put me in the infantry... I asked the captain and the boy came along with me.

LARRA: What?

PEDRO: As a drummer-boy.

LARRA: He was just a child!

PEDRO: How could I leave him behind? There was nobody else. And there were others like him in the army. Even the children of officers... *(Losing himself in memory.)* He was killed by the tiger.

LARRA: Cabrera?

PEDRO *(Nodding.):* He trapped us in Nogueruelas and we had to surrender. He'd promised to spare us. But as soon as we appeared with the white flag he started shooting. Just as we did at other times...

LARRA: Have you ever been in a firing squad?

PEDRO: Ever? We had no choice. *(LARRA sits down beside the*

velador.)

LARRA. Sigue. (*Confusas voces, fuego graneado.*)

PEDRO. ...A los que quedamos en pie nos reservó Cabrera para dar fiesta a sus lanceros. Nos mandó desnudarnos... ¡Él, él mismo, con aquellos ojos de gatazo!... Mi Juanín temblaba. Me puse de rodillas ante Cabrera pidiéndole la vida de mi hijo. Y me dice riendo: ¿Y la de mi madre? A golpes me devolvieron al grupo. ¡Hala, a correr! Y la patrulla de lanceros, tras nosotros. (*Los ruidos han crecido. Gritos, risas. PEDRO se ha levantado y llega al primer término. Una luz vivísima entra por el lateral derecho.*)

CABRERA. (*Su voz.*) ¡A ellos, lanceros! (*LARRA se levanta despavorido.*)

VOCES. ¡Negros! ¡Impíos! ¡A correr! (*Carcajadas. Trote de caballos que se acercan.*)

PEDRO. (*Hacia la derecha.*) ¡Corre, Juanín! ¡Corre conmigo!

JUANÍN. (*Su voz.*) ¡Padre! (*PEDRO cae bajo un lanzazo invisible. El trote es ya un ruidoso galope. Por el lateral aparece corriendo el muchacho semidesnudo que muestra en su cuerpo la terrible herida de la lanza. Nada más entrar, JUANÍN cae al suelo. PEDRO lo incorpora y, conteniendo sus propios dolores, lo lleva aprisa y medio a rastras hacia la escalera izquierda soportando el prolongado alarido del hijo. Se desploman ambos sobre las gradas. El escándalo de las risas, los gritos, los cascos, llega al máximo. JUANÍN agoniza. Apenas se le oye.*) ¡Padre!...

ADELITA. (*Su voz.*) ¡Papá!... (*LARRA mira espantado a la puerta del fondo, donde surge y se apaga el resplandor. El estruendo de los lanceros se va alejando. En el fondo sigue brillando la noche estrellada. La claridad del lateral se extingue. Silencio.*)

PEDRO. (*Sin moverse.*) Cuando me volvieron las luces toqué y toqué a mi Juanín. (*Lo hace.*) Estaba muerto. (*Levanta un poco la cabeza.*) Y pensé, enloquecido y lleno de odio, que era como si me lo hubiesen violado. Y que Cabrera había querido que lo pensásemos así para ofendernos más... Había otros muertos cerca, todos traspasados. (*Se incorpora.*) Aupé a mi hijo... (*Lo levanta en brazos con gran esfuerzo.*) ...deseando morir. (*Se yergue, con el cuerpo en sus brazos, y mira al frente. Un foco lo ilumina.*) Caminé... hasta que se me fue otra vez el sentido. (*Breve silencio.*) Desperté en una carreta de heridos y ardía de fiebre... No sé si a Juanín lo enterrarían... Alguien me tocó y dijo: no durará esta noche. Pero llegué vivo al hospital y en tres meses casi curé.

occasional table.)

LARRA: Go on. *(A clamour of voices accompanied by a sudden barrage of shots.)*

PEDRO:... Those of us who were left standing were given by Cabrera to his lancers as a special treat. He ordered us to strip... Cabrera himself, with his wildcat eyes!... My little Juan started to shake. I knelt down in front of Cabrera and begged him for my son's life. And he just laughed and said: "And my mother's?" They beat me back into the group. Go on, start running! And the troop of lancers on our heels. *(The noises have grown louder. Screams, laughter. PEDRO has stood up and moved forwards. A very bright light shines from the right-hand side.)*

CABRERA *(Voice off.)*: Get them, men! *(LARRA stands up in fear.)*

VOICES: Run, you heathen! Masons! *(Guffaws. The sound of horses' hooves trotting closer.)*

PEDRO *(Towards the right.)*: Juan, son, run! Keep up with me!

JUANIN *(Voice off.)*: Father! *(PEDRO falls, the victim of an invisible lance. The trot has now become a thundering gallop. The half-naked boy runs on from the side, the terrible wound from the lance clearly visible on his body. He immediately falls to the floor. PEDRO tries to lift him and, although in great pain himself, half-carries, half-drags him as quickly as he can towards the left-hand stairs, ignoring the boy's prolonged shriek of pain. They both collapse on the stairs. The tumult of laughter, screams and pounding hooves reaches a crescendo. JUANIN is dying. He can hardly be heard.)* Father!...

ADELITA *(Voice off.)*: Papa!... *(Frightened, LARRA looks towards the door at the back, where the glow appears once again and then subsides. The clamour of the lancers grows distant. The star-studded night still shines in the background. The light from the side goes out. Silence.)*

PEDRO *(Motionless.)*: When I came to, I touched him again and again. *(He does so.)* He was dead. *(He raises the boy's head slightly.)* And I went crazy with hate, and I thought that it was as if they had raped my son. And that Cabrera had wanted me to think that so as to make it worse... There were bodies all around, all of them run through. *(He stands up.)* I took my son in my arms... *(He lifts him with great difficulty.)* ...all the time just wanting to die. *(He straightens up with the body in his arms, and faces forward. He is lit by a single spot.)* I walked... until I lost consciousness again. *(Short pause.)* I woke up in a cart full of wounded men, burning with fever... I don't know whether they would have buried Juanín... Somebody touched me and said: "He'll not see the night out". But I was still alive when they got me to hospital, and three months

Me licenciaron. Y aquí estoy. Siempre con mi hijo a cuestas. (*LARRA baja la cabeza. PEDRO vuelve la suya hacia él.*) No piense tanto. No hay que enrabiarse. ¡Hay que apretar los dientes y vivir! (*Se encamina despacio hacia el fondo. Se vuelve hacia LARRA.*) Hay que vivir. (*Sale por el hueco izquierdo con el muchacho en brazos.*)

LARRA. (*Con profunda emoción.*) Sí. Para escribir y para defenderos. (*Va a su bufete, escoge algunos papeles, se encamina a la escalera derecha.*) Ésta es mi guerra. (*Se ilumina el bloque. El escritor empieza a subir. Un hombre trabaja en la mesa. No se le ve la cara, pero se advierte que no es DON HOMOBONO. LARRA llega a su nivel y se acerca, intrigado.*) Disculpe, señor. ¿Puede atenderme? (*Como quien esperaba la visita, el censor levanta la cabeza sin girarla.*) Usted, ya veo que es nuevo... De parte de don Andrés Borrego, traigo un par de artículos míos para «El Español». (*El censor se levanta despacio y se vuelve hacia LARRA. En su enmascarado semblante, una turbia sonrisa. Es CLEMENTE DÍAZ. A LARRA se le descompone todo el rostro; no ha podido evitarlo.*)

DÍAZ. Celebro verle, señor de Larra.

LARRA. (*Retrocede un paso.*) ¿Usted?

DÍAZ. Clemente Díaz, para servirle.

LARRA. ¡Usted... abominaba de la censura!

DÍAZ. Porque es abominable. Pero la de los gobiernos reaccionarios o... moderados. No la nuestra.

LARRA. (*Se ha sobrepuesto con gran esfuerzo.*) Usted lo pase bien, señor Díaz. (*Va a irse.*)

DÍAZ. ¿No me da sus artículos?

LARRA. (*Con triste sonrisa.*) Le ahorraré trabajo.

DÍAZ. Me está ofendiendo. Soy un funcionario del Gobierno y procederé en conciencia.

LARRA. Pues mi enhorabuena, señor Díaz. Le auguro largos años de plácidas y bien remuneradas tachaduras.

DÍAZ. Sus ironías me resbalan. Ya no está a la izquierda, sino a la derecha. A mí no me va a engañar, ni siquiera por esas argucias satíricas de las que tanto abusa.

LARRA. Justo. Ni-por-ésas. Andrés Niporesas le saluda y desaparece. (*Inicia la marcha.*)

DÍAZ. (*Sardónico.*) ¡Vuelva usted mañana! (*Torna a sentarse, en tanto que LARRA baja los peldaños lentamente. La luz abandona el bloque.*)

ater was all but cured. They released me. And here I am. Still carrying my son. *(LARRA looks down. PEDRO turns towards him.)* Don't brood on things so much. There's no point in rage. Just grit your teeth and get on with it! *(He walks slowly towards the back. He turns to face LARRA.)* You've got to live your life. *(He exits through the left-hand gap, his son hanging limply across his arms.)*

    LARRA *(Profoundly moved.):* Yes. So that I can write and defend others like you. *(he goes to his bureau, selects some papers and walks towards the right-hand staircase.)* This is my particular war. *(Light falls on the rostrum. The writer begins to go up. A man is working at the desk. His face cannot be seen, but it is clearly not DON HOMOBONO. LARRA reaches the floor where he is working and approaches him with curiosity.)* Excuse me, sir. I wonder if you can help me. *(As though expecting the visit, the censor raises his head without turning round.)* I see that you're new to this office... On behalf of don Andrés Borrego, I've brought a couple of articles of mine for "The Spaniard". *(The censor slowly rises and turns to face LARRA, a dark smile on his masked face. It is CLEMENTE DÍAZ. Taken by surprise and unable to prevent it, LARRA's face crumples in dismay.)*

    DÍAZ: I'm delighted to see you, Señor de Larra.

    LARRA *(Stepping backwards.):* You?

    DÍAZ: Clemente Díaz, at your service.

    LARRA: You... detested censorship.

    DÍAZ: It's a detestable thing. When it's in the hands of reactionaries or moderates. Ours is different.

    LARRA *(Controlling himself with a great effort.):* I hope you enjoy yourself, Señor Díaz. *(He makes to go.)*

    DÍAZ: Aren't you going to give me your articles?

    LARRA *(With a sad smile.):* I'll save you the trouble.

    DÍAZ: I find that offensive. I am a servant of the government and I shall follow the dictates of my conscience.

    LARRA: In that case, you have my congratulations, Señor Díaz. I predict that you will enjoy many years of quiet and richly-rewarded erasure.

    DÍAZ: I'm impervious to your jibes. You are no longer on the left, but on the right. And you won't convince me otherwise, not even with the sarcastic chicanery which so pleases you.

    LARRA: Indeed. Not-even-so. Andrés Notevenso salutes you and takes his leave. *(He begins to leave.)*

    DÍAZ *(Sardonically.):* Call back tomorrow! *(He ret   to his seat as LARRA slowly goes down the steps. The light leaves the rostrum.)*

LARRA. (*Mientras baja, su voz en el aire.*) «Coja usted un hombre (si es usted ministro (...), porque si no, no sale nada) (...) déle usted (...) un ligero barniz de nombramiento, y ya le ve usted irse doblegando (...), reír a todo lo que usted diga: y ya tiene usted hecho un ministerial.» (*Un foco saca de la sombra a PEDRO, de nuevo vestido y sin máscara.*)

LARRA. Estoy perdido.

PEDRO. ¡Ánimo! (*Torna a oírse en el aire la voz del escritor.*)

LARRA. (*Su voz.*) «... Tenemos hecha la maleta para la primera remesa de deportación (...) Declaramos (...) vivir en la calle de Santa Clara (...) número 3 (...) donde se nos puede prender por la mañana (...), que tanto en aquella casa (...) como fuera de ella, admitimos anónimos (...), desafíos, puñaladas, órdenes de destierro, ministros (esto es, alguaciles, que a los otros no recibimos, aunque en el día todos prenden)...»

PEDRO. ¡Ánimo! (*LARRA se acerca al velador y contempla la pistola.*) ¡A la calle! ¡A distraerse! Estamos en Carnaval. (*Muy suavemente, al tiempo que se retira.*) Hay que vivir. (*El foco se apaga y el criado se va en silencio por un hueco del fondo. El escritor toma su sombrero y avanza hacia el frente. Se detiene, absorto.*)

LARRA. «... Hay máscaras todo el año; aquel mismo amigo que te quiere hacer creer que lo es, la esposa que dice que te ama, la querida que te repite que te adora, ¿no te están embromando toda la vida? ¿A qué, pues, esa prisa de buscar billetes? Sal a la calle y verás las máscaras de balde... *El mundo todo es máscara: todo el año es carnaval.*» (*LARRA baja el escalón y se encamina, lento, hacia la derecha. Se oyen cascos de caballo y las ruedas de un tilburi. LARRA lo sigue con la vista y se abalanza de pronto hacia el frente.*)

LARRA. (*Con su boca.*) ¡Dolores! (*El coche está pasando. LARRA va hacia la izquierda y grita.*) ¡Dolores, si no paras, me oirá toda la calle! (*Cesa el ruido del vehículo. Una pausa. Con aire furtivo, DOLORES aparece por la izquierda. Cubre sus galas una larga capa azul. Sobre su máscara, un antifaz bordeado de encajes. LARRA se descubre.*) Sabía que estabas en Madrid.

DOLORES. (*Inquieta.*) Sólo un momento, Mariano. (*Señala levemente a la izquierda.*) Temo que él baje del coche.

LARRA. ¿Quién es?

DOLORES. Un primo de mi esposo.

LARRA *(As he descends, voice off.):* "Take any man (but only if you are a minister of the crown (...) because, otherwise, you'll get nowhere) (...) give him (...) a light varnish of mandate, and watch how his will gradually bends (...) how he laughs upon command: and there you have him, a minister's man". *(A light picks out PEDRO, dressed, but not wearing a mask.)*

LARRA: There's no hope.[57]

PEDRO: Don't give up! *(The writer's voice sounds in the air once again.)*

LARRA *(Voice off.):* "...We have our bags packed and ready to take our place among the first deportees (...) We declare (...) that our place of residence is No.3 (...) Calle Santa Clara (...) where we can be apprehended any morning (...) that both indoors or out we accept anonymous letters (...) challenges, daggers drawn against us, orders of exile, ministers (or rather, their constables, for we are not at home to ministers, although on their day they all apprehend)..."

PEDRO: Don't give up! *(LARRA goes over to the occasional table to contemplate the pistol.)* Go out for a while! Enjoy yourself! It's Carnival. *(Softly, as he draws away.)* You've got to live your life. *(The light goes out as the servant silently exits through one of the gaps at the rear. The writer takes his hat and walks forward. He stops, lost in thought.)*

LARRA: "... There are masks all year round; that selfsame friend who wants to have you believe that that's exactly what he is, the wife who says she loves you, the lover who swears she adores you, are you not their constant butt all life long? So, why rush to buy tickets? Just go out into the street and you'll see the masks for free... The whole world is a mask: Carnival lasts all year round".[58] *(LARRA steps down from his study and walks slowly towards the right. The sound of horses' hooves and the wheels of a carriage are heard. LARRA follows it with his gaze and suddenly rushes forward.)*

LARRA *(Speaking normally.):* Dolores! *(The carriage is passing by. LARRA moves to the left and shouts.)* Dolores, unless you stop the whole street will hear me! *(The sound of wheels stops. Pause. DOLORES enters furtively from the left. Her dress is covered by a long blue cloak. Over her mask, she is wearing another smaller one, bordered with lace frills. LARRA removes his hat.)* I'd heard you were in Madrid.

DOLORES *(Nervously.):* I daren't stop, Mariano. *(She gestures fleetingly towards the left.)* I'm frightened he might get out of the carriage.

LARRA: Who is it?

DOLORES: A cousin of my husband's.

LARRA. ¿Disfrazado de Luis XV?

DOLORES. Ha querido llevarme al baile para que me distraiga un poco.

LARRA. Le conozco aunque lleve antifaz. Es Bertodano: un mequetrefe a quien me presentaron en tu salón.

DOLORES. Es pariente lejano de mi marido.

LARRA. Es tu cortejo.

DOLORES. Son infundios...

LARRA. (*Ríe.*) ¿Niegas la evidencia? Salís juntos a divertiros.

DOLORES. (*Visiblemente nerviosa.*) ¡No hay nada entre él y yo! Te lo juro... por nuestro amor.

LARRA. ¿Amor? Te he enviado varios recados. No has contestado.

DOLORES. Hay un cerco en torno a mí... que no puedo burlar.

LARRA. ¡Vente a vivir conmigo! ¡Ahora! ¡Atrévete y ya no habrá cercos para nosotros!

DOLORES. Déjamelo pensar.

LARRA. (*Le toma las manos.*) ¡Ahora, Dolores!

DOLORES. ¡Por favor! (*Libera sus manos.*) No provoques un incidente.

LARRA. ¿Por qué no? Si tú tienes miedo, yo no temo nada. (*Da un paso hacia el coche invisible. Ella lo retiene.*)

DOLORES. ¡Así no, Mariano!

LARRA. ¿Cómo, entonces?

DOLORES. Hablaremos.

LARRA. Mañana a las siete iré a tu casa.

DOLORES. ¡Imposible! Estoy vigilada.

LARRA. ¡Y qué importa!

DOLORES. Mariano, bien mío, ¿por qué no quieres comprender?

LARRA. Porque estoy desesperado. Porque te necesito, y tú a mí.

DOLORES. (*Tras una mirada de soslayo al coche.*) Iré yo a visitarte.

LARRA. (*Se le ilumina el rostro.*) ¿Mañana?

DOLORES. Sí.

LARRA. ¿Me lo juras?

DOLORES. (*Asiente.*) Por nuestro amor.

LARRA. (*Muy nervioso.*) ¿A qué hora?

DOLORES. Te lo diré en un billete.

LARRA. (*Le toma una mano con suavidad.*) Si vienes, ya no saldrás de allí. (*Le besa la mano.*)

DOLORES. Pudiera ser... Hasta mañana.

LARRA: Disguised as Louis XV?

DOLORES: He wanted to take me to the ball, to take my mind off things.

LARRA: I recognise him, even through his disguise. It's Bertodano: a good-for-nothing I was introduced to in your salon.

DOLORES: He's a distant relative of my husband's.

LARRA: He's courting you.

DOLORES: That's just lies and rumours...

LARRA *(Laughing.):* Can you deny the evidence? You're going out together to enjoy yourselves.

DOLORES *(Visibly nervous.):* There's absolutely nothing between us! I swear it... on our love.

LARRA: Love? I've sent you various messages. You didn't reply once.

DOLORES: They keep me like a prisoner... I can't do anything.

LARRA: Come and live with me! Now! Have courage and there'll be no more prisons for either of us!

DOLORES: I need time to think.

LARRA *(Taking her hands.):* Now, Dolores!

DOLORES: Please! *(Freeing her hands.)* Don't cause a scene.

LARRA: Why not? Even though you're afraid, I'm not. *(He steps towards the invisible coach. She stops him.)*

DOLORES: Not this way, Mariano!

LARRA: How then?

DOLORES: We'll talk.

LARRA: I'll come to your house tomorrow at seven.

DOLORES: Impossible! They watch me all the time.

LARRA: What does it matter?

DOLORES: Mariano, my darling, why do you refuse to understand?

LARRA: Because I've got nothing left. Because I need you, and you need me.

DOLORES *(After glancing quickly in the direction of the coach.):* I'll come to you.

LARRA *(His face lights up.):* Tomorrow?

DOLORES: Yes.

LARRA: You swear it?

DOLORES *(Nodding.):* On our love.

LARRA *(Very nervous.):* What time?

DOLORES: I'll send you a note.

LARRA *(Gently taking her hand.):* If you do come, you'll never leave. *(He kisses her hand.)*

DOLORES: Perhaps... We'll see each other tomorrow.

LARRA. Hasta mañana, Dolores. (*DOLORES sale por la izquierda.* *Vuelve a oírse el ruido del coche que se aleja. LARRA sube al gabinete, donde crece la luz.*) ¡Pedro! ¡Pedro! (*Se quita el sombrero y el frac. El criado reaparece.*)

PEDRO. ¿Señor? (*LARRA le da las dos prendas.*)

LARRA. Mañana quiero todos los braseros bien encendidos y en la chimenea, un buen fuego. ¡Y flores! Al peluquero le avisas para las diez. (*Va al escritorio.*)

PEDRO. Sí, señor.

LARRA. (*Abre un cajón.*) Queda bastante dinero. Le llevaré a mi difunta: ahora menos que nunca debe tener queja de mí. Visitaré también a mi editor. (*Cierra el cajón.*) Volveré a reimprimir artículos: eso no podrán prohibirlo. Y empezaré a torear al marrajo de Díaz. Tampoco él va a vencerme. (*Corre el sillón y se deja caer en él.*) ¡Ah!... Estoy cansado. Y contento.

PEDRO. Más vale así.

LARRA. Había olvidado lo que es la alegría. Me voy a la cama. Dile a María que prepare mañana un chocolate, bollos... (*Se le cierran los ojos.*)

PEDRO. Sí, señor.

LARRA. Esta noche sí dormiré.

PEDRO. Y el señor se fue a su cama. Y soñó.

LARRA. (*Angustiado.*) ¿También el sueño? (*El criado asiente y se retira por el fondo. LARRA se levanta muy alterado. La argentina risa de su niña suena tras la puerta de cristales, donde se enciende el extraño fulgor. LARRA huye hacia el frente, denegando en silencio. La risa infantil vuelve a sonar. El soñador se vuelve despacio hacia el fondo. La negrura estrellada azulea. La puerta se abre y por ella se filtra una luz muy alta, fría y casi cegadora. En el umbral, dos raras figuras. El hijo de PEDRO reaparece tal y como se mostró anteriormente: desnudo, salvo el mugriento calzón que conserva en las caderas, y con su herida sangrante. Cuidadosos, sus brazos sostienen una especie de marioneta repulsiva, ataviada con andrajos de colorines entre los que emergen sus secos miembros de madera. El rostro es atroz, como el de algún ídolo toscamente tallado y ennegrecido. El cabello, de espesa estopa amarillenta, le cuelga por los lados. Petrificado, LARRA observa a la pareja.*)

JUANÍN. (*Al muñeco.*) ¿Cómo se dice? (*La risa de la niña se desgrana en el aire, mientras JUANÍN manipula al muñeco para que avance con rígidos pasos.*)

ADELITA. (*Su voz, en el aire.*) Buenas noches, papá... (*Llegan*

LARRA: Until tomorrow, Dolores. *(DOLORES exits from the left. The noise of the departing carriage is heard once again. LARRA steps up into his study, which is now brightly lit.)* Pedro! Pedro! *(He takes off his hat and evening coat. The servant reappears.)*

PEDRO: Sir? *(LARRA hands him both items.)*

LARRA: Tomorrow, I want the whole house warm, with a blazing fire. And flowers! Tell the hairdresser to come at ten. *(He goes to his writing desk.)*

PEDRO: Yes, sir.

LARRA *(Opening a large box.):* There's enough money left. I'll take some to my dead wife: she has even less cause for complaint now. And I'll go and see my editor. *(He closes the box.)* I'll reprint some articles: they can't prevent me from doing that. And I'll take on Díaz, like a bullfighter with a stiff-necked bull. He won't get the better of me either. *(He runs to the chair and drops into it.)* Ah!... I'm tired. And happy.

PEDRO: All the better.

LARRA: I'd forgotten what happiness was. I'm going to bed. Tell María that for breakfast I'll have chocolate and cake... *(His eyes are closing.)*

PEDRO: Yes, sir.

LARRA: I'll certainly sleep tonight.

PEDRO: And so you went to bed. And then the dream.

LARRA: *(With anguish.):* The dream as well? *(The servant nods and leaves by the back. LARRA stands up in great agitation. The silvery laughter of his young daughter filters through from behind the glass door, where once again the strange glow is discernible. LARRA hurries away towards the front of the stage, shaking his head. The girl's laughter sounds again. The dreamer turns slowly towards the back of the room. The starry blackness gains a bluish hue. The door opens and through it shines, from above, a cold, almost binding light. Two strange figures stand in the doorway. PEDRO's son is as he last appeared: naked save for the grimy undergarment clinging around his waist, his bloodstained wound clearly visible. He is carefully holding a repulsive kind of puppet, dressed in coloured rags, from out of which emerge its crude wooden limbs. The face is repellent, like that of some roughly carved, blackened idol. The hiar, of thick yellowish flax, hangs lankly. Transfixed, LARRA watches them both.)*

JUANÍN *(To the doll.):* What do you say? *(The young girl's laughter bursts in the air as JUANÍN works the doll so that it walks stiffly forwards.)*

ADELITA *(Her voice, in the air.):* Good night, papa... *(They reach

junto a LARRA, quien se mueve levemente para evitar su roce.)
JUANÍN. Buenas noches, papá. *(Suena la galopada de los caballos.)*
LARRA. *(Su voz, en el aire.)* Yo no soy tu padre.
JUANÍN. Los lanceros ya se van. Usted curará.
LARRA. *(Su voz.)* A mí no me han herido. *(JUANÍN ríe. La risa*
de la nena le acompaña.)
JUANÍN. ¡Pa...pá!
ADELITA. *(Su voz, al mismo tiempo.)* ¡Pa...pá!... ¿No me da un
besito? *(LARRA deniega.)* Pues vendrán los lanceros. Déme un besito...
Verá qué sorpresa. *(Asustado, el escritor se inclina despacio para besar al*
espantajo. Risitas cómplices de JUANÍN y ADELITA. LARRA besa la
madera del rostro. Risas muy divertidas de ADELITA y JUANÍN.) Así
se quedará sin sorpresa. Béseme... en la orejita.)
JUANÍN. *(Reprime su risa.)* En la orejita... *(LARRA se inclina de*
nuevo, receloso, y JUANÍN separa los cabellos de la marioneta.
Horrorizado, LARRA se incorpora: en el lugar de las orejas hay dos
agujeros negros y sangrantes. ADELITA y JUANÍN rompen a reír.)
ADELITA. *(Canturrea su voz.)* ¡Le hemos engañado! ¡No hay
orejas! ¡Hay ojeras! ¡No hay orejas! ¡Hay ojeras!
JUANÍN. *(Canturrea.)* ¡Se las comió el tigre!
ADELITA. *(Su voz.)* ¿Las ojeras?
JUANÍN. *(Canturrea.)* ¡Se las comió el gato!
ADELITA. *(Su voz.)* ¿Las orejas?
JUANÍN. ¡Y las ojeras!
ADELITA. *(Su voz, misteriosa.)* ¡Un gatazo verde se comió la oreja
y con su gran lanza me pintó la ojera! ¡Lanzazo va, lanzazo viene y
lanzazo va! *(En un susurro.)* Si papá no me quiere besar, todos los
lanceros me atravesarán.
LARRA. *(Retrocede.)* ¡Basta! *(Vuelve a oírse la galopada.)*
JUANÍN. ¡Los lanceros!
ADELITA. ¡Vamos a buscarlos! *(JUANÍN maneja el muñeco y*
torna con él presuroso a la puerta, por donde sale. La puerta se cierra y
se oscurece. La galopada se acerca. Antes de salir JUANÍN, dos focos
crecieron en el bloque sobre CALATRAVA y DÍAZ. Ambos se han
levantado y miran hacia el durmiente mostrando en sus manos sendas
navajas. Con ellas bajan las escaleras y la luz los sigue. Entre golpeteos
de cascos y relinchos, el ruido de los caballos se detiene muy cerca
CALATRAVA y DÍAZ se sitúan a los dos lados del escritor
Bruscamente, le obligan a volverse de espaldas.)
CALATRAVA. Saque la lengua el pobrecito hablador.

LARRA's side. He moves slightly to avoid their touch.)
JUANÍN: Good night, papa... *(The sound of galloping horses.)*
LARRA *(His voice, in the air.):* I'm not your father.
JUANÍN: The lancers are going. You'll get better.
LARRA *(Voice off.):* It wasn't me they wounded. *(JUANÍN laughs, as does the little girl.)*
JUANÍN: Pa...pa!
ADELITA *(Simultaneously, voice off.):* Pa...pa!... Won't you give me a kiss? *(LARRA shakes his head.)* Then the lancers will come... I've got a surprise for you. *(Frightened, the writer slowly leans forward to kiss the ragged doll. Conspiratorial laughter from JUANÍN and ADELITA. LARRA kisses the wooden face. The laughter intensifies.)* You won't get the surprise that way. Kiss me... on the ear.
JUANÍN *(Stifling his laughter.):* On her little ear. *(LARRA reluctantly bends forward again, and JUANÍN lifts the puppet's hair. LARRA straightens up in horror: instead of ears there are two blackened, bleeding holes. ADELITA and JUANÍN burst into laughter.)*
ADELITA *(Voice off, in singsong tones.):* We fooled him! No ears... just holes! No ears... just blackholes!
JUANÍN *(In a singsong voice.):* The tiger gobbled them up!
ADELITA *(Voice off.):* The holes?
JUANÍN *(In a singsong voice.):* The cat gobbled them up!
ADELITA *(Voice off.):* The ears?
JUANÍN: And the holes!
ADELITA *(Voice off, mysteriously.):* A big green cat gobbled up my ear and painted a black hole with his great big lance! Pushing his lance here, pushing his lance there! *(In a whisper.)* If papa won't kiss me, then the lancers will stick their lances right through me.
LARRA. *(Stepping backwards.):* That's enough! *(The sound of galloping hooves is heard once again.)*
JUANÍN: The lancers!
ADELITA: Let's go and meet them! *(JUANÍN manoeuvres the doll to hurry back out with it. The door closes and the glow subsides. The sound of galloping comes closer. Before JUANÍN leaves, two spots have picked out CALATRAVA and DÍAZ on their rostrum. They have got to their feet and now look over at the sleeping writer, both of them holding knives. They walk with them down the stairs, followed by the light. Amidst the clattering of hooves and whinnying, the horses stop close by. CALATRAVA and DÍAZ position themselves on either side of the writer. They roughly force him to turn round.)*
COLATRAVA: Hold out your tongue, poor babbler.

LARRA al sufrir las mutilaciones.)

DÍAZ. Ahora podrás hablar y escribir según lo mandado. (*LARRA se encoge bajo el dolor y toma su brazo mutilado con el otro. El ministro y el censor se encaminan a los huecos del fondo, llevando con solemnidad sus trofeos. El escritor gime. Ellos se vuelven y le sisean, ordenándole silencio. Y desaparecen. La luz normal se reinstala y el fondo estrellado palidece. Como si despertara, LARRA se estira. PEDRO entra por la puerta del fondo con una bandeja y la levita de su señor.*)

PEDRO. Buenos días, señor. ¿Ha descansado bien?

LARRA. No.

PEDRO. ¿De levita, señor?

LARRA. Sí. (*PEDRO deja la bandeja sobre el bufete y le pone la levita. Después recoge la bandeja y se la tiende.*)

PEDRO. Han traído este billete, señor. (*LARRA toma la esquela, se vuelve hacia el frente y la abre.*)

LARRA. (*Resplandeciente.*) ¡Pedro, todo dispuesto para las siete y media!

PEDRO. Bien, señor. (*Al escritor se le nubla otra vez el semblante y se guarda el papel.*)

LARRA. ¡Para qué seguir! Eso ha sucedido esta misma mañana.

PEDRO. Así es. La mañana del 13 de febrero de 1837.

LARRA. (*Va hacia la pistola.*) Bórrate.

PEDRO. Entonces, usa la pistola. La tienes en la mano desde que la cogiste. (*El suicida se mira las manos y mira, desvalido, al criado.*) Bien. Visitaste a tu editor y a tu difunta. Después, a Mesonero. Parecías alegre pero estabas tenso como un arco. (*Se retira por el hueco derecho. Mientras hablaba, MESONERO ha entrado por el hueco izquierdo, en bata, y aguarda risueño. La luz se dora. MESONERO viene enmascarado. Se miran. MESONERO avanza.*)

LARRA. Don Ramón, vengo a proponerle algo insólito. Tengo la idea completa de un drama que, a mi juicio, podría insuflar sangre joven en nuestro depauperado teatro.

MESONERO. ¡Mi felicitación anticipada! ¿Cuál es su asunto?

LARRA. Quevedo. Con su grandeza de poeta y con algunas de sus miserias.

MESONERO. Casi un héroe trágico.

LARRA. (*Asiente.*) Un héroe vencido al fin por la tiranía.

MESONERO. Ninguna pluma mejor que la suya para ese proyecto.

DÍAZ: Stretch out your arm, Andrés Notevenso. *(LARRA obeys. With clean precision, CALATRAVA catches his tongue and slices it off. DÍAZ cuts off his right hand. A prolonged, muted groan from LARRA as he suffers these mutilations.)*

DÍAZ: Now you can babble and write as you're told. *(LARRA shrinks beneath the pain and nurses his injured arm with the other. The minister and censor walk towards the gaps at the rear, solemnly carrying their trophies. The writer moans. They turn round and hiss at him to be silent. Then they disappear. The light returns to normality and the starry background pales. LARRA stretches as though he had just woken up. PEDRO comes in through the door at the back, carrying a tray and his master's frock coat.)*

PEDRO: Good morning, sir. Did you sleep well?

LARRA: No.

PEDRO: Your frock coat, sir?

LARRA: Yes. *(PEDRO sets the tray down on the bureau and helps him on with the coat. Then he takes the tray and offers it to him.)*

PEDRO: This note came for you, sir. *(LARRA takes the envelope, turns to face the front and opens it.)*

LARRA *(Delightedly.):* Pedro, have everything ready for half past seven!

PEDRO: Yes, sir. *(The writer's face clouds over once more and he puts the letter away.)*

LARRA: What's the point in going on? This happened just this morning.

PEDRO: That's right. The morning of the 13th of February, 1837.

LARRA *(Going towards the pistol.):* Just disappear.

PEDRO: Then use the gun. You've been holding it ever since you picked it up. *(The suicide looks at his hands and then, dejectedly, at his servant.)* All right. You went to see your editor and your dead wife. Then, Mesonero. You seemed happy, but you were tense, like an overstrung bow. *(He goes out through the right-hand gap. While he is speaking, MESONERO has appeared through a gap on the right-hand side. He is wearing a dressing gown, and stands waiting cheerfully. The light is golden. MESONERO, masked, walks forward.)*

LARRA: Don Ramón, I've come with a novel proposition. I've worked out a play which, I believe, could pump new blood into our impoverished theatre.

MESONERO: I congratulate you in advance. What's it about?

LARRA: Quevedo.[59] In all his grandeur as a poet, and some of his suffering as well.

MESONERO. Casi un héroe trágico.

LARRA. (*Asiente.*) Un héroe vencido al fin por la tiranía.

MESONERO. Ninguna pluma mejor que la suya para ese proyecto.

LARRA. Ninguna no, don Ramón. La tarea es tan difícil... que necesitaría dos plumas.

MESONERO. ¿Me está proponiendo una colaboración?

LARRA. Sí. Y su nombre iría el primero.

MESONERO. (*Pasea.*) El tema es muy suyo, no hay duda. Pero no mío... Discúlpeme... Y muchas gracias.

LARRA. Don Ramón...

MESONERO. ¡Querido Fígaro! Ninguno de los dos es un niño. Usted no solicitaría colaboración de nadie sin razones poderosas...

LARRA. No iba a ocultárselas. He venido a hablarle sinceramente del temor que me mueve a suplicar su ayuda.

MESONERO. ¿Temor?

LARRA. Desde la subida al poder de Calatrava... apenas me dejan publicar.

MESONERO. Eso es transitorio. No podrán con usted.

LARRA. Sé lo que digo. Clemente Díaz es ahora censor y me ha hablado muy claro. Es como si me hubiesen cortado la mano y la lengua. Por eso recurro a su amparo. Usted es muy respetado. Si colaboramos, aprobarán el drama. Si lo firmo yo solo, no. Tiéndame su mano de amigo.

MESONERO. Me duele decirle que no... Pero yo no sabría colaborar en un «Quevedo» como el que usted quiere. Y créame que usted tampoco debería hacerlo... Acepte de nuevo mi más desinteresado consejo: haga costumbrismo, como yo.

LARRA. (*Lo observa fríamente por un instante.*) No.

MESONERO. ¡Le destruirán!

LARRA. Ya me han destruido, pero a usted lo destruyeron mucho antes. Por eso quiere que me transforme en otro manso cordero. Si no hay rebeldes, usted está justificado.

MESONERO. (*Seco.*) Larra, le ruego...

LARRA. No me señale la puerta. Me voy en seguida. Otra persona me dará su apoyo, y me basta con ella para seguir luchando. Yo no me dejaré dominar por la obsesión de aumentar mis comodidades aunque sea

MESONERO: Virtually a tragic hero.

LARRA *(Nodding.):* A hero finally conquered by tyranny.

MESONERO: I can think of no pen more capable than yours of writing such a work.

LARRA: Not one, no, don Ramón.   The task is such a daunting one... that it needs two pens.

MESONERO: Are you suggesting we collaborate?

LARRA: Yes. With your name given precedence.

MESONERO *(Pacing to and fro.):* The subject is an excellent choice for you, of that there can be no doubt. But it is not for me. I'm sorry... Thank you anyway.

LARRA: Don Ramón...

MESONERO: My dear Figaro! Let us not be naive. You would not wish to work with anyone unless you had very powerful reasons for doing so...

LARRA: I had no intention of hiding them from you. I have come here to talk to you openly of the fear that brings me to ask you for help.

MESONERO: Fear?

LARRA: Since Calatrava has taken power... I am barely permitted to publish.

MESONERO: That won't last. They won't get the better of you.

LARRA: I say this with good reason. Clemente Díaz has become a censor and he has made himself perfectly clear. It's as though they'd cut off my hand and ripped out my tongue. That's why I've come to you to shield me. You're well respected. If we collaborate, they'll approve the play. But if my signature alone appears on it, they won't. Give me your hand as a friend.

MESONERO: I'm sorry to say that I can't... I wouldn't be able to work on the type of "Quevedo" you envisage. And let me tell you that you shouldn't countenance it either... Please accept my most disinterested piece of advice: describe the traditional life and customs of our country, as I do.

LARRA *(Staring at him coldly for a moment.):* No.

MESONERO: They'll destroy you!

LARRA: They've destroyed me already, but they got you a long time ago. That's why you want me to become just another meek little lamb like you. If no one rebels, then you feel justified.

MESONERO *(Drily.):* Larra, I beg you...

LARRA: There's no need to show me out. I'm going. Somebody else will give me their support, and that will be enough to give me the strength to fight on. And I won't allow myself to become obsessed with

a costa de la miseria ajena.

MESONERO. ¿De qué habla?

LARRA. De seguros contra quintas, por ejemplo.

MESONERO. (*Se inmuta y reacciona.*) Ha oído algo. Bien. Pero no lo entiende. Sería un negocio caritativo: una ayuda para muchos desdichados labriegos.

LARRA. Negocio y caritativo. Es fantástico. Adiós, Mesonero. (*Se levanta.*) Mi vida no será como la suya.

MESONERO. ¿Más corta? (*Se despoja de su máscara.*)

LARRA. (*Ríe.*) ¡Pienso vivir muchos años!

MESONERO. Usted ha escrito: «Mil veces desdichado (...) quien no viendo aquí abajo sino caos y mentira, agotó en su corazón la fuente de la esperanza.» Y otras cosas parecidas que... nos preocupan a sus amigos.

LARRA. Las circunstancias han variado desde ayer. Adiós.

MESONERO. Adiós. Cuídese. (*Se va, lento, por el hueco izquierdo. Mientras sale, entra PEDRO por el derecho. En el gabinete aumenta la luz.*)

LARRA. Y al fin aquí. Contigo.

PEDRO. No. El criado está abajo y despide a las señoras. Estás contigo mismo. Por poco tiempo. Hasta que apures el recuerdo. (*Se acerca a la puerta del fondo y la abre. Muy conmovido, LARRA se yergue.*) Las señoras han llegado.

LARRA. (*Sorprendido.*) ¿Las señoras? Sólo esperaba a una.

PEDRO. Vienen dos.

LARRA. (*Para sí.*) ¿Alguna amiga? (*Va a la puerta, aparta a PEDRO y sale. Se le sigue divisando de perfil.*) ¿A qué ha venido usted?

M. MANUELA. (*Su voz.*) Caballero, Dolores no podía verle sin una compañía respetable.

DOLORES. (*Su voz.*) Mariano, es mi cuñada María Manuela..

LARRA. (*Su voz. Seco.*) Ya lo sé. ¡Debiste venir sola!

M. MANUELA. ¡Caballero, usted me ofende!

LARRA. ¡Yo soy el ofendido! Pasa, Dolores. (*Se aparta. Entra DOLORES, enmascarada y con muy recatado atavío. LARRA se interpone en la puerta.*) ¡Usted no, señora mía!

M. MANUELA. (*Su voz.*) ¡Yo debo estar presente!

LARRA. ¡Usted no entra!

my own comforts at the expense of others.

MESONERO: What are you talking about?

LARRA: Insurance against conscription, for example.

MESONERO *(His expression changes before he has time to reassert control over himself.):* You've heard something. Very well. But you don't understand. We;re talking about a charitable enterprise: bringing help to many workers sunk in misery.

LARRA: Enterprising and charitable. Unbelievable. Goodbye, Mesonero. *(He stands up.)* My life won't be like yours.

MESONERO: Shorter? *(He removes his mask.)*

LARRA: *(Laughing.):* I intend to live a good few years yet!

MESONERO: You once wrote "A thousand times unhappy the man (...) who seeing down here only chaos and deceit, has exhausted the fountain of hope in his heart". And other similar things which... have worried those of us who are your friends.

LARRA: Circumstances have changed since yesterday. Goodbye.

MESONERO: Goodbye. Take care. *(He slowly leaves through the left-hand gap. As he does so, PEDRO enters from the right. The light in the study grows.)*

LARRA: And so this is the end. Here. With you.

PEDRO: No. Your servant is downstairs seeing the ladies out. You're alone with yourself. For just a short time. Until you've drained the final memory. *(He goes to open the door at the back of the room. Deeply moved, LARRA stands erect.)* The ladies have arrived.

LARRA *(Surprised.):* Ladies? I was expecting only one.

PEDRO: There are two of them.

LARRA *(To himself.):* A friend perhaps? *(He goes to the door, moves PEDRO aside and goes out. His silhouette is still visible.)* What are you doing here?

M.MANUELA *(Voice off.):* Sir, Dolores could not visit you unless respectably accompanied.

DOLORES *(Voice off.):* Mariano, this is my sister-in-law María Manuela...

LARRA *(Voice off. Abrupt.):* I know who she is. You should have come alone.

M.MANUELA *(Voice off.):* Sir, I find your attitude offensive!

LARRA: I am the one who has been offended. Come inside, Dolores. *(He moves aside. DOLORES comes in, masked and very discreetly dressed. LARRA stands in the doorway.)* Not you, madam.

M.MANUELA *(Voice off.):* I insist on being present.

LARRA: You will remain outside.

DOLORES. ¡Por favor, María Manuela! Déjanos solos. Te aseguro que no sucederá nada impropio. (*LARRA la mira, estupefacto.*) Espérame ahí, te lo ruego.

M. MANUELA. (*Su voz.*) Confío en ti. Si me necesitas, me llamas. (*Con un cabezazo, LARRA le indica a PEDRO que se retire. El criado sale por la puerta y la cierra. DOLORES se adelanta al primer término.*)

LARRA. (*La observa con encendidos ojos.*) No me digas nada. Vienes a romper conmigo.

DOLORES. Mariano, te ruego que comprendas...

LARRA. (*Va hacia ella.*) Lo comprendo muy bien. Yo no estaba tu lado y has sido débil. La parentela de tu marido te habrá ido ahormando día tras día.

DOLORES. Te engañas. Han sido muy considerados.

LARRA. Sin duda. Hasta te dejan concurrir a saraos con Bertodano. Saben que tu galán se aviene a gozar de tus favores sin escándalo.

DOLORES. Te repito que nada le he concedido a Bertodano.

LARRA. (*Después de un momento.*) Eso quiero creer... todavía. (*Se acerca más.*) Como quisiera creer que aún me amas.

DOLORES. Mariano, ayúdame...

LARRA. ¿Me amas?

DOLORES. (*Vacila. Con la voz velada y sin mirar a su amante.*) Sabes que sí.

LARRA. ¡Dolores! (*La abraza y besa con ardor. Ella le responde con tibieza. Se deshace el abrazo y quedan cogidos de las manos.*) ¡No hay más que hablar! Ahora abrimos esa puerta y le dices a tu cuñada... (*Ella se turba.*) Pero no. Te ahorraré ese embarazo. Yo le diré en tu nombre que te quedas para siempre. (*Se dirige a la puerta.*)

DOLORES. ¡No, Mariano!

LARRA. (*Con una penetrante mirada.*) ¿Prefieres hacerlo tú?

DOLORES. Antes... hemos de hablar. (*LARRA frunce las cejas. Se acerca ella.*) ¿No me ofreces asiento?

LARRA. (*Le indica fríamente una silla.*) Por favor. (*Se sienta ella. Él se sienta a su lado.*) Habla. ¿Es que dudas de mí?

DOLORES. Dudo... de mí misma.

LARRA. Sigue.

DOLORES. Mi pobre Mariano... Nos hemos equivocado. (*Él va a hablar.*) Yo no soy la mujer que tú sueñas. Creí serlo... y me engañaba.

DOLORES: Please, María Manuela! Leave us together. You have my assurance that nothing improper will occur. *(LARRA looks at her in astonishment.)* Wait for me here, if you don't mind.

M.MANUELA *(Voice off.):* You have my complete trust. If you need me, you have only to call. *(LARRA nods to PEDRO to indicate that he may retire. He leaves through the door, closing it behind him. DOLORES moves forward to the front of the stage.)*

LARRA *(Watching her with burning eyes.):* There's no need to say anything. You've come to finish it.

DOLORES: Mariano, please try to understand...

LARRA *(Going towards her.):* I understand very well. I wasn't at your side and you have been weak. Your husband's tribe will have been working on you day in and day out.

DOLORES: You're wrong. They've been very kind.

LARRA: I don't doubt it. They even allow you to sport in public with Bertodano. They know that your gallant is prepared to enjoy your favours without causing a scandal.

DOLORES: I insist that I have shown no favour whatsoever to Bertodano.

LARRA *(Pausing.):* I want to believe that... still. *(He draws closer to her.)* Just as I would like to believe that you love me... still.

DOLORES: Mariano, help me...

LARRA: Do you love me?

DOLORES *(She hesitates. In muted tones, and without looking at her lover.):* You know I do.

LARRA: Dolores! *(He embraces and kisses her passionately. Her response is lukewarm. They break off their embrace but remain holding hands.)* There's nothing more to say. We'll open that door now and you can tell your sister-in-law... *(She looks upset.)* No, no. I'll spare you that embarrassment. I'll tell her on your behalf that you will be staying here for good. *(He goes towards the door.)*

DOLORES: Mariano, no!

LARRA *(Looking at her sharply.):* Would you prefer to do it?

DOLORES: We must talk first. *(LARRA frowns. She goes over to him.)* May I sit down?

LARRA: *(He coldly points to a chair.):* Please do. *(She sits down. He sits beside her.)* Tell me now. Do you have any doubts about me?

DOLORES: I have doubts... about myself.

LARRA: Go on.

DOLORES: My poor Mariano... We've made a mistake. *(He makes to speak.)* I'm not the woman of your dreams. Oh, I thought I was... but I

Te pido perdón. Hemos pecado...

LARRA. ¿Pecado?

DOLORES. Contra mi marido y contra tu esposa.

LARRA. Sí. ¡Pero mientras les mentíamos! No después.

DOLORES. (*Después de un momento.*) José María me ha escrito que me perdona... si me reúno con él en Manila. (*Abre su bolso y busca algo.*)

LARRA. (*Amargo.*) No necesito leer su carta.

DOLORES. (*Saca un paquetito de cartas atadas con una cinta azul.*) No es su carta. Son las tuyas... Te las devuelvo. (*Deposita el paquetito sobre el velador. LARRA se ha levantado.*)

LARRA. (*Grita.*) ¡No! (*Ella se levanta.*) ¡No!

DOLORES. ¡Mariano!

LARRA. (*Muy fuerte.*) ¡Te estás mintiendo a ti misma! ¡Tú no puedes hablar así! ¡Ah, el daño era mayor de lo que pensaba! ¡Pero yo te salvaré! (*Una sombra femenina golpea en los cristales de la puerta.*)

M. MANUELA. (*Su voz.*) ¡Caballero! ¡Exijo que me deje entrar!

DOLORES. (*Eleva la voz.*) ¡No es nada, María Manuela! ¡En seguida salgo!

LARRA. ¡Tú no te vas!

DOLORES. ¡Devuélveme mis cartas! (*Él la mira, deshecho.*) ¿Qué esperas? (*LARRA se dirige a su escritorio, abre un cajón, saca un paquetito atado con cinta rosa, vuelve al velador y deposita las cartas junto al otro paquetito.*)

LARRA. (*Con aparente calma.*) Aquí las tienes. Ahora, escúchame. (*Pasea.*) Si sales por esa puerta, ya nunca más serás Dolores. Serás la señora de Cambronero: una mentira. Reirás, te divertirás..., olvidarás. Pero estarás muerta. Muerta entre muertos.

DOLORES. ¿Qué dices?

LARRA. Todos en el cementerio de España. Mascaritas que ríen y parlotean, peroran en las Cortes, hacen sus negociejos, prohíben libros, asisten a la ópera..., mientras se van pudriendo. Sal por esa puerta y no vuelvas. (*Se acerca y baja la voz.*) Pero, si quieres vivir..., no salgas. Yo soy la vida.

DOLORES. ¿Tu querida a la luz del día, para que nadie me salude ni me reciba? ¿Es ésa la vida?

LARRA. ¿Qué te importa ese mundo de cadáveres?

DOLORES. ¡Deja de soñar! (*Se desprende en un arranque de la careta: bajo la endrina negrura de sus cabellos aparece el rostro de PEPITA WETORET.*) Los que tú llamas cadáveres son los que están

as simply fooling myself. I'm sorry. We've sinned.

LARRA: Sinned?

DOLORES: Against my husband and against your wife.

LARRA: Yes. But only while we were lying to them! Not afterwards.

DOLORES *(After a moment.):* José María has written to tell me he forgives me... if I go to him in Manila. *(She opens her bag and searches for something.)*

LARRA *(Bitterly.):* I have no desire to read his letter.

DOLORES *(She pulls out a small bundle of letters bound with a blue ribbon.)* This isn't his letter. They're yours... I'm returning them to you. *She leaves the bundle on the occasional table. LARRA has stood up.)*

LARRA *(Shouting.):* No! *(She stands up.)* No!

DOLORES: Mariano!

LARRA *(Very forcefully.):* You're lying to yourself! It's not like you to be speaking like this. The damage must have been greater than I thought. But I'll help you. *(A woman's silhouette raps on the glass door.)*

M. MANUELA *(Voice off.):* Sir! I demand to be let in!

DOLORES *(Raising her voice.):* It's nothing, María Manuela. I'll be out directly.

LARRA: You won't go anywhere.

DOLORES: Give me my letters back! *(He looks at her in despair.)* What are you waiting for? *(LARRA goes to the bureau, opens a drawer, takes out a small bundle bound with a pink ribbon, returns to the table and puts the letters down beside the other bundle.)*

LARRA *(With apparent calm.):* Here they are. Now, listen to me. *He paces to and fro.)* If you go through that door, you can never be Dolores again. You'll be Cambronero's wife: a lie. Oh, you'll laugh, you'll enjoy yourself..., you'll forget. But you'll be dead. Dead among the dead.

DOLORES: What do you mean?

LARRA: All in the cemetery of Spain. Little masks that titter and chatter, that make speeches in Parliament, make their sordid little business deals, ban books, go to the opera..., and all the while slowly rot. Go through that door and don't come back. *(He draws close to her and lowers his voice.)* But, if you want to live..., then stay. I'm life.

DOLORES: Your mistress dragged out into the open... so that no decent person would receive me in their home, or even acknowledge me. Is that what you call life?

LARRA: Why concern yourself with a world of corpses?

DOLORES: Stop dreaming! *(She snatches off her mask: under the silky blackness of her hair appears the face of PEPITA WETORET.)* The people you call corpses are the ones who are really alive. It's you who's

vivos. ¡El muerto eres tú, y siempre lo has sido! (*Recoge sus cartas y la* *guarda en el bolso.*) Volveré con mi marido y te olvidaré. ¡En una sociedad mentirosa, sí! La vida no es otra cosa ni puede serlo. ¡Y yo tengo muchas ganas de vivir! Adiós. (*Se encamina a la puerta.*)

LARRA. (*Ríe débilmente.*) Tonto de mí. ¿Cómo pude creer que tú no llevabas máscara? (*Ella se detiene y lo contempla sorprendida.*) Al fin te veo tal y como eres. Y eres... Pepita. Sois la misma.

DOLORES. ¿Estás loco?

LARRA. Quizá es pronto. Nosotros no podemos ser hombres y mujeres verdaderos. Acaso mañana los haya. (*Toma el paquetito de sus* *cartas.*) Éstas son las cartas de un necio. Mira qué hago con ellas. (*Va a* *la chimenea y las arroja al fuego.*) ¿Quemo las tuyas?

DOLORES. Prefiero llevármelas.

LARRA. Entonces puedes irte. Ya no te amo.

DOLORES. No vas a persuadirme con palabras hábiles...

LARRA. (*Muy tranquilo.*) Te he dicho la verdad. Te he visto de pronto desenmascarada y mi pasión se ha apagado.

DOLORES. ¡Deja de fingir!

LARRA. ¿Crees que te estoy haciendo una escena de teatro? No. Esto no es un drama romántico. (*Corta pausa.*) Si un día te dicen que Larra se quitó la vida, no pienses que lo hizo por amor, sino porque.. todo es irremediable. Adiós, Pepita.

DOLORES. ¿Pepita?

LARRA. O Dolores, qué más da. Te deseo otro amante que te haga feliz en las Filipinas. En cuanto a mí, nunca he estado más lúcido: la puerta está abierta.

DOLORES. (*Mira a la puerta.*) Está cerrada.

LARRA. Cierto. (*Sonríe.*) Esa puerta está cerrada. (*Va al bufete* *y llama con una campanilla.*)

DOLORES. (*Vagamente inquieta, da un paso hacia él.*) Mariano...

LARRA. ¡Por favor! Te digo que esto no es un drama romántico. Es otra cosa que tú no entiendes. Sobra cualquier despedida sentimental. (*La sombra de PEDRO, tras la puerta. Golpecitos en el cristal. Entra el* *criado.*) Acompaña hasta el portal a las señoras.

DOLORES. (*Desconcertada.*) Adiós, Mariano. (*Se decide y sale.* *PEDRO se inclina, sale y cierra. Los cristales se oscurecen. La luz va* *menguando. Los luceros resplandecen en el cielo negrísimo. LARRA se* *acerca al tremor del fondo y se contempla.*)

ead, and you always have been! *(She picks up her letters and puts them nto her bag.)* I'll go back to my husband and I'll forget you. A world of lies, yes! That's all life is, all it can be. And I so much want to live! Goodbye. *(She walks towards the door.)*

LARRA *(He laughs weakly.):* I've been a fool. How could I ever have believed that you weren't wearing a mask? *(She stops and looks at him in surprise.)* At last I can see you as you really are. You're... Pepita. You're one and the same.

DOLORES: You've taken leave of your senses!

LARRA: Perhaps it's still too soon. We can't be real men and women. Not yet. Maybe one day... *(He lifts the small bundle of letters.)* These are the letters of a fool. And this is what I think of them. *(He goes to the fireplace and throws them into the fire.)* Shall I burn yours?

DOLORES: I would rather take them with me.

LARRA: Then you can go. I have no love left for you.

DOLORES: You needn't think you can cajole me with clever words...

LARRA *(Very calmly.):* I've told you the truth. Your mask has dropped and quite suddenly all passion has gone.

DOLORES: Don't pretend!

LARRA: You think I'm just playing out some role? No. This is no scene from some romantic drama. *(Short pause.)* And if some day you hear that Larra killed himself, don't think he did it for love, but because... everything is beyond hope. Goodbye, Pepita.

DOLORES: Pepita?

LARRA: Or Dolores, there's no difference. I hope you find another lover to keep you happy in the Philipines. But as far as I'm concerned, I've never seen things so clearly: the door is open.

DOLORES *(Looking towards the door.):* It's closed.

LARRA: Indeed. *(He smiles.).* That door is closed. *(He goes to his desk and rings the small bell.)*

DOLORES *(Vaguely uneasy, she takes a step towards him.):* Mariano...

LARRA: Please. I've told you already... this is no romantic drama. It's something else, far beyond your understanding. Any touching little farewell would be superfluous. *(PEDRO's silhouette appears behind the door. He knocks gently and enters.)* Show the ladies to the door.

DOLORES *(Disconcerted.):* Goodbye, Mariano. *(She makes up her mind and leaves. PEDRO bows, goes out and closes the door. The glass panels grow dark. The light gradually fades. The stars glisten in the pitch-black sky. LARRA goes to the mirror at the back and contemplates himself.)*[60]

LARRA. Y éste..., ¿quién es? No lo sé. Ahora comprendo que también es una máscara. Dentro de un minuto la arrancaré... y moriré sin conocer el rostro que esconde..., si es que hay algún rostro. Quizá no ha ninguno. Quizá sólo hay máscaras. (*Permanece de espaldas. El bloque derecho se ilumina. CALATRAVA y DÍAZ están de pie en sus sitios mirando al suicida. El bloque izquierdo se ilumina también. En él, de pie, el GENERAL CABRERA y el BRIGADIER NOGUERAS. Por ambos laterales del primer término aparecen MESONERO, BRETÓN DE LOS HERREROS, ANDRÉS BORREGO, el PADRE FROILÁN, DON HOMOBONO. Todos, menos los dos militares, con la cabeza descubierta. Las caras, ocultas por sus caretas. Sin volverse, LARRA nota su espectral presencia, aún más afantasmada en las borrosas imágenes que acaso ve en el espejo. Sigilosos, van bajando por las escaleras los que están en los bloques. Los demás suben al gabinete y se sitúan a ambos lados. La luz general es extraña, desigual y vagarosa, como acaso lo sea en algún otro planeta.*) Ya no os necesito.

CALATRAVA. Sí, mientras nos piensas.

ADELITA. (*Su voz, acompañada del resplandor tras los cristales.* ¡Papá!... ¡Buenas noches! (*LARRA se estremece y mira a la puerta, que se ha vuelto a oscurecer. Con careta, DOLORES entra por el hueco izquierdo. LARRA la mira y se vuelve hacia el frente. BORREGO se acerca al velador, toma la pistola y se la tiende.*)

LARRA. ¿También Andrés Borrego? Claro. Y Carnerero. Cuando me regaló las pistolas, sabía lo que hacía. Gracias. (*Se acerca y empuña la pistola. BORREGO-CARNERERO se retira a sus espaldas. DON HOMOBONO se acerca y le levanta un poco la mano.*)

LARRA. (*Sin mirarlo.*) Adiós, mascaritas. (*DON HOMOBONO se reúne con BORREGO-CARNERERO. El PADRE FROILÁN se acerca entretanto y levanta un poco más la mano armada. Después se aleja hacia el fondo, mientras BRETÓN se acerca y eleva un poco más la mano. Casi al tiempo, se adelanta CABRERA y la levanta otro poco; el BRIGADIER NOGUERAS agarra el brazo entero del escritor y lo sube algo más. El ritmo gana rapidez; todos, después de su contribución al suicidio, se apostan en el fondo. Tras NOGUERAS le toca el turno a CALATRAVA, quien conduce la mano armada hasta cerca de la sien.*) ¿Calatrava?... O Mendizábal, o Istúriz, o Martínez de la Rosa, o Cea Bermúdez... O Calomarde. Tanto da. Yo os desenmascaré a todos. Pero pronto os

LARRA: And this face... who does it belong to? I don't know. But I do know that it's a mask as well. And in a short minute's time I'll tear it off... and I'll die without ever knowing the face hidden behind..., if there is a face. Perhaps there's nothing. Nothing but masks. *(He remains standing back to the audience. The right-hand rostrum lights up. CALATRAVA and DÍAZ are standing in their places, watching the man about to take his life. The left-hand rostrum is lit as well. Standing on it are GENERAL CABRERA and BRIGADIER NOGUERAS. From both sides downstage appear MESONERO, BRETÓN DE LOS HERREROS, ANDRÉS BORREGO, FATHER FROILÁN, DON HOMOBONO. With the exception of the two soldiers, they are all bare-headed, their faces hidden behind masks. Without turning round, LARRA becomes aware of their eerie presence, made even more ghostly by the shadowy forms he perhaps sees reflected in the mirror. Those on the rostra stealthily descend the stairs. The others move up into the study and gather on both sides. The general lighting has a strange quality, unequal and diffuse, as it might well be on some other planet.)* I don't need any of you any more.

CALATRAVA: You do. For as long as you keep us in your thoughts.

ADELITA *(Voice off. As she speaks light glows behind the glass panels.):* Papa! Good night! *(LARRA shudders and looks towards the door, which has fallen into darkness again. Wearing her mask, DOLORES enters through the left-hand gap. LARRA looks at her and turns towards the front. BORREGO goes to the dresser, takes the pistol and offers it to him.)*

LARRA: Andrés Borrego as well? Of course. And Carnerero. When he gave me those pistols he know exactly what he was doing. Thank you. *(He walks over to take the pistol. BORREGO-CARNERERO withdraws behind him. DON HOMOBONO approaches and raises LARRA's hand slightly.)*

LARRA *(Without looking at him.):* Goodbye, all of you, with your shoddy little masks. *(DON HOMBONO rejoins BORREGO-CARNERERO. Meanwhile, FATHER FROILÁN draws nearer and raises LARRA's armed hand slightly higher. Then, as he moves away towards the back of the room, BRETÓN approaches and lifts the hand even more. CABRERA steps forward almost at the same time to raise it further. BRIGADIER NOGUERAS takes LARRA's whole arm and forces it upwards. The rhythm intensifies; each one, after his contribution to the suicide, stations himself at the back. After NOGUERAS it is the turn of CALATRAVA, who draws LARRA's armed hand towards his forehead.)* Calatrava? Or is it Mendizábal, or Istúriz or Martínez de la Rosa, or Cea Bermúdez... Or Calomarde. It makes no difference. I unmasked you all.

disfrazáis de nuevo... Sois tenaces. (*PEPITA-DOLORES se acerca y aproxima un poco más el arma a la cabeza. Inmediatamente actúa MESONERO, que ya aguardaba. Muy turbado y mirando hacia otra parte, mueve presuroso la mano de LARRA y escapa. CLEMENTE DÍAZ, ya junto a él, empuja enérgicamente la mano odiada hasta que la pistola se sitúa muy cerca del cráneo.*)

DÍAZ. (*Al tiempo que lo hace.*) ¡Dispara! (*Va hacia el fondo. Todos espían a LARRA. La sombra invadió la escena; un poderoso foco alumbra al joven de 27 años que va a morir. En su cara, los ojos dilatados anuncian la inminente decisión. Así permanece un instante, hasta que cierra los ojos y oprime bruscamente la pistola contra la sien. Al disparar nada se oye, pero la escena entera se sume de pronto en absoluta oscuridad. Momentos después se ilumina despacio la figura de PEDRO, erguido en la parte derecha de la escena. Las estrellas reaparecen en el fondo. PEDRO es ahora un anciano de más de 75 años, con todo el cabello blanco. Sus ropas son modestas.*)

PEDRO. Era un señorín... Yo vi que su cara se volvía blanca al decirle que ellos no iban a la guerra... A veces pienso si no lo maté yo. Pero yo... le quería bien... Cualquiera sabe lo que pasaría por su cabeza en aquellos minutos. (*Suspira.*) Luisín creyó que había heredado aquel talentazo. Baldomerita nos ha salido prestamista. Y Adelita, la que le encontró con aquel agujero negro en la cabeza, la nena que decía: Papá... Listísima que es, sí, señor. Cuarenta años tendrá ya y el rey Amadeo la ha hecho su querida. Y los tres más muertos... que mi pobre rapaz. Barrunto yo que aquel hombrín se dio cuenta de que no podría salvar de nada a sus hijos... y que eso también le amargó. No acertó a aprender lo que yo ya me tenía bien sabido desde antes de conocerlo: que es menester un aguante inagotable. Murió por impaciente. (*Muy despacio, le abandona la luz mientras habla. Otro foco empezó a iluminar, en el gabinete, la erguida e inmóvil figura de LARRA, con la pistola en la diestra y los ojos fijos en el vacío. El criado sigue hablando y el escritor empieza a elevar la mano armada. PEDRO se lleva los puños al pecho.*) Pero nosotros siempre hemos sido muchos, y ahora lo empezamos a comprender. (*Se pasa la mano por la frente.*) Es curioso. Tantos disparos y cañonazos que he oído en mi vida, apenas los recuerdo. Y aquella detonación que casi no oí, no se me borra... (*Se enardece.*) ¡Y se tiene que oír, y oír, aunque pasen los años! (*Pausa.*) ¡Como un trueno... que nos despierte! (*La luz le abandona del todo. La pistola está, de nuevo, muy cerca de la sien del suicida, que semeja una pálida estatua.*

But you soon cover up again... You all cling on so greedily. *(PEPITA-DOLORES approaches and draws the pistol closer to LARRA's head. MESONERO, who has been waiting, immediately makes his move. Clearly disturbed and looking away, he hurriedly shifts LARRA's arm and leaves. CLEMENTE DÍAZ, close behind him, forcefully pushes the hand of his hated rival until the pistol is right beside the skull.)*

DÍAZ *(As he does so.)*: Shoot! *(He goes to the back. They all watch LARRA intently. Shadow has invaded the scene; a powerful single light illuminates the young man who is about to die. His dilated eyes reveal that his decision is imminent. He stands like this for an instant, then closes his eyes and brusquely presses the gun to his forehead. When he pulls the trigger no sound is heard, but the whole scene is suddenly plunged into absolute darkness. Shortly afterwards the figure of PEDRO, standing on the right-hand side, is slowly lit up. The stars reappear at the back. PEDRO is now an old man of more than 75, his hair completely white. He is dressed modestly.)*

PEDRO: He was a young gentleman, too much of a one... I watched how his face drained when I told him that wars weren't for the likes of him. Sometimes I wonder if it was me who killed him. But I... I was very fond of him. Who can tell what went through his mind in those final moments? *(He sighs.)* Luisín thought he'd inherited his marvellous talent. Baldomerita has gone and become a moneylender. And Adelita, the one who found him lying with that black hole in his head, the little one who called out: Papa... Oh, yes, she's got all her wits about her. She must be about forty now and King Amadeo has made her his lover. And the three of them every bit as dead as... my own poor lad. I dare say that even so young he knew he couldn't do anything at all for his children... and that made him even more bitter. He never managed to learn what I had known even before I met him: the need for an unending endurance. He died because he was impatient. *(Very slowly he leaves the light as he speaks. Another spot has picked out the erect and unmoving figure of LARRA in his study, pistol in his right hand and his eyes staring into space. The servant continues speaking as the writer begins to raise the pistol. PEDRO lifts his fists to his heart.)* We have always been many, and now we're beginning to realize it. *(He passes his hand over his brow.)* It's strange. So many shots from guns and cannons that I've heard in my life, and I barely remember any of them. And yet the sound of that shot, which I hardly heard at all, still rings in my head... *(With passion.)* And it must be heard and heard again. Rolling across the years! *(Pause.)* Like thunder... to wake us all! *(He is left in darkness. The pistol is, once again, very close to the forehead of the suicide, who stands like a pale statue. The faint glint of

El débil fulgor de las estrellas brilla en la noche.)

TELÓN

The pistol with which he took his life, from a display cabinet in the Museo Romántico, Madrid. (Photo, courtesy of José Luis Antigüedad)

the stars shines through the darkness of the night.)

CURTAIN

Larra points the pistol at his head. *(Photo by Gyenes, courtesy of Antonio Buero Vallejo)*

"The face of a man with few friends"

*Contemporary portrait of Bretón de los Herreros,
housed in the Museo Romántico, Madrid
(Photo, courtesy of José Luis Antigüedad)*

Notes to the Play

1. Calle Santa Clara still exists, in the heart of the so-called Madrid de los Austrias, between the Plaza de Oriente and the Calle Mayor. Items of interest linked to Larra's life, including the actual pistol with which he took his life, are housed in the Museo Romántico in Calle San Mateo.

2. Adjoining the Teatro del Príncipe, later re-named the Teatro Español, and situated in the Plaza Santa Ana in the centre of Madrid. Sadly, the café no longer exists.

3. It is virtually a commonplace to draw attention to the fact that Buero's detailed stage directions are the sign of a man of the theatre whose creative imagination is geared more towards the play as performance than as literary text. Nevertheless, it is particularly important in the case of *La detonación* to remember that many of the stage directions refer to the dramatization of Larra's own life that is taking place within his mind.

4. Due to his liberal French sympathies, Larra's father was forced to leave Spain when the French troops were finally defeated on Spanish soil in 1813. Although it is commonly believed that Larra spent all four years of the family's exile in a boarding school in Bordeaux, as Buero seems to be suggesting, it is much more likely that he actually only spent seven months there, before moving with his parents to Paris. The point, however, is that Larra's liberalism was a product of his French education.

5. Francisco Tadeo Calomarde, Conservative Minister of Justice from 1823 to 1833. After incurring the wrath of Fernando's widow and daughter in 1833 (hence the later reference to the famous "slap"), he went into voluntary exile and died in France.

6. With admirable economy Buero sketches in both the history of the Larra family and the immediate history of the country. The family had been permitted to return to Spain in 1818 after Larra's father, a well-known doctor, had attended the King's brother, don Francisco de Paula, in Paris. The conversation between Larra and his father presumably takes place early in 1826, at a time when King Fernando VII's reign was particularly repressive. Fernando (Ferdinand) VII who ruled from 1814 to 1833, had returned from exile as absolute monarch when Spanish liberalism collapsed with the departure of the French.

7. This incident, in which Larra's father apparently took his son's first lover as his own mistress, has never been documented, although its source was a member of the Larra family. Clearly, it would have had a profound effect on the temperament and attitudes of the young Larra.

8. This is the first indication that Pedro is not just a simple servant, but also represents an autonomous voice within Larra's consciousness. As such, Buero can make use of him virtually as a straightforward narrator without distancing the audience and so dissipating the intensity of Larra's psychological drama.

9. In the last few years of his reign, and especially after his marriage to María Cristina of Naples in 1829, Fernando VII's regime became increasingly unacceptable to extreme conservatives who looked to the King's reactionary brother, don Carlos. Here we find the roots of the Carlist Wars which raged in Spain for much of the century, and which form the violent national backdrop against which Larra's public and private agony is projected (see note 28.)

10. Ramón de Mesonero Romanos (1803-1882), considered one of Spain's leading practitioners of "costumbrismo", the picturesue depiction of national traditions and customs. After Larra's death Mesonero distanced himself from a writer he clearly considered subversive, and actually published pieces attacking Larra's value and originality.

11. José de Espronceda (1808-1842), unquestionably Spain's most significant romantic poet and a committed radical who was no stranger to brushes with authority.

12. Major Riego y Núñez, a military radical, who organised a short-lived liberal revolt in 1820. The name of the "Numantinos" comes from Numancia, a city of ancient Hispania celebrated for its stout resistance to Roman rule.

13. Ventura de la Vega (1807-1865), dramatist whose work moves from early romanticism to a later more realistic vein. A follower of the "Spanish Molière", Moratín, Vega's theatre was overshadowed both in his own lifetime and in subsequent reputation by the work of the more conservative Manuel Bretón de los Herreros (1796-1873).

14. Clemente Díaz, the self-styled poet whose sense of political outrage prevents him from publishing under censorship, is a necessary foil to draw out Larra's views on the role of the writer in times of oppression. He is remembered today virtually only on account of the letter addressed to him and signed by Andrés Notevenso (one of Larra's several pseudonyms), published in *The Poor Little Babbler* in 1833.

15. José María Carnerero, influential editor who presided over the group of writers who met regularly in Little Parnassus.

16. Juan Bautista Arriaza. Largely forgotten neo-classical poet.

17. As director of the Príncipe Theatre Juan de Grimaldi wielded much influence in the literary world of the time. He originally came to Spain with the so-called "one hundred thousand sons of St. Louis", French troops sent by Louis XVIII to support Fernando VII in his struggle against the liberal rising of 1820 (see note 12).

18. The Batuecas area in the province of Salamanca, traditionally a very backward area, was used by Larra as an indirect means of both speaking about Spain and alluding to its anachronistic structures and customs.

19. The change in lighting here suggests an emotional shift in Larra's subjective recreation of past experiences. In other words, it is a stage direction which refers wholly to the drama within the drama.

20. Mariana Pineda, executed for her adherence to the liberal cause, later became the eponymous heroine of a play by Federico García Lorca.

21. The changes from the polite to familiar forms of the second person are notoriously difficult to translate convincingly. In this case, the shift is very significant in that it serves further to blur the master/servant relationship of Larra and Pedro.

22. Larra's only wholly original play, banned until after the death of Fernando VII, eventually receiving its first performance in 1834. It is generally held to be of interest principally for the insights it gives into Larra's own view of himself as reflected in and through the character of the poet who is the eponymous hero of the work.

23. Larra was, above all else, a journalist. This was his first venture in this field, and the publication ran to a total of five issues with eight articles in all.

24. Larra's first published work, appearing in 1827. A poem inspired by an industrial exhibition and universally acknowledged a failure, even by its author.

25. Although there is no documentary proof for this visit, it is generally accepted that Carnerero's rancour at Larra's attacks was, in great part at least, responsible for the eventual prohibition of Larra's first venture into journalism.

26. An echo of one of Larra's most famous articles, "Come back tomorrow", published in *The Poor Little Babbler* in 1833. The title of this piece has now passed into the Spanish language as a way of describing the intractable world of bureaucracy. *The Poor Little Babbler* was to last barely a year, but in that time published fourteen issues which contain some of the finest pieces of satirical writing in the Spanish language. The title of the journal suggests someone who talks nonsense or who can find nobody to listen to him.

27. Larra married Josefina (Pepita) Wetoret in August 1829. The temperamental and intellectual differences that Buero has clearly shown were responsible for one of his most famous articles, "Marry in haste, repent at leisure", published in *The Poor Little Babbler* in 1832.

28. In order to protect the rights of succession of her daughter Isabella, Queen María Cristina persuaded Fernando to abolish the so-called Salic Law which decreed that only men could take the throne, thereby disinheriting Fernando's brother Carlos at a stroke. Carlos's faction had only agreed to Fernando's rule in the first place on the understanding that Carlos would inherit the crown upon his brother's death. The seeds of civil war were hereby sown (see note 9).

29. A lightweight farce adapted by Larra at the suggestion of Grimaldi from Scribe's *Les adieux au comptoir*. It is important to notice that here, as in other aspects of Larra's life, Buero does not simply pass over his character's weaknesses and mistakes in silence.

30. Fernando's illness in September 1832 gave María Cristina the opportunity to secure her political influence. Larra's response here provides a clear echo of Franco's apparent deathbed recovery in the autumn of 1974. Both Larra's society and that of Buero were on tenterhooks awaiting the death that could herald a new era.

31. This was a frequent charge laid at Buero's door by those who believed that the success of a theatre of protest was possible only through the protection afforded by someone close to the source of power. Buero's response here has the simple ring of truth.

32. Social criticism through letters sent between fictional characters had been fashionable in Spain since Cadalso's *Moroccan Letters*, published in 1789. These are two of Larra's fictional correspondents. He himself frequently took the role of the Graduate.

33. The pistol, both in its real form and as a symbol, is constantly present throughout the play, rather like the knife in Lorca's *Blood Wedding*. In both works these weapons create a heavy sense of fatalism presiding over the action.

34. Francisco Cea Bermúdez, Secretary of State from 1832 to 1834, who undertook certain mild reforms after the departure of the authoritarian Calomarde. To Buero's contemporary audience this would reflect the beginning of the process known as "apertura" or "opening up", which took its first timid steps in the final stages of the Francoist regime.

35. These words were appended to the end of "Come back tomorrow" and announced the official